## Critical Acclaim for *The Pink Triangle*

"A strong book, not easy to put down . . . Mr. Plant writes convincingly, keeps clear of sentiment, and lays bare a particularly fearful corner of mid-twentieth century inhumanity."
—*The Economist*

"A wrenching, highly readable study . . . recommended for both its personal insights and scholarship."
—*Kirkus Reviews*

"Using many documents and studies available only in German and augmenting them with . . . his own interviews with survivors, Mr. Plant . . . has begun to shed light on this obscure and nasty byway of National Socialism."
—*The New York Times Book Review*

"A well documented, controlled, and compelling account."
—*Books for Young Readers*

"An impressively researched, often moving book. Its subject matter is also, sadly, still too relevant to our times."
—*San Jose Mercury News*

# THE PINK TRIANGLE

## The Nazi War Against Homosexuals

### RICHARD PLANT

A HOLT PAPERBACK

A NEW REPUBLIC BOOK

HENRY HOLT AND COMPANY / NEW YORK

Holt Paperbacks
Henry Holt and Company, LLC
*Publishers since 1866*
175 Fifth Avenue
New York, New York 10010
www.henryholt.com

A Holt Paperback® and ® are registered trademarks
of Henry Holt and Company, LLC.

Library of Congress Cataloging-in-Publication Data
Plant, Richard.
The pink triangle.
"A New Republic book."
ISBN-13: 978-0-8050-0600-1

1. Homosexuality, Male—Germany—History—20th century.
2. Concentration camps—Germany—History—20th century.
3. Germany—Politics and government—1933–1945.
4. Homosexuality—Law and legislation—Germany.
I. Title.
HQ76.2.G4P55   1986      306.7'662'0943      86-346

Henry Holt books are available for special promotions and
premiums. For details contact: Director, Special Markets.

Originally published in hardcover in 1986 by
New Republic Books / Henry Holt and Company

First Holt Paperbacks Edition 1988

Designed by Robert Bull

Printed in the United States of America

50  49  48  47  46  45  44  43

*To Eric and all those who did not get away*

# CONTENTS

# ACKNOWLEDGMENTS

I had the good fortune to receive encouragement from many women and men who saw me through long years of work and worry. Four men have gone out of their way to help me; I will list them in the order in which they have entered my life and this book:

New Republic Books editor Marc Granetz, who let me, so to speak, into the house and gave me the first valid directions.

My assistant, Hugh Murray, who never tired of checking esoteric data in various libraries. His broad knowledge of European and American history provided an invaluable perspective for my project and spurred me on to explore those murkier aspects of German history that I had feared defied transfer into English.

Andrew Rubenfeld, whose kind heart did not keep him from using several red pencils and sharp scissors whenever he thought I was deviating from the main road. He also prevented the footnotes from overgrowing and choking the text. Finally, he held steady when I despaired of ever being able to accommodate the abundance of material. As a native-born American, he conveyed an unobtrusive optimism that restrained my Central European philosophizing and excessive *Weltschmerz*.

Last, but definitely not least, I am indebted to my new editor, Steve Wasserman, who, although he inherited me and was faced with an enormous task, i.e., to ready a large, complex manuscript for publication within a short time, displayed not only a never-flagging goodwill but a scholar's knowledge of German politics and metapolitics which sometimes stunned me, but which vastly benefited the book.

Among the women and men who stood by me, I want to mention the following: Iska Alter, Achim Besge, Zenos Booker, Alois Brands, Peter Chatel, Albert de Cocatrix, Charles Creegan, Richard Deppe, Page Grubb, Richard Hall, Gert Hekma, Erich Henschel, Winfried Hohmann, Justus Imfeld, Mrs. Kirsten Michalski-Kalow, Simon Karlinsky, Jonathan Katz, Hubert Kennedy, Mrs. Felix Kersten, Gary Krawford, Siegfried Kuhn, Jon Klysner, Rüdiger Lautmann, Bill Long, David Marans, Lawrence Mass, Mrs. Elisabeth Meter-Plaut, Klaus Milich, Mrs. Peggy Richard, Heinrich Siebel, Charles Simmons, James Steakley, Thomas Steele, Paul Tankersley, James Tierney, Stephen Worley, John Yancey.

And I would like to thank Randy Schein for his expert typing of the final manuscript.

# THE

## PINK

## TRIANGLE

# PROLOGUE

I fled Frankfurt am Main on February 27, 1933, the day the Reichstag went up in flames. I was fortunate. My father, however, a physician, a veteran, a Socialist, and a Jew, had been arrested several weeks earlier. Because a few of his patients, though nominally members of the Nazi Party, intervened in his behalf—this was possible during the early years of the Third Reich—he came home after only one month of imprisonment. He insisted I leave Germany as quickly as possible for Basel, Switzerland, and enroll at the university there. After encountering many obstacles, I succeeded in obtaining a passport, an object that had suddenly acquired enormous value. I gathered a few belongings and some luggage, and rushed to the Frankfurt railroad station to take the earliest train to Switzerland.

Only years later did I realize how lucky I had been. Although the anti-Jewish and the anti-gay laws became officially part of the Nazi onslaught of terror in 1934–35, the crusade against various minorities had really begun long before. Brown-shirted gangs of trigger- and hammer-happy youths, in an outbreak of "spontaneous" national outrage, had vandalized Jewish stores or thrashed the patrons of the few timid gay bars in Frankfurt. By June 1933, a few Swiss newspapers had reported with near incredulity that Hitler's threats in *Mein Kampf* to expunge his enemies had not been empty posturing—that Jews, liberals, Social Democrats, Catholics, and labor leaders had been arrested or murdered; that, in short, a revolution was rocking Germany to its already shaky foundations. The Swiss never alluded to the Nazis' anti-gay crusade—in part because this movement began in full only in June 1935, but also because in the 1930s no self-respecting publication would dare to discuss such a delicate subject. To what length the Nazi regime was prepared to carry the war against "non-Aryans" no Swiss newspaper could foresee. Yet another agency concerned with the public good, the Swiss Foreign Ministry in Berne, did exhibit a knack for anticipating Hitler's moves.

A few weeks after my arrival in Basel, I had gone to the university, a sixteenth-century fortress overlooking the Rhine, to register as a graduate student in history and literature. About six months later the Foreign Ministry struck, ruling that foreign students could not attend classes in Switzerland unless they had been in the country for a certain length of time and had been given a provisional permit of residence. Fortunately, because I had registered in February, I was safe.

By the time I was ready for my first class at the fortress, I had found a place to stay in the eccentric household of Gabrielle Gundermann, a very unmarried old lady, tiny and vivacious, a former coloratura soprano and telephone company employee. She insisted I call her "Miss Gaby." I tried to settle down to the life of a financially insecure alien student. Like other fugitive German students I met, I had few forebodings of what was going to happen in Germany, though I harbored a profound worry. I spent some nights sleepless with anxiety. Certain events in Germany gradually made the situation clearer. The *Frankfurter Zeitung*, for example, one of the better liberal German dailies, not only acquired a new editorial staff, but its tone began to change markedly. Jewish names disappeared from the masthead. The paper now seemed to speak in code. In contrast, the small local liberal daily, the *Basler Nationalzeitung*, began to print more and more news about Germany, most of it shocking. Throughout the Nazi years the paper resisted the pressure put on it by German interests and compliant Swiss officials to change its anti-Nazi bias. Meanwhile, my father kept writing guarded letters to me. But he did not mention that one day the SS had put a uniformed guard in front of the door of every Jewish physician. This I heard about late one night on Basel radio.

I had left friends behind in Frankfurt. Ferdi Strom, an old classmate, had shared my brief tenure in one of the youth groups known as the Rovers. The leader of such a group usually expected the members, as his disciples, to be loyal if not devoted. Soon I discovered that a Rover leader had his favorites. Whether this went beyond arm-on-the-shoulder familiarity I could not tell then. In such brotherhoods a few adolescents had little affairs, misty and romantic sessions around a blazing fire in the dark of the forest. Other boys, more down-to-earth, talked openly about "going with friends" and enjoying it. The leaders of these groups tended to disregard the relationships blossoming around them—unless they participated—just as they paid scant attention to the ideological debates that regularly erupted while we sat and talked around the campfire. I left the Rovers, a vaguely romantic association of mostly middle-class Protestants and Catholic teenagers, and a similar Zionist brotherhood when, as an older teenager, I fell in love with the cinema. From Ferdi's letters I learned what happened to the youth groups. After 1933 the Nazis forcibly dissolved all independent youth organizations, even the Catholic ones, hurled accusations of "homosexual degeneracy" against their leaders, and embarked on a campaign to enforce strictly heterosexual behavior.

By this time Ferdi, too, had left the Rovers. He also quit school. It was Ferdi who had explained and demonstrated the mysteries of sex to me and my friends. He was basically a street kid, tough, truculent, and wise. But he did not hold it against me that he had a menial job at a pharmacy while I went to the university. I had not kept in touch when he joined the Communist Youth League. On the night in 1933 when Hitler was inaugurated as chancellor, Ferdi phoned me very late, and his curses sounded drunk. A few weeks before my journey to Switzerland, I had gone to the pharmacy where Ferdi worked, and where I often picked up medicine for my father. I was shocked to see Ferdi wearing a brown shirt with a red, white, and black swastika armband, and I yelled at him. To Ferdi the brown uniform meant only that he could get a better job. He urged me to "get away from this mess," and it was he who provided the useful channels for obtaining that indispensable passport. He never wavered. After I had settled in Basel he started sending me unsigned postcards with badly spelled messages that I could not always decipher, though mostly they concerned acquaintances who had disappeared or been taken to jail.

From the summer of 1935 on, Ferdi's messages betrayed their meanings more clearly. Hans K. had "gone on a long vacation," and someone nicknamed Veidt had been "transferred to Berlin." I did not know then about the new anti-gay legislation that had been introduced. Soon I began bombarding my father with letters urging him to leave Germany, even if it meant abandoning his patients and his valuable library.

He did not listen to my pleas. My mother had died earlier, of cancer; my sister, a musician, had found refuge in Holland—for a while. During my first term at Basel I had looked up distant relatives who lent support in many ways. For my part, I tutored reluctant children in German and Latin and wrote short articles on books and films (under a pseudonym) for the *Basler Nationalzeitung*. By this time the entire world had heard about the 1935 Nuremberg laws concerning "racial purity," and about the confiscation of "non-Aryan" properties and the edicts that made Jews into nonpersons. Yet the impact of the state action against gays did not really hit me until much later. Had I looked through the pages of the easily available *Völkischer Beobachter*, I might have encountered the various announcements of the Führer's measures to cleanse the brave new Germany of criminal sexual deviants. But neither I nor anyone I knew took the trouble to study the *Völkischer Beobachter* because its headlines trumpeted a political ideology that I refused to take seriously even in 1935.

One day, in an envelope without a return address, I received a letter from another friend in Frankfurt, Eric Langer. Eric had been my main ally in my school years, and my one true friend. His father had also been a physician, practicing in the nearby village of Cronberg. During World War I, both of our fathers had worked in a hospital near Cracow, Poland. Toward the war's end both were wounded; my father recovered from a splintered kneecap, but Dr. Langer died of an infection shortly before the armistice. Hilda Langer, his wife, managed to keep the family going in Cronberg. Small, with dark eyes that seemed to give more compassion than they accepted, Hilda was always in repose; she resembled a Dürer woodcut without the harshness that those prints often convey. My parents did whatever they could for her. Eric, a half-year older than I, spent as much time at our house on Reuterweg in Frankfurt as I did at his farm in Cronberg. We attended the same school and considered ourselves cousins. The farm was my haven from the busy Frankfurt house and office where my father practiced, and I did not mind the exercises that Eric insisted I must do to get stronger and overcome my stuttering. I sense now that Hilda secretly furthered the friendship between Eric and me. She was aware that I cared more for him than I could admit. Until I reached puberty I was a loner, and I stuttered with a vengeance. Whenever tension attacked me from within, the words left my mouth crippled, and I expected, and probably invited, my peers to make fun of me. But from early on, Eric never giggled; he tried to persuade me that I was silly to worry about my handicap. In high school, the venerable Goethe Gymnasium, I was nicknamed the Stick because I was undernourished and a poor athlete. Eric's unruly blond hair earned him the nickname of Lion. I was dimly aware that Eric restrained his urge to protect and dominate me. Essentially, we had liked and understood each other from the day we first met at the Cronberg farm.

At school, Eric excelled in all subjects. I faltered in some—math, physics, chemistry—while in others I had no trouble—history, Greek, Latin. Somehow we managed to keep the class bullies at a distance, and, not surprisingly, developed an aversion to the conservative patriotic clubs that the school promoted among the pupils, in opposition to the supposedly liberal ideas of the post–World War I Weimar democracy. As it was, few of these ideas ever threatened the stuffiness of our institution. Eric was never fooled by false prophets or hyperbolic sloganeers of any denomination. He did not feel comfortable with the Rovers and soon quit. I meandered first to a Zionist brotherhood and then devoted most of my time to the film club. And although we talked for hours about sexual riddles, we never crossed a certain unspoken barrier; Eric could not abide Ferdi and his insatiable sexual pursuits.

Eric was not in Frankfurt when my world collapsed in January 1933. During a visit to his mother's family in Holland he had fallen seriously ill, and returned to Frankfurt only after I had escaped to Basel. Later I discovered that all his notes mailed to me before I finally settled at Miss Gaby's had gone astray. But now, in September 1935, my landlady placed several envelopes on the all-purpose table of the one-room enclave that was my home for those years, giving me a smile of conspiracy as if to say, You see, at my house, you will get your interesting letters punctually. Eric wrote:

Before I come to what has happened to some of our acquaintances, here is some news not published by anybody in Frankfurt. Have you heard about the Roehm murders? With that it started, the rounding up, the closing of the bars, and so on. No place is open here in Frankfurt. In return we are blessed with new sex laws. Our old buddy Harold said they can get you if you smile at another boy. This he told me before he went underground—I have no idea where he is. If he is alive. Remember the G.G. brothers? Arrested a week ago, put into Preungesheim jail. Remember Max? Supposedly in Dachau, near Munich. What little contact I had with Ferdi is lost but I'm afraid his SA uniform is no protection with Roehm gone. A few he seduced on his endless expeditions would rat on him quickly. Richard, you could never guess how many told on their former friends when they were thrown in jail and "reeducated" by the bullies. Kurt, the pharmacist near your house, was dragged out of bed at 5:00 A.M. They found his address book—the fool didn't burn it or throw it in the river. What happened at headquarters I can only guess—I haven't seen him and don't have the nerve to ask his mother. Oh, yes, you remember Bert? You will not believe it, he joined the SS gang, displays his elegant penmanship in their main office, and looks the other way when he spots me. By the way, my mother told me to assure you that your father still has a practice but is preparing to leave. She sees him twice a week, at least. Now don't worry about me. I'm going to enlist in the navy. Yes, I know, I should stay with you in Basel and perhaps later we could get away from all this, far away, to Australia, Canada, or California. Mother wants me to, but how can I leave her?

There followed some stern warnings. Under no circumstances should I consider visiting Frankfurt. For once, Eric insisted, I should think ahead without worrying. But my situation in Basel was shaky too. The Swiss authorities in Berne were not friendly to emigré students. Not only were they not friendly—they wanted us out and they absolutely did not care to have new ones. By some bureaucratic passport trick, Eric had heard, the Swiss could prevent Germans from entering as "tourists." Didn't I have family in the United States? I should start communicating seriously with them. What bothered Eric most was that I would not be able to reach him after he began his naval training. He suspected that all mail would be censored. He promised to send anonymous cards whenever he found a chance. I could mail unsigned messages to his mother, and when—not *if*—I reached America, I must give an address. He would telephone her regularly; they had already worked out a private code.

For a while Eric sent noncommittal postcards from northern German cities, but beyond the fact that he had joined a mobile naval training unit, they revealed little. I could not call Hilda in Cronberg. The journalists on the *Basel Nationalzeitung* reported that people in Germany had been summoned to Gestapo headquarters because they had received calls from outside the Third Reich. When I finally left for New York, I was cut off altogether from Eric and his mother. In an important way it was the memory of Eric that kept urging me on, decades later, to search out that rather little-known area of the swastika tyranny, the hounding and slaughter of homosexuals under the Third Reich.

At the end of the last letter I received in the packet, Eric indicated that one of our classmates, someone he identified only by the nickname Loko Buff, would visit me in Basel. Could I put him up? As it happened, Loko Buff, whose real name was Robbi Becker, showed up in the winter of 1936. Miss Gaby rang my bell, shouting that there was someone waiting for me. When I got downstairs, I did not recognize Robbi and couldn't muster a welcoming smile. Apparently he had lost so much weight that his face had shriveled. His blond hair had been clipped convict-style. As he climbed the narrow stairs, he appeared old and numb. Miss Gaby knew this visitor could not pay much—he carried only a small leather overnight bag—but she let him have one of the four tiny attic rooms and did not ask him to sign the register, as was required by law.

But first we went to my room. When I finally settled Robbi into my best chair—faded red plush from Miss Gundermann's coloratura days—he began to talk, but at first only of how he had managed to slip into Switzerland. His father, the chief of the German locomotive workers' union, had mobilized some members who worked and lived in Lörrach, the German village facing the Swiss border near Basel. Somehow they had managed to sneak Robbi across the border, and from there he had simply taken a streetcar to my neighborhood. Exhausted, Robbi fell silent and I decided to take him up to his room, so he could gather himself.

Only after he had been with me for a few days and had made friends with Miss Gaby, who even persuaded him to take some specially prepared food, did Robbi finally tell me what had happened to him. In September 1935 he was arrested and jailed together with his father. At first the Gestapo authorities tried to make him testify that his father had printed anti-Hitler leaflets. Later, when they added charges of "homosexual indecencies," Robbi suspected that somebody had denounced him. He was sure the police had used the charge of "deviant sexual actions" to obtain further proofs against his father, a staunch Social Democrat. Although Robbi's alleged sexual sins had taken place before the 1935 injunctions against homosexual activities were issued, this did not make him less guilty; when it suited them, the Nazi legalists declared their laws to be retroactive. Robbi was never allowed to confront his partner in crime, or to have legal counsel.

After Robbi had spent a few weeks in Preungesheim jail, a high-ranking SS officer in the Frankfurt power structure bribed some lower SS officers and Robbi was dismissed with a stern command never to talk about his stay. Immediately he had someone gather a few of his clothes from home. Every second night he slept in a different place; he never visited his family again. And then, reluctantly, he showed me all the still-visible bruises and burns on his body. Because he would not rat on someone else, a guard had rammed an iron bar into his rectum, damaging his sphincter. Robbi could have saved himself much trouble if he had asked for medical help earlier. But he would not go to a Basel hospital—officials might ask for papers he did not have.

Fortunately, among the Swiss students I had met, there was one who was close to completing his medical finals. From the day I encountered Justus, he had always shown great concern for us foreigners, and I confided in him. Justus promised to look for a surgeon who would not ask questions, and a place where he could operate undisturbed. It was, he added, tougher than getting an abortion. While Justus and his friend worked out the arrangements, Robbi and I talked about what could be done. One of his father's brothers had emigrated to São Paulo and Robbi knew the address by heart—he had had enough sense to get rid of his address book well before he was arrested. After long weeks of waiting, we received a reply from São Paulo. The Brazilian uncle wondered why his nephew wished to leave a newly liberated and strong Germany, but he nevertheless promised to help.

Justus also came through with a classmate willing to operate and a safe operating room. How they overcame paperwork and avoided keeping records, I do not know. The operation went well, and Robbi recuperated under the care of Miss Gaby, who had grown fond of him, although she never asked the nature of his surgery. Justus next enlisted the aid of another Swiss student, who was going to Frankfurt. After making sure the apartment was not being watched, he visited Robbi's mother to collect some clothes and, above all, those papers precious to bureaucrats worldwide. He also learned that Robbi's father was still in jail. As Robbi recovered and lost his air of depression, I heard from him too the details of the Roehm massacre, the new anti-gay rulings, and the subsequent persecution. The São Paulo uncle finally mailed the steamship ticket plus some spending money. We waited weeks for the Brazilian consul in Zurich to grant a visitor's visa. Finally, all was set. Robbi left for Genoa to board an Italian freighter bound for South America. Miss Gaby cried during those last days of preparations, sure that the steamer would sink—and besides, who ever heard of anyone going to such a place as Brazil?

Those four rooms in Miss Gaby's attic were rarely left empty. Again and again, Jewish, Catholic, gay, and generally anti-Nazi friends and friends of friends would stay there for a while until they could find refuge elsewhere. The wealthier ones, or those with sure contacts in Canada, America, Australia, or South America, usually succeeded in obtaining visas—though these were often dubious. In the larger Swiss cities and in France, a black market in passports and visas began to develop, so that, for instance, a Jewish businessman from

Frankfurt might find himself traveling to Santo Domingo with a Panamanian passport. Or a gay opera singer with a Paraguayan passport might book a berth on an English steamer bound for Shanghai. To manage all this, to dominate this theater of the absurd and the blackly comic, demanded patience and a certain grit and toughness not granted to everyone. The Swiss authorities would frequently not permit the refugee to stay longer than three weeks, but it usually took at least six months to negotiate the necessary papers. To my recurring dismay and horror, many friends had no choice but to return to Germany. From there, few managed to keep in touch or survive—I simply lost them.

After Robbi had reached São Paulo, I received a few letters from him, but we lost contact when I emigrated to America. Fortunately, I took notes during our talks and remembered well what he wrote in his letters—my first interview, as it were, with a gay survivor.

# INTRODUCTION

This book seeks to throw some light in a corner of modern history that has thus far remained too much in the shadows: the persecution of homosexuals under the Third Reich. Even today, four decades after Hitler's defeat, many facets of the Nazi regime have not received full popular and scholarly attention; they have been crowded out, so to speak, by the horror of the major atrocity, the extermination of the Jews. The attempted systematic destruction of other, numerically smaller groups also caught in the maw of the Nazi terror, such as the Jehovah's Witnesses, the Gypsies, antifascists of all shades, and nonconforming clergymen can only be presented marginally in this study. Fuller presentation must be consulted elsewhere, or, in many cases, left to future researchers.

The period directly following the collapse of Hitler's Germany offered much immediate relief for most of the regime's persecuted victims, in addition to giving them a platform to air to the world their undeniable grievances—but not so for the gays. For one thing, the climate of the Cold War and the conservative moralism of the Adenauer administration was not conducive to eliminating all traces of Nazi jurisprudence, including the 1935 antihomosexual laws, which remained in effect until 1969. For another, the nature of their "crimes" was so intimate that very few wished to publicize such a sexual preference or life-style. Finally—and perhaps most curious of all—the mortality rate for homosexuals incarcerated by the Nazis was, it appears, relatively higher, in the camps and after their release, than that of other persecuted groups. Researchers learned that the gays, marked by pink triangles, were a relatively small minority in the camps but had a proportionately higher mortality rate than, for example, the more numerous political prisoners, who wore red patches. As with all of those who survived the jails, forced labor camps, and death camps, a large number died shortly afterward. Of those gays with whom researchers were able to make contact in the 1960s and 1970s, an unusually high number died before initial interviews, and many did not live to complete correspondences or accounts of their personal histories.

Thus it is no accident that the first full-length report by a gay ex-inmate, Heinz Heger's *The Men with the Pink Triangle*, appeared late, in 1972, followed in 1977 by the now classic investigative report, *Homosexuality and Society*, conducted by a team led by Rüdiger Lautmann of Bremen University. This work offered the first truly reliable statistics on the persecution, arrest, imprisonment, and fate of German and Austrian homosexuals in various concentration camps. Although a few historians, notably Eugen Kogon in his pioneering *Der SS Staat* (1946), had called attention to the existence of gay inmates in various camps, especially Buchenwald, it remained for Lautmann and his associates to make known to a larger public the results of his definitive study— carried out in part in the vast archives of the International Tracing Service at Arolsen, West Germany.

In 1980, Heger's memoirs were translated and published in the United States and Britain. Unfortunately, they were generally ignored. On the other hand, Martin Sherman's play *Bent* (1979), which based some of its plot on material in Heger's book, was widely discussed. *Bent* opened the forbidden closet a crack and put the world on notice that indeed the Nazis had hounded all contragenics,* that gays had been classified with criminals, asocials, and Jews as deviant subhumans, the cosmic lice that Hitler and Himmler had vowed to exterminate.

One might be tempted to conclude that before the late 1970s writers interested in tracing the Nazi persecution of homosexuals had little source material to draw upon. But this temptation must be resisted. For historians able to read German there was ample evidence available to prove that Himmler's storm troopers were as eager to get rid of the gays as they were to expunge other contragenics. In fact, even for those who could read no German there was a sufficient amount of statistical material and documentation on the subject—if they had wanted to focus on it.

For a long time German historians also failed to discuss the plight of the gays during the Third Reich. Quite to the contrary, a few writers such as Konrad Heiden, with a sort of coy horror, offered hints that Hitler himself might have been a homosexual or at least some kind of sexual deviant. The technique of homosexualizing the enemy, employed by some emigré authors, can be understood as a thirst for revenge, but it does not excuse such gleeful illogic—they simultaneously depict Hitler as wickedly effeminate but stop short of proving that he was homosexual. What they did was to indict him by association. Because SA chief Ernst Roehm was admittedly an active homosexual, these writers concluded that the dictator himself and all of his top henchmen must have shared Roehm's inclinations. Luchino Visconti's

---

*Contragenics* is a term the linguist Richard J. Deppe has coined to encompass all those groups the Nazi regime resolved to eliminate: Jews, antifascists, gays, Jehovah's Witnesses, nonconforming clergymen, Gypsies, etc.

cinematic fantasy *The Damned* (1969) was among the worst offenders in this regard. The movie featured a number of senior storm troopers in drag, thus popularizing the image of a homosexual Nazi elite. More tendentiously, the film promoted the theory, believed by many intellectuals, that the incomprehensible Nazi crimes could be easily explained: the Nazis were simply homosexual perverts. (The tenacity of this view is exemplified by Bernardo Bertolucci's *The Conformist* [1971], based on the 1951 novel of the same name by Alberto Moravia.) Nor was this theory new in the postwar period. A Soviet film made in 1936 stressed the same point. Gustav von Wangenheim's *The Fighters* purported to tell the true story of the 1933 burning of the Reichstag. It depicted the Nazis as homosexuals—the official Communist Party line about the German fascists. Soviet officials quietly shelved the film in 1939 after Hitler and Stalin signed the nonaggression pact. The film has never been publicly screened in the West.

But this theory offers no explanation of why writers and historians have never fully addressed themselves to the Nazis' apparent homophobia—a fear that early on considered the gays as subhumans to be weeded out, root and branch, as Himmler put it. Take, for example, an avowedly conservative biographer, Joachim Fest. In his excellent study of Hitler and his courtiers, Fest omitted a critical historical incident. On May 6, 1933, a gang of "outraged students" stormed the famous Institute for Sexual Research, directed by Magnus Hirschfeld, the father of the new science of sexology. For three decades Hirschfeld and his team of legal and medical associates had assembled an invaluable collection of documents, photographs, treatises, and statistics about sex. For the Nazis, Hirschfeld—a Jewish physician, a homosexual, and a liberal propagandist—was an ideal target. The fascist press had denounced him with lavish insults for many years.

The eager fascist students rummaged through the building, throwing books, photos, paintings, and files into the yard; around the growing fire they sang patriotic songs about Germany's awakening. Four days later they returned and put the ransacked building to the flame, and with it the bust of their patron-Satan, Dr. Hirschfeld. Out of the country on a lecture tour, Hirschfeld never returned to Germany. He died in France in 1935.

Fest mentions Hirschfeld's name only once, in passing, in his 764-page study of Hitler. In an earlier study, the shorter *The Face of the Third Reich*, Fest does justice to Roehm and his execution, but in neither work are Hirschfeld, his institute, or his writings and priceless research ever discussed.

The same omission can be found in nearly all major histories of the Third Reich; this holds true for the work of journalists, too. Consider William Shirer, the one reporter who, through his radio broadcasts and writings, presented the most penetrating image of Nazi Germany to the American public before, during, and after the war. In *The Rise and Fall of the Third Reich* (1959), Shirer paints a picture of Germany in the 1930s that dominated American understanding of the Nazi regime for many years. Shirer's observations and perceptions of the destructive power of the political volcano whose eruptions he witnessed show a clear appreciation of events and personalities. Yet in none of his major works dealing with the Third Reich does Shirer call attention to Hirschfeld's pioneering studies, the early German gay rights movement, or the subsequent Nazi crusade against the gays. Shirer's sins of omission are matched by sins of commission. In discussing Hitler's indifference to criminals on his staff, Shirer notes: "No matter how murky their past or indeed their present . . . Murderers, pimps, homosexuals, perverts or just plain rowdies were all the same to [Hitler] if they served their purpose."[1] In *The Nightmare Years*, his published diaries for 1930–40, Shirer is honest enough to admit how naïve he had been in accepting his assignment in Germany, how many errors of judgment he had committed, and how often he had closed his eyes to the truth because it was too painful. Although the diaries cover the year 1933, when the incineration of the Institute for Sexual Research made headlines in the fascist press, Shirer ignores the incident. Further, while he reports in detail the intrigues leading to the purge of Roehm and his followers on June 28, 1934, he has no space to spare for the new antihomosexual laws published pointedly a year later on June 28, 1935.

It would be unjust to single out Shirer, who alerted Americans to the true threat of the swastika revolution. Yet while putting together his compendious 1959 study, he could easily have consulted two volumes written not by concentration camp survivors or gay propagandists, but rather by someone clearly involved. Rudolf Hoess, a high Nazi official, in his *Kommandant in Auschwitz* (1959), elaborately recounted how he attempted to "reeducate" decadent homosexuals by assigning them to the toughest work details and by forcing them to visit female prostitutes. Also available in the 1950s were the indispensable reminiscences of Himmler's private physician, translated into English as *The Memoirs of Dr. Felix Kersten* (1957). In this work there is an entire chapter devoted to Himmler's obsession with eliminating the gays. There is simply no excuse for the widespread silence on what was clearly an important aspect of Nazi ideology and action. Only Erich Fromm seems to have understood the importance of the subject. Although he did not make use of the Hoess and Kersten books, Fromm pointed out in *The Anatomy of Human Destructiveness* that for an understanding of the homophobic strain in Germany, we must reach back to the mid-nineteenth-century homosexual emancipation movement that flourished at the same time that various strains of xenophobia developed, mixing in their wake in the German consciousness a hatred of racial and sexual minorities such as Jews and homosexuals, along with a yearning for some charismatic figure to lead the "real" German people to victory over the problems and crises caused by these insidious threats.

One can only conclude that, for most historians, there was and still is a taboo in effect. The territory of gay history is strewn with such taboos. This book seeks to end the silence toward the fate of homosexuals under the Third Reich. That their story is an integral part of German history will, I trust, be only too evident.

# 1

# BEFORE
# THE
# STORM

THE NAZI WAR AGAINST GERMANY'S HOMO-
sexuals, to be properly understood, must be seen against the
backdrop of the terrible tensions and social traumas that
ultimately were to cause the collapse of the Weimar Republic.
For the severe economic depression, widespread unemployment, galloping inflation, and bitter civil strife that were to
engulf Germany in the wake of World War I also consigned
the country's small but vigorous homosexual-rights movement to oblivion. That movement, which began around the
turn of the century, would reach its peak in the early 1920s,
under the remarkable leadership of Dr. Magnus Hirschfeld.
It would enjoy its greatest influence at precisely the moment
that the larger society whose prejudices it sought to change
began to spin out of control. To understand the fate of Germany's homosexuals it is necessary to grasp not only the
specific events and warring ideologies that destroyed the Weimar Republic and created the conditions that permitted the
rise of the Nazis, but also the general atmosphere of Germany
between 1919 and 1933.[1]

The anxiety and insecurity that would come to grip all
social classes by 1933 began with the shock of military defeat
at the end of World War I. It was a war that had left 1.7
million German soldiers dead and another four million
wounded. The returning veterans, convinced that they had
been betrayed, claimed to have been "stabbed in the back."

Most Germans agreed. How was it possible for the Kaiser's mighty army to have been defeated? Only days before the end, hadn't the army's own press releases promised the certain victory of the "sacred German cause"? What the man in the street suspected, what the popular press trumpeted, was that traitors at home had caused the great catastrophe. War profiteers, foreigners from the East, Communists and Socialists, the Jews—all were to blame for Germany's humiliation.

A tidal wave of shame and resentment, experienced even by younger men who had not seen military service, swept the nation. Many people tried to digest the bitter defeat by searching furiously for scapegoats. The belief that internal enemies had brought down the Empire, the Kaiser, and the "Golden Age of German Power" was widespread. Enraged ex-soldiers and younger men formed violent bands that roamed Germany. A palpable yearning could be felt on all levels of society, from farm and factory workers to middle-class businessmen and big-city intellectuals, for security and vengeance. The old guard of the Empire had never given up their positions of privilege and power, and no truly democratic government ever really grew strong enough to dislodge them. Arch-conservatives still held most of the leading positions in the army and navy, the universities, the civil service, and especially the courts. Long before Adolf Hitler entered politics, long before anti-Semitism and antiliberalism had become battle cries for the Nazis, the Weimar Republic's experiment in democracy and social tolerance was steadily undermined by distrust, injustice, and violence. One is almost tempted to say that Hitler did not bring the Republic down; he merely saved it from suicide by murdering it himself. It was bankrupt long before he appointed himself as Germany's savior.

The social hurricane at the heart of the Weimar Republic was prompted and complicated by five factors: (1) fear of revolution; (2) racist and xenophobic paramilitary groups; (3) unprecedented inflation; (4) extreme unemployment; and (5) the Nazi Party.

First, directly after World War I, many older people were frightened by the specter of revolution. The Bolsheviks had accomplished it in Russia, and they had counted on the spreading of revolution in Europe to ensure their survival. The revolt in Munich in 1918 seemed to many to be but the opening shot in a class war. German newspapers were soon filled with hysterical reports of famine in the Ukraine. Many people feared that a Socialist triumph in Germany would doom the country to Russia's plight.

Second, dozens of racist and virulently nationalistic groups began to flourish in this climate, each more fanatical than the other. Many participated in the civil strife that began to break out sporadically all over the country. These guerrilla skirmishes especially alienated those Germans (the majority, it is safe to say) who wanted an orderly society in which to live and work.

A third factor cracked open the thin walls of stability and did more than any other to destroy trust and hope: the mammoth inflation of 1922–23. In just sixteen months the German mark soared from 192 marks to the American dollar to a staggering 4.2 *trillion* marks to the dollar.[2] The financial faith of the country was shattered beyond repair. The middle class lost its savings and its confidence in government. Persons on fixed incomes, such as pensions, war bonds, and annuities, found their dreams drowned in monetary quicksand. An incomprehensible economic sickness infected everyone, diminishing all salaries and gobbling up savings. Everywhere, pawnshops were packed, and relief rolls lengthened. The labor unions, too, in which many had put their trust, failed. Since the unions' funds were gone, they could no longer resist the demands of employers: the ten-hour day returned to many industries. Unions began to lose members. Death and suicide rates rose; many children suffered from malnutrition. Those who had left the unions—and there were hundreds upon hundreds of thousands—found themselves politically adrift. Neither the left-wing Social Democratic Party (to which most labor unions belonged) nor the liberal or right-wing parties offered any prescriptions to cure this epidemic.

That the middle classes and the workers lost faith in both the state and the economy is not surprising. When money loses its value, then government is robbed of its authority. As Alan Bullock, the distinguished British historian and biographer of Hitler, has observed, the "result of the inflation was to undermine the foundations of German society in a way that neither the war nor the revolution of 1918 nor the Treaty of Versailles had ever done. The real revolution in Germany was the inflation."[3] Berlin, the capital of the country, became the object of hatred for many Germans. A wave of anti-Berlin sentiment, always dormant on many levels of German society, swept through the provinces. Berlin, it was said, was different; it was evil, dominated by Jews, homosexuals, Communists.

A fourth factor compounding the deepening crisis was the rapid rise in unemployment, especially after the 1929 New York Stock Exchange crash, which toppled half of the financial institutions of Central Europe. Austrian banks collapsed first, then a number of leading German banks. In January 1930, the number of unemployed workers rose from 1.5 million to 3.2 million. Some economists estimate the actual number to have been more than six million by 1933. Many of the unemployed were teenagers or in their early twenties; they waited in endless lines before the welfare agencies to receive their meager welfare stamps worth less than twenty dollars a month. On every corner, peddlers offered trinkets nobody wanted; street singers and itinerant musicians played endlessly in courtyards for people who could not afford to drop a few pennies into their empty caps. Many young men, without hope, sullen and bewildered, were filled with a rage that knew no release. Many began to join the extremist parties of both the left and the right; many joined first the left, then the right. The promise of dramatic change suddenly made sense. Men were hungry too long, and now they were angry and desperate.

Into this social cauldron was added the fifth and most poisonous ingredient: the Nazi Party. As the numbers of unemployed rose, the Nazi membership rolls grew. To be sure, just before Franz von Papen maneuvered Hitler into the chancellorship in 1933, the Nazis had lost quite a few members. Still, the rise in unemployment and the growing strength of the Nazis were indissolubly linked. The Nazi Party not only provided food, weapons, and a splendid uniform, it proclaimed a new purpose, a new faith, and a new prophet. Inflation and unemployment catapulted into power a man who promised rebirth to all "Aryan" Germans, regardless of status. Hitler vowed to avenge the injustices of the Treaty of Versailles, and to punish the culprits who had been responsible for Germany's defeat. As was so often the case, Hitler's rhetoric was littered with sexual metaphors. Jews and other minorities, for example, were guilty of the "syphilitization of our people." In 1935, Nazi lawyer Hans Frank would warn that the "epidemic of homosexuality" was threatening the new Reich.[4] America, too, was an enemy, a "niggerized Jewish country"[5] where women painted their faces—a practice that enraged Nazi moralists. Heinrich Himmler, head of the SS, would later boast that no Aryan woman he knew ever used lipstick. It was Himmler who would mastermind the attacks on homosexuals, whom he endowed with the same subhuman, dangerous qualities as were ascribed to Jews, Communists and Gypsies.[6]

During the Weimar Republic, the homosexual subculture had managed an uneasy coexistence with the larger heterosexual society surrounding it. Of course, those in the spotlight—famous actors, designers, dancers, doctors, politicians, directors, and lawyers—had to live with a certain amount of abuse. But many had acquired power, money, and even connections to the Weimar government, which served as protection. The average gay man could live unnoticed and undisturbed unless he fell victim to police entrapment or blackmail. The average lesbian enjoyed a kind of legal immunity. During the Weimar years, organized lesbian costume balls were held; luxurious lesbian bars and nightclubs flourished. Their owners never feared a police raid. The reason: neither the Second German Empire nor the Weimar Republic had ever promulgated laws forbidding or punishing sexual acts between women. Lesbian magazines enjoyed healthy circulations, some even featuring personal ads, and a few lesbian plays achieved widespread popularity.[7]

But the sexual tolerance so often associated with the Weimar Republic began to disappear as rapidly as Germany's economy began to crumble. (The unemployed are generally less tolerant of contragenics.[8]) Germany, it must be remembered, had never been an ethnically pluralistic society. Almost all German churches were state churches. There were no large ethnic groups or religious sects other than the Jews, the Gypsies, and the Jehovah's Witnesses—the latter relatively small in number. Homosexuals were an obvious, if largely invisible, scapegoat.

The years from 1929 to the end of the Weimar Republic were years of mounting tension. The Brown Shirts, or SA,

under the leadership of Ernst Roehm, who was himself homosexual and would later be the target of Hitler's wrath, became
even more brutal and more repressively efficient. Hitler had
promised Germany's youth life as an endless military parade,
replete with dashing insignia, badges, and banners. He invented special ranks for SA recruits and later for the SS. He
proffered the vision of a brave, sunny world of soldiering for
those who had given up hope. His enemies he threatened with
war and extinction. They would be eliminated "ruthlessly"
(his favorite word), and "heads would roll." His various adversaries were united in nothing but blindness. Only when it
was too late did some grasp that Hitler's program of wholesale destruction would indeed be carried out, its scope wid-
ening year after year. The initial misreading of the implications
of the Nazis' policy of systematic violence was shared by
almost all of those who were their victims: union leaders,
shrewd politicians of the center and the right, Marxists, Jewish scientists, writers, lawyers, and, of course, homosexuals
of all professions and educational levels. To be sure, a small
minority did read the omens correctly and managed to leave
Germany before it was too late; but many stayed behind to
face their doom uncomprehendingly.[9]

▽

It is in this context that the successes and failures of the
homosexual-rights movement in Germany must be measured.
The movement began long before World War I, during the
reign of Kaiser Wilhelm II, but didn't assume the proportions
of a significant reform movement until the arrival of Magnus
Hirschfeld (1868–1935). It would be hard to overestimate
Hirschfeld's importance. The attacks on his person and on
his life's work anticipate the wholesale horror that was to be
unleashed once Hitler had consolidated his rule.

Hirschfeld, a Jew, a homosexual, and a physician, was a man possessed of enormous energy, imagination, and ambition. He became the leader of several psychological and medical organizations, the founder of a unique institute for sexual research, and the organizer of numerous international congresses dedicated to research on sexual matters and to the promotion of policies that would lead to an acceptance of homosexuals by society. In his celebrated study, *Homosexuality in Men and Women*, Hirschfeld optimistically declared that 90 percent of the German people would vote to repeal the nation's antihomosexual laws if only they had a chance to learn the truth.[10] His optimism would later prove to be unfounded, even after Hitler's defeat in 1945. Hirschfeld's motto was "Justice Through Knowledge." He was not alone in his belief that progress could be made through the exercise of reason. Other doctors and psychiatrists, such as Richard von Krafft-Ebing, Albert Moll, and Alfred Adler, shared this belief even as they contested Hirschfeld's ideas while respecting his research.

Consumed by a kind of missionary zeal, Hirschfeld wrote book after book, polemic after polemic, pamphlet after pamphlet. His total output (nearly two hundred titles) is staggering: *Natural Laws of Love* (1912), *Homosexuality in Men and Women* (1918–20), *Sexual Pathology*, three volumes (1920), *The Science of Sexology* (1920), and *Sexual Knowledge*, five volumes published from 1926 to 1930, are his major works. Most of the books were quite lengthy; for example, the second edition of *Homosexuality in Men and Women* stretches to more than one thousand pages. In addition, Hirschfeld composed scores of articles, book reviews, political pamphlets, and petitions to government agencies. He also founded the *Yearbook for Intersexual Variants*, which he edited until 1923, and was published, with a few interrup-

tions, until 1932–33. The yearbooks addressed legal, historical, medical, and anthropological aspects of homosexuality.
They presented lengthy discussions with psychiatrists who
disputed Hirschfeld's work. For a long time Hirschfeld had
believed that homosexuals formed a third sex. (He would
abandon this notion in 1910.) He considered the archetype
of the totally masculine male and the totally feminine female
as unchanging throughout history, a law of nature as firmly
rooted in reality as the laws of mathematics. He was convinced that homosexuals constituted a biologically distinct
gender—a human being between male and female. He devoted much thought to establishing fine differentiations within
this third sex. (The "third sex" thesis, however, would in-
advertently help the Nazis in their crusade against homosexuals, as will be explained below.)

Hirschfeld repeatedly tried to reform Germany's laws, particularly the notorious Paragraph 175. This national law,
enacted in 1871, stipulated that "A male who indulges in
criminally indecent activities with another male or who allows
himself to participate in such activities will be punished with
jail." That such a law should have been passed is no surprise. Legal authorities in Germany had been obsessed with
sexual practices for several centuries. In the seventeenth century, for instance, the German legalist Benedict Carpzow,
in a legal commentary of 216 pages, condemned not only
bestiality, masturbation, coprophilia, homosexuality, and intercourse with virgins, but sexual relations between Jews
and non-Jews as well. Since the Jews were not human but
animals, Carpzow reasoned, intercourse with them should
properly fall under the legal category of the crime of sodomy-
bestiality.[11]

With the rise of the nation-state, homosexuality was regarded as particularly dangerous, although, as James D. Steakley

points out in his important study on the origins of the homosexual emancipation movement, "In France, the revolutionary Constituent Assembly had enacted a penal code in 1791
that removed homosexuality from the list of punishable offenses. This action was reaffirmed in the Napoleonic
Code. . . ."[12] French thinking on this matter was to have a
liberalizing influence on several of the German states, especially Bavaria. Even Prussia was not immune. Still, Eduard
Henke, in his influential *Handbook on Penal Law and Penal
Policy* (1830), asserted that "sodomy damages the state—to
be sure indirectly, but still in a disadvantageous manner. For
it renders those individuals who practice it incapable of ful-
filling their duties as citizens for the purpose of the state. This
is due to several reasons: active sodomites waste their pro-
creative powers instead of producing future subjects for the
state. They weaken themselves through their debaucheries,
whereupon, first, they cannot serve the state properly; second,
they will finally be unable to take care of themselves and thus
become an additional financial burden to the government.
Furthermore, their bad example corrupts other citizens. The
state must vigorously oppose this vice in the interest of its
other citizens."[13]

Others found this too harsh. Carl von Westphal, for example, published in 1869 what is probably the first psychiatric
look at homosexuality. He wrote that homosexuality "occurs
more frequently than is realized," and thought it a problem
more for medicine than for the state. He sought the repeal
of Prussia's antihomosexual laws, hoping that when "the specter
of prison no longer appear[s] as a threat to the confession of
perverse inclinations, such cases will certainly come to the
attention of *doctors*—in whose area they belong—in greater
numbers."[14] His view found an echo in the work of Richard
von Krafft-Ebing, the leading psychiatrist of the late nine-

teenth century. In his book *The Deviant Sexual Male Before the Court of Justice* (1894), he concluded: "Such degenerates have no right to existence in a well-regulated bourgeois society, and they have no gift for doing so. They endanger society to a high degree and they do so as long as they live. Medical science has found no way to cure these victims of an organic disturbance. They should be put away for life; however, they should not be branded as criminals—they are unfortunates, deserving pity."[15] At least Krafft-Ebing tempered his attitude with a measure of charity. Refusing to stigmatize homosexuals as criminals was some improvement from the common practice in the seventeenth century, when Germany imprisoned convicted homosexuals with pickpockets, murderers, thieves, and the "work-shy." Indeed, over the course of many years, there had been a marked lessening of the punishment prescribed for homosexuals. In Prussia, the most homophobic of all the German states, homosexuals had risked burning at the stake until 1794, and imprisonment followed by banishment for life until 1837.[16] Later, sanctions would be relaxed even further.

But only in Bavaria and three other German states (out of twenty-five) had a truly tolerant view prevailed. In 1813, under the combined influence of the Enlightenment and the French Revolution, and upon the urging of Anselm von Feuerbach, an influential liberal jurist, Bavaria liberalized all laws concerning sex, including those penalizing homosexual acts between consenting adult males.[17] Hannover followed suit a generation later, in 1840, when it repealed its antihomosexual legislation.[18] But the old prejudices were ultimately to prove too strong. In the end, von Feuerbach recanted and reversed himself, condemning "indecencies of the coarser type, illicit licentiousness and bestiality."[19] In 1851, Prussia enacted Paragraph 143, which outlawed "unnatural sexual acts between men, and men and beasts," and promised imprisonment for up to four years for violators.[20] This law served as the legal basis for Paragraph 175, passed by the newly united Germany of 1871.

In 1898, Magnus Hirschfeld circulated a petition to abolish this law. He obtained the signatures of prominent writers, lawyers, politicians, and church dignitaries. The petition was discussed by the Reichstag and rejected. Only the Social Democratic Party, under the guidance of August Bebel, pleaded for reform.[21] Most deputies were outraged and did not hide their abhorrence. All the old arguments of the past were marshaled: homosexuality corrupts a nation; it breaks the moral fiber of the citizens; it is un-Germanic; it is connected with dangerously corrosive left-wing and Jewish elements (this from the right), or it is typical of the dissolute aristocracy and high bourgeoisie (this from the left). Above all, the spread of homosexual behavior would lead to Germany's decline, just as it had always spearheaded the ruin of great empires. Such arguments, recycled and sometimes imbued with Himmler's special brand of crackpot fanaticism, would later reappear in numerous Nazi directives.[22]

Despite the setback in 1898, Hirschfeld refused to give up. Soon afterward, he issued one of his many pleas for understanding, an appeal entitled *What People Should Know About the Third Sex*. By the outbreak of World War I, more than fifty thousand copies had been distributed. Hirschfeld's tireless efforts, while in many respects enlightened, nevertheless did much to establish the notion of homosexuals as a medically defined, vulnerable, and official minority. Like many turn-of-the-century psychiatrists, he wanted legal punishment to be replaced by treatment of patients who deserved to be pitied and helped rather than censured and ignored. He followed the conventions of his time when he sought the key to homosexuality by measuring the circumferences of male pelvises and chests in an attempt to define a physiologically recognizable "third sex." Only after the Nazis had turned his lifework into ashes did he concede that, on the one hand, he had failed to prove that homosexuals were characterized by distinct and measurable biological and physiological qualities and that, on the other hand, he had unwittingly deepened popular prejudices by endowing male homosexuals with "feminine" characteristics. This had only served to confirm the prevailing assumption that because homosexuals were "not really men," they were therefore inferior.

The notion of homosexuals as "basically different" permitted the left as well as the right to revile them whenever it was politically expedient to do so. The very word *homosexual* could be used as an epithet and a term of opprobrium. For example, Hirschfeld's main political ally, the Social Democrats, deserted him during a famous scandal that rocked Germany during the reign of Kaiser Wilhelm II. Alfred Krupp, who had refused to sign the Hirschfeld petition, was heir to the giant munitions fortune. Wealthy, right-wing, moving among the nobility, he had been caught with a few young men on the island of Capri and in a Berlin hotel. He committed suicide a week later.[23] The Social Democratic newspapers could not pass up the chance to twit the upper class, just as, years later, they could not resist exploiting the revelations about the homosexual activities of Hitler's deputy, Ernst Roehm, chief of the SA. In the Krupp affair, the party's hacks reveled in phrases like "capitalist culture in garish colors," "fateful errors of nature," "gratifications of a certain sickness." Similar phrases were served up during an even more notorious and publicized affair, that of Prince Philipp von Eulenburg and Count Kuno von Moltke, both members of the Emperor's inner circle. Hirschfeld's hopes for sexual tolerance would founder the moment accusations of homosexual conduct were used to blacken an opponent's reputation.

The rank and file of the two labor parties (Communist and Social Democratic) probably did not care one way or the other what happened to homosexuals. The leaders, however, wanted to have it both ways. Officially, they fought to overturn Paragraph 175, and when speaking before special legislative committees or in the Reichstag, they often voted for Hirschfeld's petition, which, by 1913, had been debated five times by special councils. But in the sordid world of party rivalry, the charge of homosexuality was a useful weapon.[24]

Among those who repeatedly rose to speak on Hirschfeld's behalf was August Bebel, the respected leader of the Social Democratic Party. As early as 1898, he had taken the petition to the floor of the Reichstag. He argued that because so many gays were to be found in all levels of society, the government would have to build countless new jails if the police were actually to prosecute every violation of Paragraph 175. When he encountered acute opposition from the Catholic Center Party, Bebel pointed out that thousands of people from all walks of life were probably homosexual. Should the truth of this social reality be known, he emphasized, the ensuing scandal would make the Dreyfus affair look like "kid stuff."[25] Bebel's remarks were virtually ignored by his aristocratic and middle-class fellow legislators in the Reichstag.

Like Anselm von Feuerbach before him, Bebel also favored a more conservative position. In his famous study, *Women and Socialism* (1883), Bebel sounded the by now standard view that sexual indulgence inevitably leads to impotence, spinal paralysis, and idiocy. Young men, he wrote, today age prematurely, become "roués," and demand ever new forms of titillation. True, some people are homosexuals from birth, but others indulge in it because it offers new thrills. Bebel called it "Greek love," which included "Sappho's love," prevalent among the better classes of Berlin and Paris, and among prostitutes. In a footnote added in the 1907 edition, Bebel paid tribute to the von Eulenburg–von Moltke scandal and suggested that homosexuality was more frequent among the military and the upper middle class—thus confounding his earlier view that love among men reached equally into every sector of society.[26]

The same confused mix of liberal sentiment and traditional intolerance is exemplified by Bebel's contemporary, Eduard Bernstein, the prominent theoretician and right-wing socialist, a man bitterly attacked for his revisionism. In the Social Democratic Party's theoretical magazine *Neue Zeit*, Bernstein covered the Oscar Wilde trial (1895), and later wrote a revealingly muddled commentary on homosexuals.[27] He begins by expressing his disapproval of the spirit of decadence, so apparent in Wilde's circles. He discovers in this spirit an affinity to Baudelaire and French aestheticism. Still, he repeatedly deplores those who would use the word "unnatural" (*widernatürlich*) for Wilde's activities. He pleads against punishment of people attracted by their own sex. Yet he speculates that homosexual activities probably begin when heterosexual outlets are unavailable. A few lines later he challenges the popular notion that Greece fell because of pederasty. He recognizes that throughout history the treatment of women and sexual minorities stems from the same sociocultural perception. He acknowledges that punitive proceedings against homosexual acts are carried out rarely, perhaps in only one out of a hundred cases. He approvingly quotes Richard von Krafft-Ebing to the effect that homosexuality is a sign of pathological disturbance, that it should not be punished, and that it is not always the consequence of a hedonistic, thrill-seeking life-style. What most people think about such sexual practices does not matter to Bernstein; most people are prisoners of ancient prejudice. Toward the end of the essay, he seeks a connection between the structure of society and the development of homosexuality. He writes that "as long as social conditions, which, so to speak, threaten natural sexual pleasure with punishment, as long as our entire way of life does constant injury to the requirements of health and body and spirit—then so long will abnormal sexual intercourse not cease. On the contrary, it will reveal a tendency to become the norm."[28] Therefore, he concludes, homosexuality is but a symptom of "our entire way of life." It does not arise from a lack of discipline; it is rooted in a defective society.

In Bernstein we encounter the Marxist version of the theory of "degeneracy," only the emphasis has shifted. Conservative German legislators, politicians, and clergymen had always insisted that homosexuality inevitably brought about the dissolution of marriage, the decline of morals, and the ruin of the body politic. Marxists, on the other hand, had generally regarded homosexuality as a consequence of the antisexual, repressive nature of society; homosexuals were, so to speak, not the pathogenic agents of the "fatal disease" but its victims.[29]

Marx and Engels, unfortunately, were not of much help in guiding the average socialist of the period through the thicket of these contending theories. None of their major published works addresses in a systematic manner the problem of homosexuality. Repeatedly, Marx and Engels analyzed the structure of the nuclear family and the change in the family's role brought about by capitalism. They regarded sexual phenomena only within the framework of their materialism. However, Marx and Engels express themselves quite candidly in their correspondence. There they occasionally crack jokes about "warm brothers," a derogatory German phrase for homosexuals. They entertain each other with vitriolic sketches of allies and enemies.

In 1896 a quarrel erupted at the Universal Congress of German Workers held in Eisenach. Here the Social Democratic Party was founded; its platform and bylaws were formulated. The essential features had been worked out beforehand by August Bebel. But followers of the populist leader Ferdinand Lasalle, headed by Jean-Baptiste von Schweitzer, tried to sabotage the congress. Thirty-four years before, von Schweitzer, a lawyer, had been indicted for "public indecency" with a boy and had been jailed.[30] Engels, recalling this incident, used it to make a number of acid remarks about the effeminate disciples of Lasalle who were threatening to wreck the congress. And, in a letter to Marx discussing a book by Karl Heinrich Ulrichs (1825–95), an early pioneer of homosexual emancipation, Engels wrote:

> The pederasts start counting their numbers and discover they are a powerful group in our state. The only thing missing is an organization, but it seems to exist already, though it is hidden. And since they can count on important personalities, in all old and even new parties, their victory is assured. Now the motto will be "war against the frontal orifices, peace to those behind." How lucky we are that we are both too old—otherwise we might have to submit personally to the victors. But the younger generation! Really, it can only happen in Germany, that such a no-good can transform lechery into a theory and invite us to "enter." Unfortunately, he hasn't the courage to openly confess what he is and is forced to operate in full view of the public, though not "frontally" as he once called it by mistake. But just you wait until the North German legislation has recognized the "rights of the behind," then he'll sing another tune. We poor frontal fellows with our childish passion for women, will have a bad time.[31]

Despite such bigoted witticisms in the correspondence between Engels and Marx, the Bolsheviks were to take a forthright stand in favor of homosexual rights when they took power in 1917. They quickly abolished the Czarist antihomosexual laws two months after the storming of the Winter Palace.[32] Only under Stalin in 1934 were antihomosexual laws reintroduced.[33] Until then, Communist parties hewed to the liberal Soviet stance. The German Communist Party's official position toward homosexuality was clearly summed up by one of its more prominent lawyers, Felix Halle:

> The class-conscious proletariat, uninfluenced by the ideology of property and freed from the ideology of the churches, approaches the question of sex life and also the problem of homosexuality with a lack of prejudice afforded by an understanding of the overall social structure. . . . In accordance with the scientific insights of modern times, the proletariat regards these relations as a special form of sexual gratification and demands the same freedom and restrictions for these forms of sex life as for intercourse between the sexes, i.e., protection of the sexually immature from attacks . . . control over one's own body, and finally respect for the rights of noninvolved parties.[34]

As we have seen, however, this enlightened official attitude was often considerably diluted in the party's propaganda; the Communists did not hesitate to tar their enemies with the charge of homosexuality if they thought that doing so would weaken them in the public's eyes. Ultimately the Marxist message rang loud and clear: problems of sex are secondary to the contradictions of class; they have no enduring relevance for society's workers; they will disappear come the revolution.

Before World War I the Social Democrats were the only political party willing to assist Hirschfeld in his struggle to reform Paragraph 175 and educate the German people about homosexuality. Although the party had wavered during the Krupp affair, and would betray Hirschfeld's cause during later scandals, whenever this was thought to be politically advantageous, it nevertheless backed him during the parliamentary debates over Paragraph 175, which took place until 1927–29.

▽

In 1903, after the storm over Krupp had calmed down, Hirschfeld and his Scientific-Humanitarian Committee, founded in 1897, initiated something unprecedented: they distributed 6,611 questionnaires on contemporary sex habits and attitudes to Berlin factory workers and university students. The results, published in the 1904 *Yearbook for Intersexual Variants*, surprised everybody but Hirschfeld, as he was happy to point out. On the basis of the data he had gathered, Hirschfeld concluded that 2.2 percent of Germany's males were homosexual, or about 1.2 million men.[35] (One must regard these statistics with some skepticism. Berlin had long maintained a greater degree of hospitality toward homosexuals than had most other German cities. By 1914 there were about forty gay bars in the city.[36] And the Berlin police, according to Steakley, "had a tradition of tolerance toward homosexuality which reached back to the eighteenth century."[37] Thus, there may have existed in Berlin not only a greater willingness on the part of homosexuals to profess their sexual preference openly, but also a greater proportion of the city's population may have been homosexual than that of the country as a whole.)

Hirschfeld's statistics were of no help in the Reichstag debate. In 1905 another attempt to reform Paragraph 175 was soundly beaten. Only August Bebel again dared to raise his voice in favor of total revision. Hirschfeld may have been a pioneer—after all, he probably initiated the first statistical sexual survey, nearly half a century before Kinsey—but he soon committed a political blunder. Asked to give psychiatric testimony in court during the Eulenburg proceedings, he let himself be persuaded to testify that one of the members of the Emperor's cabinet, Kuno von Moltke, was, in his professional opinion, a genuine homosexual. This mistake undid years of hard work. Prominent members of the committee deserted it, and the movement splintered.

Fortunately, Hirschfeld found some unexpected allies in the women's emancipation movement. The most active organization was the League for the Protection of Maternity and Sexual Reform, founded in 1905. Its guiding spirit was Dr. Helene Stoecker (1869–1943), an indefatigable organizer, as unswervingly optimistic as Hirschfeld, who joined Hirschfeld's committee in order to squelch attempts at making sexual relations between women a criminal offense. (The laws were never passed.) Stoecker believed, and wrote in various articles, that it was senseless to punish homosexual acts. A bond was established between the women's movement and the Scientific-Humanitarian Committee when Stoecker became one of the committee's directors. Nazi propagandists would later stress that activities for the emancipation of women and for the repeal of antihomosexual laws were part of one indivisible conspiracy. This, of course, was rubbish. What was true was the rather sudden appearance around the turn of the century of a number of independent sexual reform movements, including the movement for women's suffrage, which held its first big demonstration in Berlin in 1894. In the early twenties, a number of homosexual associations sprang up in Breslau, Frankfurt, Lübeck, and other large cities. Hirschfeld had tried unsuccessfully to unite them under one umbrella organization, but internecine squabbles made unity a mirage.

Nevertheless, cooperation among some of the movements grew over time as natural affinities came to be recognized.[38]

While Hirschfeld's Scientific-Humanitarian Committee was the largest and most influential group within the homosexual-rights movement (it had one thousand members in 1914),[39] there were others as well—for example, the Committee of the Special, founded in 1902. Headed by Benedict Friedländer and Adolf Brand, it maintained that relations between older men and younger men had contributed to the "glory of Greece"—a theory that Hirschfeld opposed.[40] Friedländer and Brand sought to refashion the image of the homosexual man as even more masculine and athletic than the heterosexual man. The ancient Greeks were cited repeatedly; it was asserted that sexual friendship between soldiers had made Sparta's armies nearly invincible. The vision of a constructive, overtly masculine society, bonded by homoerotic ties, was pursued by Hans Blüher (1888–1952) in two controversial books: *The German Youth Movement as an Erotic Phenomenon* (1912) and *The Role of Eroticism in Male Society* (1917). Blüher, originally a follower of Freud, later turned to the anti-Semitic right. He, too, ridiculed the idea of a "third sex" and adopted a contrary position. Throughout history, he wrote, the soldierly, aggressive homosexual male had fought wars, conquered nations, founded empires. Frequently he not only had a wife but kept a male lover as well. Despite Blüher's later embrace of the right, the Nazis did not hesitate to attack him vehemently, once they came to power. The *Wandervogel* movement, already riven by factionalism, was embarrassed by Blüher, and insisted that he had exaggerated the homoerotic component. In the end, the Youth Movement was first absorbed and then destroyed by Hitler Youth leaders, when its "decadent" and "elitist" homoeroticism succumbed to the "racially productive" blood-and-soil philosophy of the Nazis.

Today, Blüher's ideas may seem like pop Freudianism, spiced with homosexual imperialism and Black Forest romanticism, but to many gay Germans in the Youth Movement before World War I who felt uncomfortable at being branded as a "third sex," Blüher's views helped to impart a sense of being acceptable as men among men.

Hirschfeld's major achievement was to establish the Institute for Sexual Research, which opened its doors to the public on July 1, 1919. He amassed a unique library of twenty thousand volumes—an incomparable collection of rare anthropological, medical, legal, and social documents. He also gathered some 35,000 photographs. He employed four physicians and several assistants, and provided various research facilities. He welcomed scientists from all over the world. In addition, the attending physicians offered various kinds of sexual counseling—a practice that was considered radically reformist. His doctors also tested and treated people for venereal diseases, charging minimal fees and giving advice on abortion procedures. Eventually, Hirschfeld relinquished charge of the institute to Kurt Hiller (1885–1972), a lawyer and left-wing anti-Marxist journalist. In the 1920s a branch of the institute was set up in Amsterdam. It functioned until May 1940, when the Nazis invaded the Netherlands.

Hirschfeld's triumphant moment may have arrived in September 1921, when he organized the First Congress for Sexual Reform. Experts came from all over the world to discuss such topics as genetics, sexology, and the law. The congress was such a success that Hirschfeld was emboldened to create the World League for Sexual Reform, which at its height claimed a membership of 130,000.

Nobody has written more vividly about the institute than Christopher Isherwood, especially in his memoir *Christopher and His Kind* (1976). For a time, Isherwood lived in one of the upper rooms of the institute's buildings. Photographs in the institute's collection depicting the sexual organs of hermaphrodites shocked him, as did the drawings of one of Hirschfeld's psychotic patients, in which phalluses reigned and strange couplings took place. Isherwood reveals a more complicated reality than the one he had described earlier in *Good-bye to Berlin* (1939), in which he presented a gravely distorted vision of a city peopled by rough working men, charmed by the handsome writer from England. In 1976, Isherwood acknowledged certain brutal realities: that Hirschfeld had repeatedly been beaten up by right-wing thugs, and that he had barely escaped an assassination attempt in Vienna. What Isherwood doesn't mention is the abuse Hirschfeld suffered at the hands of the right-wing press whenever he lectured. After one physical assault, for example, a Nazi paper sneered: "It is not without charm to know that . . . Hirschfeld was so beaten that his eloquent mouth could never again be kissed by one of his disciples."[41] *Das Schwarze Korps*, the official propaganda sheet of the SS, and Hitler's personal newspaper, the *Völkischer Beobachter*, were particularly vicious. They usually varied three invectives in several combinations: Hirschfeld, the Jewish homosexual commie pervert, masquerading as a scientist, seeks only one aim—to permit homosexuality to flourish, which would mean fewer babies, and thus the German nation would be weakened.

However, neither the Nazi propaganda sheets nor the few liberal papers that took a more benevolent view of Hirschfeld had as much impact on the majority of Germans as did the mainstream yellow press. There his institute was lumped together with transvestite nightclubs, houses of prostitution, gay bars, and general rot in Berlin. The capital was Sodom anyhow, it was said; a city where bureaucrats swindled decent people out of money, a city without a soul, a city controlled by Jews and perverts. People in small provincial towns came to loathe Berlin as a center of corruption. Whatever opinions they might have held about Hirschfeld's committee weren't helped by a clumsily produced film about homosexual blackmail, *Different from the Others*, released in 1919. It starred Conrad Veidt (who became famous a year later for his portrayal of the somnambulist in *The Cabinet of Dr. Caligari*) and, in a small part, Magnus Hirschfeld. The film was banned in Munich, Stuttgart, and Vienna. In 1927 it was rereleased, but Hirschfeld's part was cut out.[42] Moreover, the problems of belonging to a "third sex" must not have seemed very compelling to the vast majority of heterosexual Germans struggling to cope with unemployment and inflation.

The film, however, was of minor importance for the homosexual-rights movement compared with the shocking murders that occurred in Hannover in 1923 and 1924, culminating in the trial of a certain Fritz Haarmann. Simply put, it was a disaster for Hirschfeld's and the committee's efforts to liberalize the law. It splintered the movement irreparably, fed every prejudice against homosexuality, and provided new fodder for conservative adversaries of legal sex reform. In addition, it pitted the Social Democrats, unwillingly, against the Communist Party. Most historians of the Weimar Republic have neglected the trial.[43] But Haarmann dominated the headlines for months, and the passions he aroused did much to weaken the struggle to abolish Paragraph 175.

The trial took place during July 1924 in Hannover, a medium-sized northern city, a place known as much for its black market as for its huge number of prostitutes and hustlers. Interestingly enough, Hannover had been the birthplace of Karl Heinrich Ulrichs, who, it will be recalled, had been among the first in the nineteenth century to urge greater tolerance toward homosexuals, writing over the course of many years a dozen books that were collectively titled *Researches on the Riddle of Love Between Men.* Until 1869, when the stringent Prussian penal code was extended, Hannover was one of the handful of German states that did not punish homosexuality.[44]

Fritz Haarmann, a homosexual small-time crook who had spent most of his life in and out of insane asylums and prisons, sold secondhand clothing and jewelry and third-rate food, mostly meat. He also acted as a police informer, which, for a time, saved him from being suspected of a series of spectacular murders. It was Haarmann's habit to pick up ("for interrogation") destitute youngsters at Hannover's railroad station or some other center of the black market. He then took them to one of his ever-changing slum apartments near the banks of the Leine River. He murdered some, but others he let go. Of those he killed, he cut off head and limbs, severed the flesh, fed it through a grinder, and sold it in small, well-wrapped packages as horsemeat. The black market absorbed all this until too many skulls and bones were found washed up on the banks of the Leine River. As more details were uncovered, it emerged that Haarmann not only carried a police badge but had founded his own phony detective agency. Haarmann, though a psychopath of low intelligence and no grasp of reality, did possess a shrewd talent for deceit, and he had actually assisted the police in solving several crimes.

He confessed readily. He did not recall details, names, faces. He remembered that sometimes, overcome by sexual rage, he bit through his victims' throats—and thus ancient tales of werewolves and vampires were thrown into the legal proceedings. Altogether, criminologists and pathologists reconstructed 147 cases of missing persons. Hirschfeld was called from Berlin as an expert witness. But he never wrote about the case. Conservative businessman Friedrich Radzuweit, head of the League for Human Rights, did. He sent a letter to the leading newspapers in which he strongly protested "the yellow press which tried to identify homosexuals with this feebleminded criminal. . . . The homosexual minority in our nation emphatically rejects these insulting remarks which equate homosexuality with criminality."[45] Haarmann admitted to 127 murders and asked to be executed. He alternated between crying and cajoling, and pleaded insanity. The court sentenced him to death.

Journalists were admonished to play everything down; the Hannover officials wanted no panic. Reporters were also encouraged not to investigate the role of the police. It was on this point that the Communists unleashed an avalanche of criticism against the hated Social Democrats. The post of police commissioner of Hannover was held by Gustav Noske, who, years before, had beaten back left-wing demonstrators by using *Reichswehr* and Free Corps troops. Officially, Gustav Noske was a Social Democrat, but he had acted with a vengeance that the radical labor rebels never forgave. He was hated as much as his superior, Karl Severing, the Prussian minister of the interior, and also a Social Democrat. Altogether, Severing and Noske had put behind bars about seven thousand workers. When the local Communist paper, the *Niedersächsische Arbeiterzeitung*, began to reveal the net of police connections Haarmann had established as a stool pigeon, its circulation jumped from 8,000 to 35,000. As soon as Noske returned from a vacation, he had the newspaper declared injurious to public safety and banned it. In Berlin, the Communist *Rote Fahne* protested "energetically the ban of the workers' newspaper. . . . It remains a scandal that the police hire such criminal stool pigeons, using them against our party. . . . It has been proven that the campaign against the Communist Party . . . has been led by stool pigeons of the

Haarmann type. . . . We demand the resignation of Police Commissioner Noske. . . . We demand the release of all victims of the Severing-Noske-Haarmann police."[46] The *Rote Fahne* then went on to speak of "Haar-men," which meant the sadistic policemen who had attacked Communist workers, and declared that "since no sane man would stoop to work for the Haarmann-Police, the system is forced to hire its tools and agents from the underworld . . . abnormal, perverted, sick people . . . the entire system is truly characterized by a mass murderer and cannibal such as Haarmann."[47] Later the Communists used expressions such as "homosexual sadists" to condemn the police, and demanded that "the police be purged of monarchist, sadist, homosexual, and fascist elements." The equation of homosexuals with criminals ran counter to the official policy of the party. But in their fervor to get even with the despised Social Democrats, the Communists did not hesitate to put the stigma of sadism, brutality, and cannibalism on all homosexuals.[48] The pitch of public hysteria mounted. Many mothers now panicked when their children did not return on time from school, which was all the more understandable because the police had begun arresting child-murderers in other cities as well. In Berlin high schools, a grim ditty made the rounds:

> *Wait with patience, little mouse,*
> *Fritz will soon come to your house,*
> *With his axe so sharp and neat,*
> *He'll make you into red chopped meat.*[49]

Hirschfeld's appearance as an expert during the Haarmann trial seems only to have deepened the public's animosity toward his committee. It infuriated the Nazis. That the main vehicles for sexual reform—the Scientific-Humanitarian Committee and the Institute for Sexual Research—were founded by Magnus Hirschfeld, a Social Democrat, a Jew, and a homosexual, and that Kurt Hiller, his administrative successor, and many other members were Jewish and liberal, made it easy for Hitler's early followers to vilify all efforts to abolish Paragraph 175. As early as 1920, Joseph Goebbels's weekly *Der Angriff* had expressed its malevolence after Hirschfeld was beaten following a lecture in Munich. The newspaper praised the students for the "sound thrashing" administered to Hirschfeld. Seven years later, Wilhelm Frick, a lawyer, later famous for drafting the anti-Jewish Nuremberg laws in 1935, denounced the Social Democrats on the floor of the Reichstag: "Your party, at its last convention, has demanded the repeal of all laws concerning adultery and homosexuality, and you seem to believe that this will contribute to a moral regeneration of the German nation. We National Socialists are convinced, on the contrary, that men practicing unnatural lechery between men must be persecuted with utmost severity. Such vices will lead to the disintegration of the German people."[50] When, in 1929, the Social Democrats and the Communists had succeeded in getting a crucial parliamentary committee to vote in favor of bringing before the Reichstag a bill to strike down Paragraph 175, Hitler's official newspaper wrote:

> We congratulate you, Mr. Hirschfeld, on the victory in committee. But don't think that we Germans will allow these laws to stand for a single day after we have come to power. . . . Among the many evil instincts that characterize the Jewish race, one that is especially pernicious has to do with sexual relationships. The Jews are forever trying to propagandize sexual relations between siblings, men and animals, and men and men. We National Socialists will soon unmask and condemn them by law. These efforts are nothing but vulgar, perverted crimes and we will punish them by banishment or hanging.[51]

Perhaps the Nazi Party's most explicit statement on homosexuality is the one it published on May 14, 1928, in response to a query about its stance toward reform of Paragraph 175. It is worth quoting in full:

> It is not necessary that you and I live, but it is necessary that the German people live. And it can only live if it can fight, for life means fighting. And it can only fight if it maintains its masculinity. It can only maintain its masculinity if it exercises discipline, especially in matters of love. Free love and deviance are undisciplined. Therefore, we reject you, as we reject anything that hurts our nation.
>
> Anyone who thinks of homosexual love is our enemy. We reject anything which emasculates our people and makes it a plaything for our enemies, for we know that life is a fight, and it is madness to think that men will ever embrace fraternally. Natural history teaches us the opposite. Might makes right. The strong will always win over the weak. Let us see to it that we once again become the strong! But this we can achieve only in one way—the German people must once again learn how to exercise discipline. We therefore reject any form of lewdness, especially homosexuality, because it robs us of our last chance to free our people from the bondage which now enslaves it.[52]

Despite these attacks, the effort to reform Paragraph 175 continued, albeit fitfully, until the end of 1929, when the Nazis gained 107 seats in the Reichstag, making parliamentary reform impossible.

On January 30, 1933, Hitler was named Chancellor of Germany. On February 23 pornography was banned along with homosexual-rights organizations.[53] As luck would have it, Hirschfeld was out of the country on a lecture trip. On March 7 the SS burst into and searched Kurt Hiller's apartment. On March 23 he was arrested and packed off to the concentration camp at Oranienburg, near Berlin. Nine months later, incredibly, he was released. He made his way first to

Prague and then to London. Hiller's arrest and incarceration was the opening salvo in the Nazi campaign to rid Germany of its homosexuals. On May 6 the full frenzy of hate was unleashed. The target: Hirschfeld's Institute of Sexual Research, condemned by the Nazis as "the international center of the white-slave trade" and "an unparalleled breeding ground of dirt and filth." A band of about one hundred young fanatics descended upon the institute, smashing everything they could lay their hands on. They confiscated more than twelve thousand books and the precious collection of photographs. Four days later, in a public ceremony, these were burned. The crowd roared approval, especially after somebody threw in a bust of Hirschfeld.[54]

By the summer of 1933, Ernst Roehm's SA goons were raiding gay bars throughout Germany. Many were closed, but others didn't shutter their doors until 1935. That was the year when the campaign against homosexuals shifted into high gear and the new Nazi laws banning such gathering places and outlawing homosexuals as "sexual vagrants" went into effect. As for Hirschfeld, he died of heart failure on May 14, 1935—his sixty-seventh birthday.

▽

After years of frustration, Nazi totalitarianism brought to the disenfranchised masses a stable, rigidly structured society and bread and circuses. Hitler's storm troopers now had their opportunity to smash their enemies: the lame, the mute, the feebleminded, the epileptic, the homosexual, the Jew, the Gypsy, the Communist. These were the scapegoats, singled out for persecution. These were the "contragenics" who were to be ruthlessly eliminated to ensure the purity of the "Aryan race." At last, shops could be looted with impunity and people could be beaten up, all in the name of the Führer's new laws.

To the rampaging fascist gangs, the Jews were money-grubbing subhumans. Many Germans knew this stereotype to be untrue. But hundreds of thousands, perhaps millions, *wanted* to believe it, or at least did not protest when the Nuremberg laws of 1935 deprived Germany's Jews of their citizenship and turned them into legal targets for persecution. Homosexuals were less easy to scapegoat and harass. Unlike the Jews, they could not be readily identified and registered—which enabled many homosexuals to "pass" undetected during the twelve years of the Third Reich.

At first the Nazi attacks against homosexuals were interpreted by many gays solely as prompted by anti-Semitism, directed at Hirschfeld and Hiller. Just as many Jews, even after the Nuremberg laws of 1935, still hoped that "things would quiet down," that Hitler would not carry out the methodical oppression he had threatened since 1925, the year *Mein Kampf* was published, most homosexuals too did not read the danger signals correctly. Perhaps some found reason for optimism in the widely known fact that one of the most influential Nazi leaders, Ernst Roehm, was himself a homosexual. Perhaps it was thought that Roehm would offer protection. If so, it was an exceedingly dangerous delusion. For it would not be long before Hitler would order Roehm's murder and the massacre of the SA's leadership. What this bloody purge meant for Germany's homosexuals needs now to be understood.

# 2

# THE
# ROEHM
# AFFAIR

"THE NIGHT OF THE LONG KNIVES"—THE popular phrase for the bloodbath that began on June 28 and lasted until July 3, 1934—saw Adolf Hitler wreck the SA militia and order the shooting of its chief, Ernst Roehm, the man who, since 1919, had been Hitler's sponsor and faithful second-in-command. Long before Hitler decided to "burn out this pestilential boil," as he later labeled the SA leadership, he had built up the SS. A black-shirted crew of tough bodyguards well experienced in street fighting, the SS, led by Heinrich Himmler and his deputy, Reinhard Heydrich, was conceived as an "elite guard" and was originally subordinate to the SA. Himmler's dislike of Roehm, his superior and a homosexual, was an open secret. While the SA had skyrocketed from 300,000 members in January 1933 to three million eleven months later, the SS, which had begun with only three hundred members in 1929, had grown to just fifty thousand by 1933.[1] Himmler's hopes for expanding the SS rested on keeping Roehm's ambitions in check. For his part, Roehm sought to replace the *Reichswehr*, or regular army, with his own SA. It was a dangerous desire. Roehm had never understood, as Hitler did, the need to avoid conflict and rivalry with the military, or any act that might provoke the army to move against the Nazi Party. Roehm didn't understand why his brown-shirted bully boys, so effective at spreading terror and intimidation when the Nazis were out of power, were now thought, after January 1933, to be an embarrassment and an obstacle. Inner-party rivalry grew more heated and bitter. Himmler, together with Heydrich and Göring, used every opportunity and means to drive a wedge between Hitler and Roehm, even going so far as to accuse Roehm, as Hitler's only serious potential rival, of planning a coup against the Führer. At long last, Hitler was forced to conclude that the SA, unruly and undisciplined, headed by a man whose objectives threatened his own, simply had to go. Operation Kolibri (German for "hummingbird") was on.

On the night of June 28, when Hitler flew to Munich, he was accompanied by his usual entourage and a small cohort of SS officers. He had alerted Adolf Wagner, the Bavarian minister of the interior, to have the local SS armed and ready. The *Reichswehr*, under the command of Colonel Werner von Fritsch, clandestinely provided arms, munitions, and transportation. Himmler, Heydrich, and Göring were put in charge of Berlin. Some weeks before, Hitler had secretly picked Roehm's successor, an obedient SA leader named Victor Lutze. The SA, Hitler would explain later, had been planning a putsch and had to be stopped by force. In fact, Hitler's overthrow was the furthest thing from Roehm's mind. Officially the SA was on vacation, dispersed all over the country. Roehm and his close followers were staying at the idyllic Pension Hanselbauer on Lake Wiessee, near Munich. A meeting between Hitler and Roehm was to take place on July 1—a last effort to iron out the problems arising from Roehm's stubborn insistence on replacing the regular army with the SA. Unaware of the web of intrigue spun by his Nazi opponents, Roehm was looking forward to a reconciliation with his old brother-in-arms.

But once Hitler arrived at the Munich "Brown House," he arrested the first two SA lieutenants he met, and ordered

Sepp Dietrich, the commander of his bodyguard regiment, to round up all the SA men he could find and take them to Stadelheim prison. Then the Führer's motorcade proceeded hurriedly to the Pension Hanselbauer in the Bavarian countryside. Without warning, the SS troopers stormed the hotel. SA Lieutenant Edmund Heines, a Nazi Party stalwart whom Hitler especially disliked, was caught in bed with his young chauffeur. When Heines protested, an SS man smashed his face. Heines was arrested on the spot, handcuffed, and, together with Roehm and five other leaders, transported to Stadelheim, now overcrowded with bruised, uncomprehending SA men. The five, including such party veterans as Hans-Peter von Heydebreck and Colonel Count Hans-Joachim von Spreti-Weilbach, Roehm's aide-de-camp, were executed the same day, together with several SA subordinates who never understood what was happening. Roehm, dazed and shaken, was left in a solitary cell.

Meanwhile, the swift purge, orchestrated by Heydrich, was taking its toll in Berlin and other German cities. About three hundred people were killed, many in no way connected with the SA but hated or feared by someone in the Nazi bureaucracy. Among them was Gregor Strasser, a veteran Nazi theoretician, suspected of leftist leanings. He was thrown in a prison cell, tortured, and then riddled with bullets. The last chancellor before Hitler assumed that office, General Kurt von Schleicher, was shot down at his home "while trying to escape arrest."

Throughout Germany, old scores were settled. For the first time the Third Reich showed its true face. In Munich, Hitler ordered the SA regulars to the "Brown House," screaming that they were all "homosexual pigs," though he well knew that only a few in Roehm's immediate entourage were homosexual. In Berlin, Göring greeted the stunned SA lieutenants with abuse, also calling them "homosexual pigs."[2]

So far, Ernst Roehm had been spared. We will never know whether Hitler was beset by any last-minute regrets about his oldest comrade. In any case, on July 1, an SS officer entered Roehm's prison cell, handed him a revolver, and said, "I'll be back in fifteen minutes. You have a choice." Roehm is supposed to have answered, "Let Adolf do it himself. I'm not going to do his job."[3] Later that same day, Roehm was finally executed by two SS hitmen, led by Theodor Eicke, later picked by Himmler to organize the proliferating concentration camps. The corpses of the Stadelheim victims were taken away in a butcher's tin-lined truck.

▽

Ernst Roehm was born in Munich on November 28, 1887, of a respected family of civil servants. Unlike other Nazi leaders, he appears to have had a peaceful childhood. In his rambling autobiography he describes his father as a "stern patriot of the old vintage," and raves about his mother, to whom he remained dedicated all his life. From the start, he wanted to be a soldier.[4]

At nineteen, Roehm gained entrance to the Tenth Regiment, named after Prince Ludwig, the Bavarian ruler. Until the end of his life he remained an admirer of all kings, especially those of the Bavarian branch. After he entered Germany's War College, he quickly rose in the ranks and was detailed to supervise the training programs for new recruits. His success was enormous. He loved turning country bumpkins into professional warriors. He also exhibited administrative abilities, becoming chairman of a committee that resolved grievances among officers. Yet his real vocation, as he insisted repeatedly, was to train "raw country youngsters."

From early on, he displayed an irreverent attitude toward those higher in rank, a trait that got him in trouble throughout his career. Later he would observe that "an intelligent, thinking subordinate is the natural enemy of his superior." Roehm often went out of his way to let his superiors know that he considered them inept. His ill-concealed contempt did not endear him to the army's high command. During his entire career Roehm battled incessantly with his higher-ups, and quickly gained a reputation for being unnecessarily abrasive.

Like many other Germans of his generation, Roehm welcomed the First World War. "With joyous pride, Germany enters the greatest war in her history," he wrote. He was never given to boasting about his career at the front, and he tended to dismiss the fact that half his nose had been shot off, leaving him scarred for life. He went back to the front until his last injury, around 1916 or 1917, made him unfit for combat. His talent for organization must have been apparent, because he won the admiration of Erich Ludendorff, the notoriously difficult administrative genius of the German army.

After the defeat in 1918, Roehm, like many other soldiers, joined one of the dozens of postwar paramilitary organizations. But, unlike others, Roehm continued to engage in secret work for the army, storing clandestine weapons at a cache in Bavaria. Still, he was drifting and he knew it. He longed to live in a truly modern state modeled after the military. Roehm was convinced that a technological monarchy was the answer to Germany's problems. He was a man in search of a king.

Roehm met his liege in 1919, when he gave a bewildered thirty-year-old veteran with an odd little mustache his first job. They had much in common. Both had been front-line fighters and both had been wounded (Hitler had been gassed). Roehm quickly became Hitler's most trusted friend. (When talking to Roehm, Hitler used the familiar form of address. Except for his chauffeurs and valets, no one else in Hitler's entourage would ever be so honored by such a gesture of intimacy—not even Martin Bormann, the "Watchdog of the Inner Chamber.") Four years after their first meeting, Roehm took part in the famous abortive Beer Hall putsch. Many of the conspirators were killed; Hitler was shot in the left arm, tried, and sentenced to one year in prison. Incarceration provided quiet and leisure. Treated more like a celebrity than a convict, Hitler began composing his political manifesto, *Mein Kampf.* Roehm, too, was briefly jailed, but the court placed him on probation.

Hitler's admiration for Roehm's organizational skills grew as Roehm built up the SA. The Führer's need for Roehm was so great that he steadily ignored every report of Roehm's homosexual activities.[5] In 1925, however, they quarreled—though not over Roehm's sexual preferences—and Roehm resigned from the SA. Roehm soon found himself embroiled in an embarrassing lawsuit against Herrmann Siegesmund, a Berlin hustler, who had somehow gotten hold of several incriminating letters. In the end, the suit was dismissed, but the damaging letters were to haunt him for the rest of his life. (In 1932 the letters were leaked to the press and proved to be a boon to his enemies within the Nazi Party. More than his homosexuality, it was Roehm's indiscretion and lack of discipline that angered many of his comrades. In a letter to Rudolf Hess, Martin Bormann wrote to express his outrage: "I have nothing against Roehm as a person. As far as I'm concerned, a man can fancy elephants in Indochina and kangaroos in Australia—I couldn't care less." But Bormann was offended by the spectacle of "the most prominent SA commander . . . slandering and denouncing people [in his letters] in this blatant manner.")[6]

In his autobiography, Roehm defended himself without apology. "Nobody can call me a puritan. . . . A so-called 'immoral' man who does something competently means more to me than a so-called 'morally' clean person who is inefficient."[7] For Roehm, a left-wing storm trooper who fought well was preferable to a fearful fascist—a sentiment he often voiced when ordering his SA subordinates to recruit among the Communists. Or, put another way, a brave homosexual was to be preferred to a cowardly heterosexual. Roehm believed that in order to be a "real fighter," a leader must remain a bachelor. His admiration for Julius Caesar, Frederick the Great, Napoleon, Prince Eugene of Saxony, and King Karl II of Sweden was unbounded: "One can barely imagine that they yielded to feminine wiles." Indeed, the last three are known to have been bisexual or homosexual. He complained vigorously about the smear campaigns against him. "It appears to me to defy all laws of common sense if the state takes it upon itself to regulate the private lives of human beings or tries to redirect these lives toward other goals." He detested the "incredible prudishness" that motivated the "guttersnipes" attacking him.[8]

Finally, Roehm left Germany and accepted a job training the Bolivian army. From La Paz, feeling banished and isolated, he poured out his heart to a gay Berlin physician and astrologer, Dr. Karl Hellmuth Heimsoth. He sorely missed Berlin's pleasures. His attempts to convert several Bolivians to his special type of eros went unrewarded, but he added in a letter to a protégé of Heimsoth's, "I will continue bravely to try and spread some culture here, probably without success."[9]

In 1929 a party squabble threatened to tear the SA apart; a rebel group under Captain Walter Stennes had started to mutiny. Stennes taunted Roehm's stalwarts at a rally, dismissing them as "sissies in frilly underwear who couldn't order their boys around." As the rebellion grew more serious, Hitler urged his old friend to return to Germany. Roehm did not hesitate to heed his Führer's call, and his armed squads quickly and ruthlessly suppressed the mutineers.[10] The "sissies," as it turned out, knew how to use their revolvers.

Roehm was made chief of the SA and went on to preside over its expansion, recruiting thousands of adoring, unsophisticated young men. He kept their loyalty until the end. According to his recollections—and even his most venomous enemies within the Nazi Party never disputed this—he never began a sexual relationship with anyone under his command. Indeed, Roehm was thirty-seven years old when he had sex with another man for the first time.[11] It must have taken a certain amount of bravado for Roehm to conduct his affairs as casually as he did. Whether this was a sign of indifference and courage or just plain foolhardiness is hard to know. What is certain is that such unabashed behavior earned him the unending hatred of Himmler and Heydrich, both still nominally under Roehm's command.

For about one year, Hitler kept faith with his second-in-command. When complaints about the blatantly open homosexual behavior of Roehm and his henchmen continued to reach him, Hitler issued an official statement: "Some people expect SA commanders . . . to take decisions on these matters, which belong purely to the private domain. I reject this presumption categorically. . . . [The SA] is not an institute for the moral education of genteel young ladies, but a formation of seasoned fighters. The sole purpose of any inquiry must be to ascertain whether or not the SA officer . . . is performing his official duties. . . . His private life cannot be an object of scrutiny unless it conflicts with basic principles of National Socialist ideology."[12]

Grateful for Hitler's support, Roehm responded by issuing an order of the day that flaunted his homosexuality and widened the gap between himself and his enemies: "I take advantage of the prevalence of these ... excrescences of prudishness ... to make it clear that the German Revolution has been won not by philistines, bigots, and sermonizers, but by revolutionary fighters. ... It is the SA's task not to keep watch on the attire, complexion, and chastity of others, but to haul Germany to its feet by dint of their free and revolutionary fighting spirit. I therefore forbid all officers and men of the SA and SS to employ their activities in this field and allow themselves to become the stooges of perverse moral aesthetes. ..."[13]

Roehm's bold declaration must have infuriated Himmler, whose loathing of homosexuals knew no bounds. But he could not act against Roehm without Hitler's permission—and that permission would not be forthcoming until the Führer was persuaded that Roehm was no longer needed. And until his 1933 takeover, Hitler had little choice but to rely upon his SA captain. Roehm's storm troopers had provided a spigot of terror that Hitler had turned on and off as the occasion demanded. The SA had cleared a path to power. By the end of 1933, Hitler had succeeded brilliantly: most important government jobs had been filled by Nazi Party members; the expulsion of non-Nazis from key positions in the judiciary, the civil service, and various bureaucracies proceeded without complication. Neither left-wing, moderate, nor conservative groups offered significant resistance. Hitler had swept everything before him. Yet some internal problems persisted. Among them, in 1934, was one that Hitler did not wish to face: what to do with Roehm and his Brown Shirts now that they were no longer needed.

To put it plainly, in 1934, this swashbuckling mercenary, father and drillmaster to his troops, straightforward and tactless, simply did not grasp Germany's political reality. Quick on the battlefield but slow in politics, Roehm never understood Hitler's renunciation of insurrection in favor of a strategy of legality to consolidate his power. Circuitous tactics in the military or political arena were beyond Roehm's imagination. Roehm was never able to understand why Hitler, now that he was chancellor, seemed so solicitous, even generous, toward the army and the *ancien regime*. For Roehm, unlike Hitler, had never learned the lesson of the failed putsch of 1923: if Nazi victory was to be achieved, it would be necessary to win the army's support, or at least its acquiescence. Hitler's embrace of the tactics of apparent accommodation, even compromise with the old order, seemed to Roehm to be a betrayal of the original ideals of the Nazi Revolution. But it was precisely these tactics that Hitler had to use to outmaneuver the barons of industry and the patricians of the army. Hitler had been elected chancellor by the slimmest of margins. Now he had to reassure the industrialists and army aristocrats that he could be trusted to pursue a course of moderation and to expel the extremists within his own party.

But Roehm kept trying to push his pet scheme: the SA must incorporate the regular army into one powerful unified force, under his command. It was, he felt, the only sure means of guaranteeing the purity of the Nazi Revolution. At first the military had welcomed Roehm, since the SA had militarized thousands of men who, because of the 1918 treaties, could not join the regular ranks. But the high command had never countenanced the possibility that a coarse homosexual Bavarian provincial should actually run the armed forces. General Walther von Brauchitsch, one of Roehm's more outspoken critics, remarked: "Re-armament is too serious and militarily important to be left to hoodlums and homosexuals like Captain Roehm."[14] But as the SA grew, Brauchitsch and other leading officers began to fear that the army might well be replaced. To General Werner von Fritsch, commander of the regular army, it was unthinkable that the ragged upstarts of the SA could be anything but subordinate to the professional military men of the *Reichswehr*. (It is one of the many ironies to be found in the Third Reich's history that von Fritsch, who conspired to smash the SA and propel Himmler's SS into power, would four years later fall victim to an SS plot in which the general's alleged homosexuality would topple him from power.)

Above all, the Führer needed a strong, devoted fighting machine. He realized that the *Reichswehr*, not the SA, was its natural nucleus. Even before the death of the aged President von Hindenburg, Hitler had made up his mind: a new war would first subdue the decadent West; then a crusade eastward would vanquish Russia and conquer Europe. To achieve these goals, Hitler had to appease the *Reichswehr* officers, to induce them into accepting him unconditionally as their leader. And thus a bargain was struck: in exchange for the destruction of Roehm and the SA, the army would swear loyalty to Hitler. This it did. Within one month after the purge, soldiers were obliged to swear personal fealty to Hitler, not to the German state. What the *Reichswehr* nobility failed to grasp was that they had made a pact with the devil. They did not foresee that "within less than ten years of Roehm's murder, the SS would have succeeded, where the SA had failed, in establishing a Party army in open rivalry with the generals' army. . . . "[15]

At the start of 1934, however, when the deal was made, the army tried to drive Hitler into speeding up the liquidation of their homosexual competitor. Hitler might have put off a decision for many weeks—he often showed a surprising and, to his staff, unnerving talent for procrastination—if events had not forced his hand. Roehm's adversaries were also manufacturing additional "events."

# The Roehm Affair

On February 28, Hitler assembled both the army high command and Roehm's executive officers. He had prepared a surprise. He announced a timetable for a new European war. Both groups were stunned. Next, Hitler laid down the law: the army was to remain the only legitimate military force. Roehm did not immediately react. Hitler then left quickly with the army high command. Afterward, Roehm exploded:

Adolf is rotten. He's betraying all of us. He only goes around with reactionaries. His old comrades aren't good enough for him. So he brings in these East Prussian generals. They're the ones he pals around with now. . . . Adolf knows perfectly well what I want. . . . Not a second pot of the Kaiser's army, made with the same old grounds. Are we a revolution or aren't we? . . . The generals are old fogies. . . . And guys like us have to cool our heels, when we're burning for action. . . . The chance to do something really new and great, something that will turn the world upside down—it's a chance in a lifetime. But Hitler keeps putting me off. . . . He wants to inherit a ready-made army all set to go. . . . He'll make it National Socialist later on, he says. But first he's turning it over to the Prussian generals. Where the hell is revolutionary spirit to come from afterwards? From a bunch of old fogies who certainly aren't going to win the new war?[16]

A shocked Victor Lutze reported the outburst to Rudolf Hess, the Führer's deputy. To make things worse, a week later Roehm gave a speech praising the valiant SA soldiers, contrasting them with the decadent bourgeoisie and its commercial values. It was an act of consummate folly. On April 20, Himmler and Heydrich were appointed heads of the Gestapo, thus giving Roehm's most implacable enemies nearly limitless powers.

On June 4, Hitler attempted to reason with Roehm. It was to be their last discussion—only Roehm did not know it. The talks lasted five hours. Later, witnesses testified that both men were exhausted and angry. On one point Roehm gave in: he agreed to send the SA on vacation in July and August. He too needed a rest; he suffered from fatigue and neuritis. Two days later his rage got the better of him and he published another reckless statement: "The SA is, and will remain, the destiny of Germany."[17]

Meanwhile, Himmler, Heydrich, and Göring were busy cooking up the "proof" that Hitler needed to make up his mind. Numerous documents containing secret SA orders to start a revolution, to march against the Führer, began to pile up in Hitler's office. Army generals found files stamped "Secret" mysteriously appearing on their desks. Inside were lists of officers to be liquidated after the new putsch had succeeded. Himmler and Heydrich had to work especially hard— even the man in the street might wonder how the SA could have prepared an uprising of such magnitude when half its ranks and almost all its leaders were on vacation.

From then on, everything conspired to drive Hitler in one direction. When visiting President Hindenburg, who clearly did not have much more time to live, Hitler met General von Blomberg of the army, who reminded him to get rid of Roehm and his ruffians. Even the fact that Hitler flew out of Berlin to attend the wedding of a minor official played into the hands of the SS. Now it could bombard the Führer by phone with faked news of streetfights, uprisings, and other ominous SA doings. On June 26, Roehm received a notice that should have put him on guard: for "behavior unworthy of an officer," he was being expelled from the prestigious Officers' League. Roehm did not let it upset his vacation plans. On June 27 or 28 he moved into the Pension Hanselbauer on Lake Wiessee and assured his staff that Hitler would hold a meeting with the SA leadership on July 1. All problems would be ironed out then.

Meanwhile, army troops in Munich went on alert; ammunition was distributed; plans were readied for occupying the railroad station where the SA leaders would arrive the next morning for the Hitler-Roehm conference. And on June 28, Hitler, surrounded by Sepp Dietrich's bodyguards, stormed into the "Brown House" and the Night of the Long Knives had begun.

▽

Roehm had made it easy for Hitler to act against him by so flagrantly flaunting his homosexuality. His unapologetic behavior had provided a convenient peg on which Hitler could hang a multitude of sins. But Roehm's sexual habits were a sideshow; they were never the real cause of his downfall. To be sure, in addition to the charge of treason, the homosexuality of some of the victims of the purge was offered as justification for their deaths. Homosexuality within the SA was used by Hitler as a ploy so that he could pose as the moral leader of the Nazi Party and the Reich. After the purge, Hitler had a directive ready:

> I expect all SA leaders to help to preserve and strengthen the SA in its capacity as a pure and cleanly institution. In particular, I should like every mother to be able to allow her son to join the SA, [Nazi] Party, and Hitler Youth without fear that he may become morally corrupted in their ranks. I therefore require all SA commanders to take the utmost pains to ensure that offenses under Paragraph 175 are met by immediate expulsion of the culprit from the SA and the Party. I want to see men as SA commanders, not ludicrous monkeys.[18]

But it was difficult to make Roehm appear as a ludicrous monkey; it was easier to make him disappear. Thus, on July 12, Roehm's name was ordered removed from those "Swords of Honor" that worthy SA men had been awarded as badges of merit. The name of the "Roehm House" was changed. All photographs of Roehm in party offices were removed and destroyed.

Neither Roehm nor his SA had ever harbored any actual plot to upstage Hitler and the army. And it was Goebbels who had suggested that Roehm had schemed to infiltrate the networks of power with his homosexual cronies. Roehm was innocent of such charges. He was a master at streetfighting, but a novice at political intrigue. The tactics of stealth were simply beyond Roehm's skills. Nevertheless, Roehm had provided as easy a target for his enemies as had Magnus Hirschfeld. He had no respect for his superiors; he was blunt and tactless when voicing his opinions; and he rarely bothered to hide his interest in muscular young men. He was the most visible homosexual in German politics, he was a Nazi, and he was doomed.

For most observers at the time, the elimination of Roehm and his SA was regarded either as an inner-party squabble, as an honest attempt by the Führer to create a morally respectable society, or as a symptom of the Nazi regime's internal weakness. Some thought that the Roehm affair meant that the Nazi Party was so riven by unrest and factionalism that it would not survive much longer. Only much later did the world realize that the true significance of the purge was the legalization of crime in the name of the state. As Karl Dietrich Bracher, one of the best-informed historians of the period, has written: "The arbitrary power of the Führer was formally turned into a principle. . . . Murder officially sanctioned and lauded became the norm for the smooth future annihilation of political enemies, Jews, and 'inferiors.' "[19] Barely two weeks after the purge, Hitler, addressing the Reichstag, declared: "If anyone reproaches me and asks why I did not resort to the regular courts of justice, then all I can say is this: In this hour I was responsible for the fate of the German people. I became the supreme judge of the German nation. . . . Everyone must know for all future time that if he raises his hand to strike the state, then certain death is his lot!"[20]

In a single blow, by eliminating Roehm and the SA, Hitler had resolved the old conflict between political and paramilitary leadership, removed a potential and embarrassing rival, gained the support of the generals, freed Himmler and the SS from their subordinate role, and bolstered his own image as a tough leader capable of imposing discipline and high moral standards on his own party. But the real meaning of the Roehm affair escaped even seasoned observers: namely, that under Hitler wholesale murder had become a permissible principle of state. This principle, embodied in the Roehm purge, was to have enormous and hideous implications for contragenics of all types—Jews, leftists, homosexuals, liberals, clergymen, Jehovah's Witnesses.

Precisely one year after the Night of the Long Knives, and shortly before the anti-Jewish laws were announced in Nuremberg, stringent new laws concerning homosexual conduct among men were promulgated. The date on which these new restrictions were made public—June 28, 1935—clearly alluded to the Roehm purge of the year before. The crusade against those dangerous contragenics, the homosexuals, was on.

3

# THE
# GRAND
# INQUISITOR

W<small>ITH</small> <small>ROEHM</small> <small>DEAD</small> <small>AND</small> <small>THE</small> <small>SA</small> <small>VAN</small>-quished, Himmler and the SS quickly emerged alongside Hitler as the true victors. Within a short time, Himmler would preside over an empire of death whose factories of mass extermination would work around the clock, turning contragenics into ash. He was now the second most powerful man in the Third Reich. And like his master, he now had the opportunity to realize his deepest obsessions. His every whim, however perverse or murderous, was regarded by his SS henchmen as law. The mammoth effort to effect Hitler's "Final Solution" for Europe's Jews would increasingly absorb his time and energy. In this, unfortunately, he was largely successful. Himmler had a special horror of homosexuals, whom he was determined to exterminate as well. In this he enjoyed only a partial success. His raging homophobia, which was responsible for a vicious campaign against Germany's homosexuals, struck fear in the hearts of hundreds of thousands of gays, and resulted in the deaths of thousands of others. In order to understand why he put such an effort into this campaign, we have to try to unravel the strands of his twisted personality.

There have always been two Himmlers: the colorless, sickly bureaucrat, hiding behind his pince-nez and his towers of alphabetized file cases, staying up late to scrutinize the family trees of prospective SS officers or the shape of "Aryan" skulls excavated in Tibet; and the ogre, the creator of the stunningly efficient Gestapo machine, the remote-control mass killer, ordering the elimination of entire populations without any visible sign of remorse. But most people who met Himmler shared the opinion of Walter Dornberger, the officer in charge of a Nazi experimental rocket base: "He looked to me like an intelligent, elementary school teacher, certainly not a man of violence. I could not for the life of me see anything outstanding or extraordinary about this middle-sized . . . man in gray SS uniform."[1]

Others, like Helmut Heiber, who collected and edited Himmler's letters, felt that "there was something threatening about his personality, something inhuman."[2] Carl J. Burckhardt, the Swiss historian and diplomat, representative of the League of Nations in Danzig, met him twice between 1937 and 1939, before most observers had any inkling of Himmler's fatal capacities. Burckhardt, an intellectual aristocrat from Basel, who seems rarely to have lost his composure, later wrote:

It has always been said that Himmler had the look of an elementary school teacher. I don't know whether one can generalize about the looks of elementary school teachers . . . one really does these people an injustice. . . . Himmler was of medium height, he had a round, pale face, a tiny, thin mouth; because of the pince-nez on his nose, his eyes looked like a caricature. . . . When he tried to imitate his master and gave his eyes a hypnotic Führer stare . . . or when, saying hello or good-bye, he attempted an expression of firm sincerity, one was tempted to think: Why all these efforts? Himmler was much more intelligent than one would conclude from his deeds and his appearance, and perhaps because of this he was essentially disloyal. . . . Nevertheless, he radiated something much more insidious than did "his Führer." Whenever I met Hitler, I always had the feeling of a certain weakness, and of being with an obsessed man. . . . Himmler didn't seem obsessed. He was sinister through the degree of concentrated subservience, through a certain narrow-minded conscientiousness, an inhuman punctiliousness about which there was something of an automaton.[3]

Himmler was obsessed, all right, but it was another type of compulsion—less visible than Hitler's, more like that of a reclusive miser constantly counting his hoard of gold. This bureaucratic side, however, was not how most of the world saw him. The world perceived Himmler as the butcher who ordered all Russian prisoners of war to be killed, and as the man who organized the destruction of European Jewry. It was Himmler's SS that set up and ran the concentration camps, beginning modestly in 1933 with a few criminals, Communists, Catholics, liberals, Socialists, Jews, and homosexuals in Dachau, and that, within ten years, had extended its network of terror over more than half of Europe. It was Himmler's "Order of the Death's Head" that supervised the gassing of inmates and the salvaging of the gold fillings in their teeth to be deposited at the federal bank in Berlin in an account credited to the fictitious "Max Heilinger."

By 1935 and 1936, when the campaign against contragenics, including homosexuals, began in earnest, Himmler's officers were legally entitled to arrest suspects on any pretext, force admission of crimes not committed, and throw the victims into camps where they were without legal recourse. Next to Reinhard Heydrich, who was assassinated in 1942, Himmler's name was the most feared throughout Germany and the occupied territories. His image was that of a monster, devoid of any shred of humanity. He did little to dispel that impression. In October 1943, for example, he told SS leaders assembled in Poznan, Poland:

What happens to the Russians, what happens to the Czechs, is a matter of utter indifference to me. . . . Whether the other peoples live in comfort or perish . . . interests me only insofar as we need them as slaves for our culture; apart from that it does not interest me. Whether or not ten thousand Russian women collapse from exhaustion while digging a tank ditch, interests me only insofar as the tank ditch is completed for Germany. . . . Most of you know what it means to see a hundred corpses lying together, five hundred, or a thousand. To have gone through this and yet, apart from a few exceptions—examples of human weakness—to have remained decent, this has made us hard. This is a glorious page in our history that has never been written.[4]

It was also at this conference that Himmler "specifically made the connection between [the Roehm purge] and the policy of annihilation and confirmed the continuity of crime as a maxim of the regime."[5]

Himmler was both too pallid and too monstrous, it appears, to captivate the curiosity of most historians. Thus, no book has been written that is equal to the many excellent biographies of Hitler. What I will attempt here is less ambitious: first, to trace Himmler's career briefly from unhappy pupil to grand inquisitor and, second, to describe his paranoid and homophobic universe of gods and devils, a universe closed to rational argument but endowed with its own peculiar logic.

▽

Heinrich Himmler was born on October 7, 1900, in Munich. His father, Gebhardt, a descendant of minor civil servants and police officers, was a pedantic, tyrannical headmaster who had met with a bit of luck: he had obtained a position as tutor to the Wittelsbach family, the rulers of Bavaria. For a while he had taught Prince Heinrich, and the prince acted as godfather to the second son, named after his father's patron. Gebhardt's first son had carried his father's name; a third son, Ernst, born five years after Heinrich's arrival, would play, so it seems, no part in the future SS leader's life. Heinrich was an ambitious, hardworking, but indifferent learner, over-awed by his stern father. He possessed average intelligence and was nearsighted, a little priggish, and unpopular in school. No matter how hard he tried, Heinrich made few friends. Poor health tormented him all his life. The outbreak of World War I filled him with patriotic ardor. He longed to emulate his older brother Gebhardt, who had joined the armed forces and become a hero. But Heinrich was too young to enlist. Still, he exulted in German victories from afar, dreamed of becoming an officer, worried about the disintegrating battle fronts, and penned a hate-poem against France.

When Heinrich graduated from high school, he was unsure of his next step. He eventually decided to pursue a career in agriculture—a step down, in his family's eyes—and found work as a trainee on a farm. An attack of typhoid fever, however, made it impossible for him to continue. He was hospitalized, enabling him to read a great deal—mostly books of the reactionary or eccentric right, which were then popular in Bavaria. Because the Imperial Navy refused men who wore glasses, he had to abandon his hopes of entering as an ensign. He then applied to the army. Although his father pulled many strings, the army, too, rejected Heinrich. He was ultimately to be accepted by a reserve unit, but did not see duty on the war front. In later years, Himmler tended to romanticize his past and regale listeners with stirring anecdotes of his "battle exploits." Finally he enrolled at the agricultural department of Munich University, where he joined several right-wing or-ganizations and a dueling fraternity. Once again, the pattern of his early school years repeated itself. Try as he might to win over his fraternity brothers by running errands, currying favor with older members, and bringing food to the sick, he remained an outsider, shunned by all. He barely managed to fulfill one ambition: when, at last, he found a dueling partner and his face was scarred, he was delighted.[6]

In August 1922, Heinrich received his diploma and took a job at a chemical factory in Schleissheim. A short time later—exactly when is not known—Himmler met Ernst Roehm, who had founded a right-wing paramilitary group named *Reichsflagge* (Federal Banner). Himmler admired the bellicose Roehm and joined up. Soon afterward he took part in the 1923 abortive overthrow of the Bavarian government, which sent Hitler and Roehm to jail. Around this time, Himmler was introduced to Gregor Strasser, an organizer of the social-revolutionary wing of the budding NSDAP, later led by Hitler. Strasser gave the eager young man a job as office worker and propaganda salesman. Himmler quit the chemical factory and began traveling on his motorbike through rural districts, pushing right-wing politics. During these months he also met and married Margarete Boden. She was a nurse seven years his senior, owner of a nursing home, and interested in some of the esoteric topics—healing herbs, spices, folk medicine—that had long intrigued Himmler.

The marriage turned sour when Himmler's party activities began to consume all of his time. He kept racing on his motorbike through Bavaria, distributing leaflets, addressing farmers' meetings, and rarely showing up at the farm in Waltrudering, near Munich, which he had bought with his wife's money. Himmler grew increasingly radical. He embraced a gospel of hate, focusing especially on Jews, loose women, Socialists, homosexuals, Freemasons, and Communists. Himmler had always been attracted by obscure political philosophies that promised simple formulas to solve life's riddles. Now he stumbled on two thinkers from whom he borrowed most of his ideological furnishings. Walther Darré, an agricultural specialist, had founded a sect called the Artaman

League. He preached a return to "blood and soil," elevating German farmers to the saviors of Europe; big cities were moral cesspools. Darré, who in 1934 was appointed agricultural minister and later directed the Central Office for Race and Settlement, wrote on the meaning of race and the ideological significance of agriculture. In *The Peasantry as the Prime Source of the Nordic Race* (1934), Darré suggested that "Semites do not understand the pig; whereas the animal occupies the first place in the cult of the Nordic people." In this and other studies he solved the mystery of the origins of all worthwhile events throughout history: they had been carried out only by men of the Nordic race.

Himmler combined these startling revelations with the concepts of Alfred Rosenberg, the Nazis' in-house theoretician. Rosenberg insisted that the vast plains in the East needed to be taken away from the subhuman Slavs and repopulated with Germanic farmer-worker-warriors. His main work of banal bunk, *The Myth of the Twentieth Century*, was considered unreadable even by ardent Hitlerites, but Himmler didn't let that deter him from gleaning what he needed to complete his vision.[7]

Strasser could not be bothered with such mystical nonsense, but Himmler believed it, and later acted on it. That he was able to make even a tenth of his fantasies come true, and to organize the wholesale killing of contragenics, has to do with historical accident and the madness of his character. Throughout his life Himmler had obediently served his superiors, particularly his later master, Adolf Hitler; he got much of what he wanted by subterfuge.[8] Himmler developed a feverish industriousness, an insatiable appetite for snooping, filing, and cataloguing dossiers not only on real and potential enemies, but also on his comrades. Hitler, whose own bookkeeping was often slack, recognized Himmler's special gifts. On January 6, 1929, Hitler rewarded him with the title of

Reichsführer SS, although the SS was then a small group of men, nominally under the command of Roehm. Himmler's zeal paid off. The ranks of the SS began to fill. Himmler carefully guided its growth; he set strict standards for candidates, such as requiring future SS bridegrooms to trace their ancestry back to the eighteenth century. All data, including the genealogy of the bride's and groom's grandmothers, had to be kept in a "clan book." For those who passed muster, Himmler and Heydrich—with whom he had become associated in 1931—built an elite training academy in the Bavarian spa of Toelz. Heydrich also talked Himmler into setting up his own intelligence network, the SD (*Sicherheitsdienst*), which was designed to spy on rival factions. Himmler and Heydrich pioneered a documentation system that soon expanded to unprecedented proportions. Any seemingly meaningless fact about the opinion or private life of anyone, whether he was working for, against, or outside the Nazi Party, was noted on color-coded file slips. Any information that one day might be used as a weapon against the person was marked down. Extra attention was given to prominent personalities in all fields. The sexual orientation of males was carefully noted. When, in 1935, the new anti-homosexual laws were put into effect, Himmler's archives were bulging with the names of thousands of "sociosexual saboteurs."

In March 1933, Himmler opened the first concentration camp at Dachau, near Munich, built to house five thousand prisoners. This penal colony—the model for all later camps—was run by a volunteer formation of the SS, called the Order of the Death's Head, which boasted a skull and crossbones on its black uniforms and caps. Himmler put in charge an old associate, Theodor Eicke, one of the two men who would later shoot Roehm. Among Eicke's assistants was an Austrian named Adolf Eichmann; another, Rudolf Hoess, would go on to become the commandant who organized the gassings in Auschwitz-Birkenau.[9]

In 1934, Himmler, as we have seen, helped to engineer the murder of Roehm, his chief competitor. A year later the SS directorates extended Paragraph 175. SS judges used the law to define as criminal even compromising letters between males, and mutual masturbation.

On June 17, 1936, Himmler was appointed chief of all SS and police forces; three months later he established the Federal Security Office for Combating Abortion and Homosexuality. In October 1938 he added another title, Federal Commissioner for the Strengthening of Germanism (*Reichskommissar für die Festigung Deutschen Volkstums*). Years later he became Minister of the Interior and Chief Minister of Prussia. This was followed in February 1944 by the takeover of both the SD, whose chief had been killed two years before, and the counterespionage operation of Admiral Wilhelm Canaris, after his dismissal. When, in July 1944, army officers failed to kill Hitler, Himmler directed the rounding up and execution of all possible conspirators. In 1945 his adolescent wish came true: he received permission to lead two regular army units—a disaster so unparalleled that he gladly handed the command over to General Heinz Guderian and retreated to a sanatorium. Himmler committed suicide on May 23, 1945, after the British troops that had captured him failed to discover a cyanide capsule he kept hidden in a tooth.

▽

The major campaign against Germany's homosexuals, which began after the Roehm purge, lasted until about 1939 or 1940, when most German men joined the armed forces. Because Himmler's Gestapo agents had no jurisdiction over the military, it offered a relatively safe refuge for most homosexuals of military age. The "ideas" that prompted Himmler to

"purify" the German people and to regulate their sexual behavior deserve examination. His worldview was endowed
with its own special logic that often found expression in his
youthful notebooks and diaries, and later in his public and
secret speeches. Himmler never followed any specific structure of thought; he simply rambled from one notion to another. He was as obsessive and illogical in private as he was
in public. His utterances, like his scattered writings, are a
jumbled but illuminating guide to the fevered fantasies that
fueled his hatreds and his hopes.

The development of Himmler's ideas, as reconstructed from
twenty-six loose-leaf notebooks kept when he was a teenager,
lay bare, on the one hand, the gradual radicalization of a
vaguely conservative adolescent and, on the other hand, a
mind-set that remained remarkably unchanged. He apparently had always borne a deep loathing for "alien" and "hostile" people, and a conviction that they should be removed.
His musings on the methods of their destruction reveal a
streak of sadism, though without any obvious sexual aspect.
Heinrich had slowly abandoned his parents' staid middle-
class standards. His readings demonstrate that he increasingly
favored books by right-wing prophets and eccentric historians
such as Houston Stewart Chamberlain, Darré, and Rosenberg. His early notes on women and both hetero- and homosexual behavior display a bent toward prudishness. At first,
religion presented a tougher problem than did politics and
sex. Both of his parents were strict Catholics; Sunday at-
tendance at church was part of the ironclad schedule that
Gebhardt imposed on his three sons. Later, when Himmler
began to persecute the Church, he never tried to turn his
mother away from her faith. Anna Himmler remained a regular churchgoer long after her son had put the Catholic Church
on his list of enemies.

What Himmler confided to his notebooks appears at first

glance drab, monotonous, and not much different from what many young Bavarians of the period would have jotted down. Nevertheless, the volcano of repressed revolt can occasionally be sensed simmering beneath the dull surface. His father had instilled in his son a respect for authority, a worship of the military, a disdain for the Weimar Republic, and—this his son does not put on paper—a pronounced fear of paternal tyranny.

Not only did Heinrich suffer from this overpowering figure who was a double authority—both father and school principal—but he also had to contend with his older brother, who was his father's favorite. His mother preferred Heinrich and tried her best never to loosen her hold on him. The junior Gebhardt outdid his younger brother in precisely those areas in which Heinrich wanted to shine—athletics and personal relationships. The diaries make plain the laborious strivings of a frightened egotist to be financially independent, to be popular, and, above all, to become a star sportsman. He failed in all three endeavors.

That his strategies to be financially independent came to nothing occurred through no fault of his own. The devastating inflation of the 1920s wiped out the middle-class Himmlers. Heinrich constantly had to beg for money. A different picture emerges, however, when we scrutinize his attempts to be a well-liked companion or to be accepted into a dueling fraternity. Whenever it appears that he had made friends, whether on the farm or at the university, he invariably reports that these companions failed him, turned their backs on him, were unworthy, talked dirty, or associated with dubious characters. These "friends" included girls. But Himmler despised "easy women," although he admits to feeling definite sexual urges—which, however, he was constrained to suppress.

What seems to have hurt Heinrich most, what elicits the most violent self-castigations, is his failure as an athlete. George W. F. Hallgarten, a classmate of Himmler's, later recalled that when Heinrich was to perform at the horizontal bar, he faltered. He could neither execute the prescribed rotations nor dismount. As his classmates shouted with glee, "he threw them a look, an expression of hatred on his face that boded no good."[10] Some years later, around 1922, their paths crossed again, when Hallgarten was elected president of the German Student Council. A jealous Himmler called him a "Jew louse." Himmler resented Hallgarten's superior social and economic station. Hallgarten's father was a wealthy, cosmopolitan, American-born German-Jewish banker who had bought a house in Munich's best neighborhood. The Hallgartens had remained "burgher aristocrats" while the Himmlers, once at the edge of the nobility, had been reduced to impoverished near-proletarians. "Out of the urge to restore the disturbed old order, Himmler created a theory of a superior race, which automatically makes him a superior member," Hallgarten later mused in his memoirs.[11] To make things worse for Heinrich, there was an upper-class clique in his school that kept strictly to itself. In the high school yearbook of 1918, which put "Himmler, Heinrich," after "Hallgarten, George," a circle of smart-looking men called "Pages" were prominently featured, distributed over different classes. These boys, youngsters from noble families, were deputized to fill various jobs in the royal Wittelsbach household. Their uniforms were narrow-legged dark trousers, dark-blue jackets buttoned at the neck, and dark-blue visored military caps. Hallgarten believed that their outfits later inspired the SS uniforms.[12] Pages enjoyed privileges denied to the other pupils: mainly, they could not be forced to repeat a class. They were sacrosanct, beyond the grasp of even Heinrich's father, the school principal. Heinrich envied them so much that he plotted to join them by using his father's Wittelsbach contacts. He was not accepted. For Hallgarten, the memory of this failure suggested another reason why Himmler, weak, nearsighted, unathletic, and utterly inept at friendship, drove so relentlessly to turn himself into the prince of a newly minted aristocracy. The SS was to be a new elite, out to conquer what the old, established Bavarian nobility had so obstinately denied him.

Perhaps, as the historian Bradley F. Smith has observed, young Heinrich's frantic maneuvers to belong to a group more powerful than the one into which he had been born explains much of Himmler's behavior. Perhaps Himmler's loathing of homosexuals had some of its roots in a deep belief that they were endowed with certain superior qualities denied to him; he often credited homosexuals with an uncanny gift for recognizing one another.[13]

Himmler worshipped authority. In one of his secret speeches, given before an audience of cadets four days after the attempted assassination of Hitler on July 20, 1944, Himmler likened schoolmasters to military officers and sovereign states. They must be obeyed under all circumstances. Neither a student nor an ordinary private can be allowed to criticize a superior. "Teachers are officers, too, and they are like gods or at least demigods and must be treated accordingly. This is the base on which our state rests. Both must be granted absolute authority."[14] Did anyone in the audience recognize that Himmler had given away more than he intended? Even then, less than a year before his suicide, he still felt compelled to square accounts with those who had rejected him: the nobles, the fraternity brothers who had remained aloof, the royal stewards who could defy his father and did not allow him to enter their magic circle.

Himmler's need to exalt authority was matched by his extraordinary meekness when in its presence. Often, for example, when he had to endure Hitler's wrath, Himmler would develop stomach cramps; but he never talked back to the Führer. His teenage diaries record no direct outbursts against his father, either, even during later years, when Gebhardt no longer checked the entries. Yet behind Heinrich's docile front, anger glowed, and the anger spawned a fierce meddlesomeness.

In 1922, when Gebhardt Himmler, Jr., was engaged to Paula, a distant relative, he wrote to his younger brother asking him to clear up a misunderstanding. He suspected Paula of infidelity. Heinrich agreed to do the favor. Paula apologized and pledged loyalty. Nevertheless, Heinrich dispatched an acid note, saying that this was not enough, that she must totally reform and control herself "with barbaric strength." Once more, Paula answered in a conciliatory tone. This did not pacify Heinrich. When rumors about Paula's behavior reached him a few months later, he resumed his attack. He badgered his mother and father to break off the engagement, and to return the presents. Paula told Gebhardt that he was being bullied by Heinrich, but Gebhardt was helpless. Heinrich then hired a private detective to watch Paula and pass on any compromising information. Nothing was found. When he heard that Paula had been talking about the Himmler family, he wrote a mutual friend that although he was usually nice, "I will be completely different if anyone forces me to it. Then I will not be stopped by any sense of false pity until the opponent is socially and morally ousted from the ranks of society."[15]

Here speaks the later grand inquisitor who never showed any "false pity." Even at twenty-three, he plotted by stealth and employed a detective to dig up incriminating evidence. Here is the Himmler whose favorite activity during his student years was "studying files." If the writings of young Heinrich often sound drab and repetitious, it is because they are so much concerned with trivia. His mania for putting everything down, for getting hold of the tiniest details, rarely subsides. In 1911, for example, whenever he took a dip in a nearby lake, he would be careful to write in his notebook: first swim; second swim; third swim, etc. Grand total: 37 swims. In June 1921, he kept a journal of expenses:

Carry over: 249 marks
June 10:
    map, 1.00 mark
    stamps, 1.20 marks
    cigarettes, 1.00 mark
June 19:
    trip to Tittmoning, 5.00 marks
    beer and sausage, 8.00 marks
    stamps and postcards, 1.80 marks[16]

As a boy, Himmler had indulged in the game of watching trains, recording every delay. He had to fit everything in its exact nook and "his pedantry went beyond absurdity."[17] As SS chief, he would keep track of every gift he had given away and how much it was worth.[18]

Perhaps the crowning achievement of his filomania was an invention he engineered with the help of Heydrich and two SS assistants. They constructed a rotating file-card box. In the early 1930s the machine was considered a miracle by the few who were allowed a glimpse of it. The giant enclosed wheel, containing thousands of index cards, was powered by an electric motor; at the touch of a few buttons, the desired card would rotate into view.[19] The dossier collection was started by Heydrich after the Roehm purge. It contained notations on all suspected enemies. No other security organization in Europe at the time, and for years to come, had a system that could compete with this monster roulette wheel.

The meticulous chronicler of his expenses for beer and sausage clearly anticipates the insatiable collector of suspects he was to become. Himmler was what Freudians would call a hoarder, and his subsequent unrivaled powers as police chief, as head statistician, and as headhunter gave him a chance to bury himself under a mountain of police blotters. Although he nourished his avenging fantasies even as a student, his scribblings reveal few sentiments of outright brutality. Only in October 1919, while visiting castles in Bavaria, did he confess that he "admired the spirit of honor, greatness, and strictness of the Middle Ages" and that he was fascinated by fortresses and torture chambers.[20]

▽

That Himmler's diaries shy away from sexual matters is understandable; after all, his father regularly reviewed the entries for years. Still, Heinrich's prudery emerges early, together with traces of anti-Semitism. He believed that Jews were capable of various sexual misdeeds. In several folk-rooted tracts Himmler found corroboration for his still-vague suspicions that Jews had corrupted German girls.[21] During his search for a better understanding of his sexual problems, young Heinrich came upon a book by Hans Wegener, *We Young Men: The Sexual Problems of the Educated Young Man Prior to Marriage* (Das Sexuelle Problem des Gebildeten Jungen Mannes vor der Ehe, 1919). He read it with fascination, praising it as "certainly the most beautiful book I have read on this problem."[22] Wegener strongly urged chastity before marriage as a way of preventing physical and moral damage. He opposed mutual masturbation, warning that loss of semen has fatal consequences. (Himmler was to grow increasingly obsessed with this notion. Later he would read the works of Albertus Magnus, who, in the thirteenth century, had thundered against homosexual relations and the deadly effects of wasting sperm.[23] Perhaps the most fanciful expression of this preoccupation was a 1939 confidential memo to the armed forces. Wherever possible, a prostitute serving men in officially supervised brothels was to quickly preserve ejaculations in special containers so that SS sperm could be analyzed for fertility and other qualities. As one might expect, the procedures were unenforceable.[24])

Heinrich went on to read "The Priest and the Acolyte," a story ascribed to Oscar Wilde. He was shocked by its idealization of homosexuality. Some time later, Heinrich summoned up the courage to discuss sex with several of his fraternity brothers. From one of them he borrowed Blüher's *The Role of Eroticism in Male Society*. It upset him greatly, but he conceded that Blüher may well have been right about the inherent dangers of the all-male commune. "In any case, the pure physical homosexuality," he wrote, "is an error of degenerate individualism that is contrary to nature."[25]

There are a few more opinions—mostly negative—on sex and women scattered throughout the diaries, but not on homosexuality. While Himmler was to change from an admirer of chastity to a promoter of "sexual assistance" for childless women, and was to organize medically supervised bordellos for the SS and the military, his hostile attitude toward homosexuals never wavered, from the 1920 diary notations to the last directives ordering extermination.[26]

▽

An important key to his cockeyed sexual cosmology is the speech Himmler delivered on February 18, 1937, in Bad Toelz, the site of his elite SS training academy.

Germany, Himmler declared, needed a "National Sexual Budget" to make up for the loss of more than a million of its soldiers killed in World War I.[27] Germany had suffered the sharpest decline in its birthrate of all European nations, reaching an exceptional low in 1933. To be sure, the battered economy probably had been the chief cause, but there were other, less obvious and more insidious reasons for Germany's weakened condition—corruption by the Weimar Republic, for instance. Venereal diseases had spread throughout the country, especially among younger people, precisely those who could produce children. In addition, the Republic had been beset by another illness; according to statistics, there were two million homosexuals. Himmler made a quick calculation: two million men killed in the last war plus two million homosexuals equaled four million German women without husbands. That, he concluded, was a catastrophe for Germany. It was even worse than the half-million babies he estimated to have been lost through abortion. Homosexuals, Himmler emphasized, corrupted other men, making them unwilling or unable to beget children. "If this vice continues," he warned, "it will be the end of Germany."

A "good race" producing few children was destined to be extinct in two hundred years, while "nations with many children can gain supremacy and mastery of the world." Sex, therefore, was a matter of public concern, not a private affair. Ancient Germany, which had always had "masculine dominance," knew this. Germany's Teutonic forebears "knew what to do with homosexuals: they drowned them in bogs. No, it should not be called punishment. It was 'extermination of abnormal existence.'" Unfortunately, the new Germany could not apply the same technique—he did not say whether this was due to a scarcity of suitable bogs—but he would see to it that "like stinging nettles we will rip them out [the homosexuals], throw them on a heap, and burn them. Otherwise, if we continue to have this vice predominant in Germany without being able to fight it, we'll see the end of Germany, the end of the Germanic world." Further, "All homosexuals are cowards; they lie just like Jesuits. Homosexuality leads to a state of mind that doesn't know what it does." In other words, homosexuals are soft and effeminate; they are not really men; they do not fight.[28] Homosexuality is a crime against nature and must be stamped out.

The Weimar Republic was guilty of criminal laxness. During a six-week period in 1934, the Berlin police and the SS arrested more homosexuals than the Weimar police did in fifteen years. Himmler proposed that any SS man caught in unnatural carnal acts with another man should be publicly disgraced, expelled from the order, put into a camp, and "shot while trying to escape." But he only issued the pertinent "Führer's Decree Relating to Purity in the SS and Police" four years later, in 1941, when the campaign against homosexuals had already been eclipsed by the effort to destroy Europe's Jews.

A former puritan who had once advised chastity before marriage, Himmler now declared prostitutes to be necessary to prevent young men from having to "turn to homosexuals for gratification," since there were often no suitable young women of "good blood" available for marriage. Himmler was not sure what was worse: a young, healthy German male seeking sexual release by turning to a woman of impure race or giving himself to a homosexual. He then sounded the two notes of what was to be a recurring rhapsody: 1) in the old days, before industrialization, everything was much better; 2) degeneracy is not practiced by the peasantry. Blood laws were strictly enforced in the villages. Even illegitimate children were accepted.[29] Himmler strove to persuade German women that it should be a point of pride to give birth to illegitimate children, that it honored the Führer and the state, that it was old-fashioned to worry about a marriage certificate. He had founded his "Spring of Life" hostels, providing homes for unmarried mothers and their offspring, to carry this through. Himmler was not optimistic about the prospects of rehabilitating men suffering from the disease of homosexuality. Perhaps a few hustlers might be salvaged, but he was doubtful about the immoral homosexual majority. Not long after, he would come to believe that the Final Solution was as inevitable for gays as for Jews and other contragenics. He

dubbed it "delousing," a term favored by other Nazi theo-
reticians as well.[30]

Himmler next confessed certain worries about the dangers
inherent in the SS project: an all-male commune, enforcing
a strictly virile code, ran the risk of glorifying the male body
and of wanting to "masculinize" women. "It would be a
catastrophe if we foolish males wanted to make women into
logically thinking instruments." Women, by nature, could not
think like men: "if we try to masculinize them, well, there we
conjure up the danger of homosexuality." Students must be
trained not only through military drill but groomed intellectually; he vented his hatred on those writers, like Blüher, who
claimed that certain military heroes were homosexuals. He
ridiculed prissy English ladies and everyday sexual life in
America. "If a man just looks at a girl in America, he can be
forced to marry her or pay damages . . . therefore men protect
themselves in the U.S.A. by turning to homosexuals . . . women
in the U.S.A. are like battle-axes—they hack away at males."
Suddenly, although he had just said that women could not
think like men, he now blamed the Catholic Church for fur-
thering "the inferiority of women," asserting that orders such
as the Franciscans had created conspiratorial sects to keep
women out. Of course, the Franciscans had another reason.
So-called celibacy was part of the homosexual conspiracy.
Throughout history, according to Himmler, monasteries were
90- to 100-percent homosexual. In 1937, the Nazi trials of
Catholic priests, mostly for illegal transfer of money and for
same-sex indecencies, were in full swing, and Himmler hinted
that his agents were able to prove these charges beyond doubt.
(As it happened, they failed.) He then elaborated upon a
sermon he frequently had preached in speeches and memoranda to Hitler Youth leaders, "Spring of Life" administrators, and SS training officers: From early on, we must introduce
male teenagers to girls. No one must ever deride a boy who

falls in love with a young girl; he asserted that this often occurred. "An adolescent male must be encouraged to fall in love with a girl of good blood; then he will turn away from homosexuals, will not participate in juvenile orgies of a homosexual nature." Himmler deplored teenagers who ridiculed an adolescent who respected his girl, his sister, his mother. "If we don't encourage this correct heterosexual behavior, we will have sexually disturbed youngsters, not the right material for the elite SS, the new Holy Order. It is essential for a nation to guide sex in the right direction."

Although this 1937 speech was the most extensive account of Himmler's ideas about homosexuals, he addressed the issue in several other speeches and memoranda. For example, in 1939, before SS leaders in Hamburg, he ranked homosexuality as one of the four illnesses, along with flight from the countryside to cities, suicide, and the decline of the birthrate, whose symptoms must be diagnosed so that the patient—Germany—could be cured.[31] It was unpatriotic to limit the family to two children, especially if the parents were well-to-do. Abortion must be discouraged; it kills living beings and makes many women sterile. All women must cultivate "joy in begetting," and barren women must accept the fact that they need children. "Spring of Life" hostels would provide these barren women with suitable quarters and conception partners. "What we need is a new respect for the illegitimate mother who has the courage to play her natural part."

These schemes often ran into trouble, however, when Himmler sought to make them real. That his proposal for a National Sexual Budget project was unpopular can be inferred from an unofficial talk defending his "Emergency Begetting Decree" (Kinderzeugungsbefehl). On October 28, 1939, he had issued a memorandum urging every SS man to sire as many children as possible, either before going to the front or when at home on furlough.[32] This apparently aroused opposition. Himmler took great pains to justify his human-breeding project. This time he spoke only of 1.5 million homosexuals unable to help patriotic German women to conceive. Because SS losses in Poland were much heavier than anticipated, the state needed more children fathered by the elite: "If both parents are pure Aryans, illegitimate children should be accepted with as much joy as legitimate offspring." That Himmler had to go on about this for some time suggests that some of his followers were not entirely happy about his propensity to issue bedroom directives.

▽

Himmler's homophobic ravings in his secret speeches and private memoranda surfaced only in 1974.[33] But his phobias and fantasies were detailed nearly thirty years before by Dr. Felix Kersten, a Finnish physiotherapist who had served as Himmler's personal physician and confidant. Kersten played a singular part in the macabre masque of the feuding Third Reich leaders. His memoirs, published in several different editions, first in 1947, then in 1955, and again in 1957, provide an unrivaled glimpse into Himmler's universe, tinctured by paranoia, filled with unsated furor against various groups, and abounding in superstitions, archaic medical theories, and grotesque misinterpretations of history.[34] Historians now agree that Kersten's memoirs are at least as astute and reliable as those of Albert Speer.

At the start of 1939, Hitler was secretly preparing to dismember Czechoslovakia, sign a peace treaty with Stalin, and invade Poland and, later, the West. Although Himmler headed all police forces, Hitler did not always turn to him for advice. Himmler did not belong to the inner circle. Most prominent in the circle was Martin Bormann, Hitler's private secretary and closest aide, who jealously guarded access to the Führer and played everyone against everyone. From 1939 on, Himmler was not often able to talk directly with his master, a fact that he frequently lamented to Kersten.

It was around this time that Kersten was recruited into the Himmler court. He obtained a privileged position in Himmler's retinue in just a few months. His rise is easily explained. Himmler had employed a regular masseur named Julius Setkorn to lessen the recurrent and debilitating attacks of muscle spasms, stomach cramps, headaches, and insomnia that afflicted him. Setkorn's methods were a failure. Nor were the injections and narcotics prescribed by previous physicians of any help. When Kersten started his treatment, consisting of what we would now term accupressure combined with yoga relaxation techniques, Himmler immediately responded, the pain vanished, and he begged Kersten to stay on, promising whatever rewards the doctor desired. Kersten was to become much more than the simple "masseur" he has been called by those critics who later tried to discredit him.

Kersten refused payment for his services. This not only continually impressed Himmler but had the advantage of making Kersten less vulnerable to the sniping of adversaries who resented his intimate relationship with the often inaccessible Himmler. Several times, Kersten wanted to quit. But officials at the neutral Finnish embassy urged him to remain so that he could funnel valuable intelligence from the heart of the SS empire to his Finnish contacts. Kersten not only agreed to provide the intelligence, but he started a one-man campaign to rescue victims from the grasp of the Gestapo.

Kersten literally held Himmler in his hands. Only when alone with Kersten did Himmler unburden himself. The corpulent, unflappable doctor had carefully kept aloof from the endless intrigues riddling Himmler's bloodstained court. He was the only person permitted to minister to the manifold

illnesses that attacked Himmler's body with increasing ferocity as he grew ever more powerful. The Reichsführer SS,
otherwise incapable of positive emotional attachment to anyone, fastened on to Kersten and spoke of him in endearing
terms and called him the "Magic Buddha." Kersten functioned not only as a healer but as a confidant. Because he
held the key to Himmler's physical well-being, Kersten learned
to manipulate his patient in many ways. How Kersten managed this feat can be seen by a short note, dated March 31,
1942, that he sent Himmler when his father died:

> I thank you for your sympathy and the flowers which we have
> put on his grave. Although my father was very old, his death
> leaves a very deep gap in my existence, and I would like to stay
> home for at least a week. . . . At the same time . . . I want to
> express my thanks for your having answered my appeal and
> granted clemency to the seven Catholic clergymen, three nuns,
> eight Dutchmen, and four Frenchmen. . . . How my father would
> have rejoiced, had he lived to see this. When Dr. Brandt [Rudolf
> Brandt, Himmler's private secretary] telephoned me, I had just
> returned from the funeral—for the one life I had to lose you
> have granted me twenty-two lives.[35]

Himmler was apparently willing to pay his physiotherapist
with human lives instead of the money that Kersten persist-
ently refused to accept.[36] Kersten repeatedly saved people
under arrest from either execution or referral to concentration
camps. In March 1941 he quashed a project leaked to him
by Brandt. Hitler had planned to force thousands of Dutch
men and women to "resettle" in the East, as punishment for
the rebellious Dutch who did not appreciate their German
invaders and who were given to frequent and disruptive general strikes. Kersten convinced Himmler that this complex
resettlement plan would consume too much of his time and
endanger his health. Himmler, in turn, repeating his phys-

iotherapist's arguments, talked Hitler into postponing his punitive action. It was never carried out. For this act alone, the Dutch government, in 1950, made Kersten a Grand Officer of the Order of Orange-Nassau.[37] In 1943, Kersten persuaded Himmler to jettison plans to make Finland expel its Jews and join the Nazi war machine. In 1944, with the help of the Swedish Red Cross, Kersten pried loose Danish and Norwegian camp inmates and had them eventually transferred to Sweden. In 1945, with the aid of one of his sympathizers at Himmler's court, the amicable but slippery Walther Schellenberg, Kersten arranged the transfer of about 1,900 Jewish prisoners from Theresienstadt to Switzerland and facilitated the rescue of Jewish and non-Jewish inmates.[38] In 1944 and 1945 he carried off another coup. Himmler had been shown a devastating report on Hitler's health. Now Schellenberg and Kersten pushed Himmler to send out, via Sweden, feelers to the Allies about ending the war in the west. Since Himmler refused to believe that Eisenhower would never accept him as Hitler's successor, the negotiations led only to the ultimate theater of the absurd: in total secrecy, Himmler received a visitor from Stockholm, Robert Masur, a representative of the World Jewish Congress.[39] Together, Kersten and Masur extracted from Himmler the promise not to blow up the concentration camps, to increase food rations, to release sick and female prisoners through the Swedish Red Cross. Kersten and Schellenberg knew, of course, that they had gambled on Himmler's fantasy of becoming the new Führer, but their tactics succeeded in saving quite a few lives. As Kersten's memoirs reveal, he gained an unrivaled glimpse into Himmler's mind.

While laboring to ease Himmler's aches and pains, Kersten was forced to listen to his patient's interminable monologues. Himmler, forever the schoolmaster, wanted to remake and reeducate the world. He told Kersten of his plans to transform his black-shirted SS men into a new nobility, replacing the former degenerate ruling classes. He dreamed of founding an empire of Nordic worker-peasants, who, after victory, would eat no white bread, but only whole grain, and smoke no tobacco or drink alcohol.[40] He envisioned his Nordic subjects living in the large territories to the east, once the Slavic sub-humans had been either eradicated or turned into illiterate slaves.[41] They would live in thatched cottages, surrounded by imported German trees, cultivating herb and fruit gardens, and producing at least four blue-eyed, blond-haired children per couple. Himmler was sure that with proper procedures, within three generations every German would be tall, blond, and blue-eyed. His eugenic utopia would be complete.

But first he had to get rid of the princes and aristocrats of Germany and, later, of all of Europe. He detested German aris-tocrats because so many had soiled themselves by going into business and industry. Sweden would lose its monarchy; the princes of Prussia and Bavaria would be hanged, as would var-ious dukes, grand dukes, and the parents of the royal house of the Netherlands. Princes were no better than Jews, he said.[42] Goebbels was to arrange the executions in front of the Imperial Palace in Berlin, while workers watched and applauded. The more important nobles would be indicted for espionage and high treason. Others would be accused of degeneracy and sexual perversion. Both charges would be easy to prove.[43]

In a guidebook distributed for the edification of SS leaders, Himmler praised two institutions as models for educating the future elite: the Prussian military academies and the public schools of the British upper class. Just as the English often elevated sons of the lower and middle classes into the higher ranks, thus adding "good new blood" to the "thin blood" of the old dynastic families, so too should capable rank-and-file Germans have a chance to become members of his projected princely caste of SS leaders. Of course, every German peda-gogue knew that homoerotic relationships flourished among the adolescents of both establishments. Even during Himmler's childhood, thinly disguised fictional and nonfictional accounts of intense friendships and same-sex scandals in the Prussian and English schools had been published. No doubt Himmler would have dismissed them as slander, just as he refused to admit the possibility that Frederick the Great might have been attracted to men.[44]

Kersten confirmed Himmler's intoxication with these fantastic projects of human engineering when he discussed them with some of the more realistic men on Himmler's staff, such as Brandt and Schellenberg. Both men had noticed Himmler's "curious blend of cold political rationalism, German romanticism, and racial fanaticism."[45] Kersten began slowly to realize that his spasm-ridden patient saw himself as a high priest, the founder of a brotherhood that was destined to change the face of Europe forever. That brotherhood would have no place for homosexuals.

Himmler spent many hours clarifying his reasons for strict measures against homosexuals, abortion, women who refused to become pregnant, and couples with fewer than four children. After the war, all marriage laws would be revised, Himmler predicted. If, within five years of their wedding, a couple had produced no children, the union would be annulled. Himmler sketched his plans for a "Women's Academy for Wisdom and Culture," where specially chosen women would be taught to ride, to swim, to speak foreign languages, to dance, and to shoot a pistol. They must be quick-witted, graceful, and, naturally, blue-eyed and blond. The graduates of such academies, when united with his SS thoroughbreds, would create the future noble generations.[46] When Kersten pointed out that even a valiant SS fighter might prefer a more pliable wife, Himmler brushed his objection aside, although he conceded that some brunettes might become "chosen women." Himmler was never able to put this plan into action.

In one particularly revealing conversation, Himmler told Kersten of the arrest, for the second time, of a respected and promising young SS leader, a blue-eyed Nordic, perfect in every respect but for the fact that he seemed to have a fatal preference for his own sex.[47] He had been charged with "carnal copulation" with another man. After the first arrest, he had been stripped of his rank and demoted to private. What should be done, Himmler complained, with such an otherwise splendid specimen? Kersten tried to play ombudsman; homosexuality, he explained, was often a medical problem, related to glandular malfunction. This, of course, was one of the approved versions of contemporary German psychiatry. Kersten saw no reason to ruin the man's life, or why "he should repent for his disposition." Himmler erupted: "We must exterminate these people root and branch. Just think how many children will never be born because of this, and how a people can be broken in nerve and spirit when such a plague gets hold of it. When someone in the Security Services, in the SS, or in the government has homosexual tendencies, he abandons the normal order of things for the perverted world of the homosexual. We can't permit such danger to the country; the homosexual must be entirely eliminated." He recalls again the Teutonic tradition of drowning homosexuals in bogs, but adds: "These wise ancestors let the Roman homosexuals go unpunished and even encouraged them. These were clever measures that we should do well to copy. The homosexual is a traitor to his own people and must be rooted out."[48]

Himmler's approval of his ancestors' decision to allow foreign homosexuals to go unpunished, even to permit them to flourish, was significantly to shape the logic of his sexual cosmology. Himmler's belief that homosexuality among subject peoples would hasten their degeneracy, and thus their demise, had important consequences for his policies of persecution throughout the Third Reich. Among Germans, homosexuality was to be eradicated ruthlessly to ensure the "purity" of the master race; among the "inferior" peoples of the occupied territories it was to be tolerated as a tactic for weakening their "vigor." A March 1942 directive by Heydrich, then ruler of Czechoslovakia, makes this plain. Heydrich suggests that it would undermine Nazi interests to promote the vital forces of alien national groups. Therefore, non-German homosexuals were not to be punished like German homosexuals, but exiled from German territories.[49] On another occasion, Himmler extended this selective principle to the problem of abortion. Unlike German women, Dutch and Slavic women should be encouraged to have abortions.[50] Within the theozoology of the National Sexual Budget doctrine, as propounded by Himmler, this principle can be said to make sense. Thus, homosexuals were the only group of contragenics not singled out for immediate extermination in countries conquered by the Nazis; only *German* gays faced certain death when caught in the maw of the Nazi machine. The only exceptions seem to have been Alsatian and Dutch gays, whose lands were considered part of the future Greater Germany. Jews everywhere, of course, were at risk.

Kersten finally managed to talk Himmler out of shipping the incriminated SS man to a camp. Instead, Kersten arranged for the culprit to be separated from his former unit and posted to Norway. Himmler next confessed to worrying about the possibility, however remote, of homosexuals having children; perhaps "the homosexual tendency would be inherited." Perhaps it would be better to have all homosexuals castrated.[51] As their talk drew to an end, Kersten told him that the accused SS officer's hero was the homoerotically inclined Prussian King Frederick II. Himmler exploded: "[People] should bow in silence before his greatness . . . if a dozen so-called proofs were put before me, I would brush them aside . . . because my feelings tell me that the man who won for Prussia its place in the sun could not have had any of the tendencies of these homosexual weaklings."[52]

Himmler knew only gods and devils. Heroes must never be doubted. Even to suspect his Prussian idol of gay leanings was tantamount to treason. If historical research contradicted Nazi doctrine, then the research must be ignored. Himmler reminded Kersten that, for the Catholic Church, respect for ecclesiastical heroes came before all truth. Suddenly the Catholic Church, the target of a vicious campaign unleashed by Himmler a few years before, had all along known the right path.

▽

The incongruous and volatile mixture that Himmler's manifold phobias present is so hard to assay because his minor obsessions often obscure the major ones with which they are entangled. Himmler's loathing of homosexuals was only one of his hatreds. Homosexuals, Gypsies, and Jehovah's Witnesses were numerically the smallest groups slated for eventual elimination. From at least 1942 on, Himmler was kept busy carrying out Hitler's Final Solution for the Jews—a larger group than any of these three. Huge numbers of Slavs had also to be either wiped out or made into helots. These mass extermination projects were of such a scale that Himmler's personal "War to Combat Abortion and Homosexuality" was pushed to the background. His campaign against Germany's homosexuals must be understood—if it is to be understood at all—as but one part of the larger war on eugenic "inferiors."

Himmler, after one has plowed through all the copious and tedious diaries, notebooks, letters, speeches, and pronouncements, remains a man of elusive, if evident, evil. Sex, as we have seen, was for him a bundle of bizarre taboos. But we will never know the precise roots of Himmler's phobias. Such speculation is better left to the more adventurous pop psychologists. What we do know, and can more accurately assess, are the murderous policies he pursued once he had obtained power. As Reichsführer SS, Himmler considered homosexuals "as useless as hens which don't lay eggs"; they were "sociosexual propagation misfits."[53] Homosexuality was to be diagnosed as a contagious disease. The plague was highly dangerous because it affected the young, precisely the group destined to bring future soldiers into the world. Himmler was repeatedly to urge chiefs of the Hitler Youth to purge former leaders of the old Rovers youth movement, which, like Blüher before him, he judged to be strongly homoerotic. In addition, homosexuals, it was thought, felt and acted like women. Even as a teenager, Himmler had held a low opinion of women: they could not think logically, they gossiped; at best, they might be useful as "warriors on the baby front."[54] Homosexuals also were supposed to prefer passive anal intercourse. This alleged preference was, it was held, analogous to the "penis-vagina" relations of the heterosexual.[55] That the so-called passive partner then was assumed to play the part of a woman, if not become a woman, seems to have been accepted folk wisdom among the rural and lower-class men of Germany.

The supposed preference for passivity left homosexuals even more open to the charge of effeminacy. How could they be true soldiers? Those who do not fight are by definition either defectors or traitors. That Roehm had been a first-rate soldier and an efficient military organizer should have puzzled Himmler; it contradicted his thesis of gays as sissies.

The facts about homosexual behavior also did not fit into the Nazi doctrine of received truths during a case—much less momentous than that of Roehm—that came before a regional court in Darmstadt in 1940. A nineteen-year-old laborer from the nearby village of Ober-Ramstadt was sentenced to five years in jail for having violated Paragraph 175. The prosecution had indicted him on more than one hundred counts of alleged indecencies with other men; fifty-one of them were proven. The court's medical advisers explained these away as adolescent aberrations—after all, the boy was hardly a legal adult. This accounts for the surprisingly mild sentence. But the Nazi press was bewildered: homosexual debaucheries might occur among the corrupt bourgeois middle class or the contaminated street urchins of big-city slums; but that a simple day laborer had seduced so many craftsmen, laborers, and their rustic offspring, that the young men of almost an entire village had given in to unnatural carnal copulation, was incomprehensible. Perhaps the culprit had Jewish blood? Himmler's comment was simple: the facts must be wrong. "The village is unacquainted with such problems."[56]

Finally, for Himmler, homosexuals were a subdivision of criminals. What linked homosexuals to the criminal classes was "moral degeneracy." For a male to be a nonmartial type was a sign of a degenerate nature. Hitler had said to Rudolf Diels, a Gestapo official, that Greece and Rome had fallen because of their degenerate ruling classes.[57] Himmler's theozoological dogma of homosexuals as dissolute, pacifist, unathletic, and therefore subversive of military traditions, was widely accepted by his contemporaries. But few of them had the chance to turn their prejudices into state policies. Himmler did.

Himmler enlarged the scope of Nazi carnage by expanding the list of groups for whom a Final Solution had to be prepared. He developed a theory based on the fiction of "pure blood," which was endangered and had to be replenished. Contragenics would have to be done away with and a warrior people carefully bred. Thus, Himmler ordered Russian prisoner officers shot so that their skulls could be transferred to medical specialists for analysis of bone structure. Thus, at

Buchenwald concentration camp, a Danish SS doctor arranged for the castration of about a dozen homosexuals who later were injected with testosterone. The aim was to see if such measures could restore potency. Himmler, however, was unable to confront personally the consequences of his destructiveness.[58] Once, when he visited Minsk and watched the execution of a group of Jewish women, he nearly fainted.[59] He visited Auschwitz only twice. He spent his time there talking about how to improve certain technical facilities; he refused to listen to Commandant Rudolf Hoess's complaints about his bloody job.

Himmler never doubted his sexual dogma. Quite late in the war, in 1943, he badgered the German military into accepting Gestapo jurisdiction over all those indicted for such crimes as insubordination, insidious slander, homosexual indecencies, absence without leave, listening to enemy propaganda, and self-mutilation.[60] Himmler's letters, demanding punishment for homosexual activities, date as late as 1943.[61] There seems never to have been any ebbing of his homophobia. In the end, the reason why he put such extravagant effort into the crusade against such a small group as the homosexuals of Germany must remain an enigma. His rage to destroy remained unchanged. It seems to have been a fundamentally different rage from Hitler's. Himmler had never experienced the near-erotic joy of Hitler, whose speeches before shouting crowds transported him into ecstasies that, in turn, intoxicated his eager listeners. In Himmler, a core of coldness was allied with a kind of controlled frenzy. While Hitler's visions of conquest possessed a certain quasi-Napoleonic grandiloquence, Himmler's eugenic utopia remained anchored in kinky inanities. For Germany's gays, it did not matter. Himmler was their most efficient and dreaded Grand Inquisitor.

# C H A P T E R

# 4

# PERSECUTION

WHEN, ON JANUARY 30, 1933, HITLER
was appointed chancellor, triumphant Nazi troopers staged
a massive demonstration, marching with torches through the
streets of Berlin, singing songs of vengeance. Still, Hitler did
not have the majority of voters needed to win an election on
March 5. Whether the Nazis really expected a Communist
uprising or whether, as often before, they camouflaged their
own wrecking methods by ascribing them to their opponents,
luck came to their assistance. On February 27 the Reichstag,
Germany's white-columned, neoclassical parliament building, went up in flames. In no time, Hitler, Göring, and Goebbels turned up among the scorched ruins. Hitler proclaimed:
"This is a sign of Providence from above. Now nobody will
dare stand in our way when we crush the Communist menace
with an iron fist." Immediately afterward, a wave of terror
swept through Germany, the first of many. Members of opposition parties found themselves on benches in the Berlin
central police station. Similar arrests engulfed cities and villages throughout Germany. The Nazis had started to settle
accounts with their enemies. When the jails proved not to be
large enough, Himmler stepped in; within less than a month
he embarked on the construction of concentration camps,
beginning with Dachau.

Among the first to be jailed were the directors of homosexual-rights organizations, which had been proscribed just

four days before the burning of the Reichstag. Hirschfeld's Institute for Sexual Research was a prime target, as were Kurt Hiller, its chairman, Felix Halle, a legal adviser, and Max Hodann, a respected sex reformer whose books on women's rights, sexual minorities, and abortion had annoyed the Nazis for years. Hiller, Hirschfeld's successor and the most prominent member of the institute, was shipped to Oranienburg, where he was repeatedly tortured. Through sheer luck he was discharged and later published a vivid account of his experience.[1] The offices of several prominent homosexual organizations were raided during these early winter weeks of 1933. Storm troopers plundered the premises of Friedrich Radzuweit, editor of *Die Freundschaft* ("Friendship"), and took his stepson to jail. Communist and Social Democratic papers were forced to stop printing. The Nazi propagandists never tired of conjuring up the smoldering debris, the smoking woodpiles, the devastated ceilings of the Reichstag, to declare that this fire was only a beginning. The Communists, they said, had destroyed the Parliament; now they would unleash a civil war. German citizens could expect the worst. Only the strongest government measures could save the nation. The strongest measures followed soon. On March 24, the so-called Enabling Law was adopted, subtitled the Law to Remove the Stress from People and State. In reality, it did away with the constitution, removed all legal restraints, and gave total control to Hitler and his thugs. It signaled the end of the Weimar Republic and the start of totalitarianism, and it remained on the books until 1945.

The blaze that consumed the Reichstag, the later ransacking of Hirschfeld's institute, and finally the notorious bookburning of May 10, during which fanatical storm troopers destroyed the works of those who had made German culture great but were now declared to be subhumans, should have been seen as a signal to every non-Nazi that an era had abruptly come to an end, that a new dark age would follow. Shortly thereafter—and nearly a year before the Roehm purge—the Law for the Protection of Hereditary Health was enacted, a barely noticed omen of mass killings to come. Here terms such as "racially inferior offspring," "deviant psychopath," "criminally insane person," and "unneeded consumers" were first introduced. Homosexuals should especially have been on their guard; as early as the fall of 1933, some were sent to Dachau and to Fuhlsbüttel, near Hamburg.[2] Yet most gays hoped they could weather the storm. Many rushed to join the Nazi Party in the belief that they could vanish among the uniformed crowds; others hoped for the best, and although bars, cafés, and dancing places catering to homosexuals were eliminated, they tried to continue their lives as unobtrusively as possible. Gradually, many realized that their existence was threatened, and they lived in constant fear of discovery. Others joined the armed forces, over which the Gestapo was never to gain complete jurisdiction. But not until Roehm and his confederates were executed did most homosexuals believe that a country like Germany could fall back into barbarism. Now, however, there could be no mistaking the murderous intentions of the Nazis. There could be no doubt any longer that the Nazis were as violently opposed to sexual deviants as they were to such racial deviants as Jews and Gypsies.

The Ministry of Justice and the Berlin headquarters of the Gestapo soon released a deluge of regulations and memoranda designed both to regulate the sex lives of German citizens and to widen the categories of crime. On October 24, 1934, for example, Himmler's still-modest Gestapo sent a secret circular letter to police headquarters throughout Germany. They were instructed to mail in lists of all "somehow homosexually active persons." If possible, political affiliations of suspects should be noted together with information on previous police records. Especially welcome were names of politically prominent personalities.[3] From the start, alleged offenses against Paragraph 175 were used as a ruse to arrest people whose politics displeased those in power.

Charges of homosexual activities were easily concocted. The authorities could always unearth an ex-convict who could be persuaded to swear that Herr X had fondled Herr Y in a bar. One might even say that the Roehm purge belongs in this category—political assassination dressed up as anti-vice action—the only difference being that Roehm had indeed been a practicing homosexual.

Two months later, on December 20, a Law Against Insidious Slander was issued to encourage relatives and neighbors to spy on one another, and it helped to breed a new class of informers, generously rewarded by the regime. More significant were two regulations, one issued in 1934, the other in 1937. The first broadened the concept of "protective custody," permitting the Gestapo to jail for an indefinite period, and without a trial, those it distrusted. Police officials had only to sign a declaration that somebody was an enemy of the state before being allowed to take him into "protective custody." In 1937, another refinement was added. People with "well-known criminal tendencies" could be arraigned, if police officers, after observation, concluded that they were a threat to the state. Two categories of suspects needed special surveillance: persons who had been sentenced to prison but were now discharged, and "anti-community-minded" people.[4] Especially dangerous were individuals who threatened the "moral fiber" of German youths, such as homosexuals, whom the decree linked together with beggars, vagrants, prostitutes, and those who refused to engage in productive labor. Thus, an efficient machinery of repression was put into motion: first, protective custody, then preventive arrest. It amounted to the same thing. A quip about Himmler's non-Nordic features, about Goebbels's philandering, or about Göring's fantasy uniforms, overheard by a neighbor, would be a violation of the Law Against Insidious Slander.

On June 28, 1935, Paragraph 175 was revised to extend the concept of "criminally indecent activities between men." It permitted the authorities to arrest any male on the most ludicrous and transparent charges. From the beginning, courts and judges took it upon themselves to decide what, in their minds, constituted criminal indecency. This meant that previous interpretations of Paragraph 175 as outlawing only actions resembling coitus were now seen as too narrow. Mutual masturbation was declared a felony; a kiss or a touch could be interpreted as criminally indecent. The specialists in the Ministry of Justice were not satisfied until anything that could remotely be considered as sex between males was labeled a transgression.

In 1935 the courts published a landmark decision to the effect that any act was punishable as a crime "if the inborn healthy instincts of the German people demand it."[5] This meant that judges could administer justice as they believed the Führer had intended it. The long-established principle of Western law—no punishment without prior law—was effectively abolished. Gradually, Third Reich jurists constructed a system of jurisprudence that was almost totally subjective and placed the power of judgment into the hands of party-appointed functionaries.

In August 1936, Himmler was compelled to suspend his assault temporarily. During the Olympic Games in Berlin, some gay bars were permitted to reopen and the police were requested not to bother visiting foreign homosexuals. But by the fall of 1936, the campaign was renewed. On October 10, Himmler delivered one of his rare public speeches. In it he sounded many of his familiar ideological formulas. Germany was "surrounded by enemies ready to destroy this heart of Europe. . . ." He was proud to report that the state had started combating homosexuality in 1934. "As National Socialists we are not afraid to fight against this plague within our own ranks. Just as we have readopted the ancient Germanic approach to the question of marriage between alien races, so, too, in our judgment of homosexuality—a symptom of racial degeneracy destructive to our race—we have returned to the guiding Nordic principle that degenerates should be exterminated. Germany stands or falls with the purity of its race. . . ."[6]

Barely two weeks later, on October 26, the Federal Security Department for Combating Abortion and Homosexuality was established in the Berlin Gestapo headquarters. It was headed by SS Captain Joseph Meisinger, an ex-policeman from Bavaria who previously had been occupied with the distribution of confiscated Jewish properties. His zeal pleased Himmler at first, but later the SS chief had to acknowledge that Meisinger's intellectual equipment was insufficient. When, in 1938, Meisinger mismanaged the von Fritsch affair, he was transferred to Poland. There, as Gestapo supervisor, he started a reign of such brutality that even his fascist co-workers denounced him. He disappeared into Japan but was surrendered by U.S. authorities to Poland, where a Polish court had him executed in March 1947 in Warsaw.[7]

The all-encompassing control of the Nazi police directorates can only be appreciated by grasping the essence of the new jurisprudence. By 1936 the traditional, more conservative police agencies were "federalized," which meant that Himmler ruled virtually unchallenged. From 1935 and 1936 on, higher legal officers were appointed by Wilhelm Frick, the Minister of Interior. Prosecutors were granted more leeway, while defense lawyers and judges lost power. The rules of factual evidence were abolished. Sentencing depended not only on the severity of the alleged criminal act but on the "psychological type" to which the offender supposedly belonged.[8] Thus, people accused of sexual deviance had little chance of avoiding conviction by a Nazi court.

The newly devised laws also were made retroactive. A Jewish man, for example, could be jailed in 1936 for having had an affair with a non-Jewish woman in 1933, before the Nuremberg laws had established the crime of "racial defilement." The same held true for homosexual practices. In addition, illegal actions, such as the 1934 Roehm purge, were now declared to have been legal. Few members of the legal profession protested; some retired, a handful braved the storm, stayed on, and tried to soften the worst excesses of Nazi-dominated courts. Still, many lawyers surrendered to Hitler's bullying as easily as did those medical doctors who helped to organize the euthanasia programs and the medical experiments on camp inmates. The Third Reich wiped out the humanization and democratization of jurisprudence that the Enlightenment had brought to Germany.[9]

Two centuries before, King Frederick II of Prussia had abolished torture as a legal instrument for extracting confessions or the names of accomplices. Now, in every large city, people were legally tortured and executed in the cellars of Gestapo buildings. No one arrested on charges of real or trumped-up homosexual activity could count on a fair trial. If, before 1933, homosexuals had been second-class citizens, now they were slowly expatriated like the Gypsies, denaturalized like the Jews. They could be doubly scapegoated, as "incurably sick" and therefore candidates for mercy death, or as "congenitally criminal deviants," to be reeducated in camps. In December 1934 the Ministry of Justice issued new guidelines stating that homosexual offenses did not have actually to be committed to be punishable; intent was what mattered. This emphasis on intent originally had been brought to bear in various cases of Jewish men accused of having had sexual relations with non-Jewish women. Since both groups were regarded as contagious subhumans, similar strategies could be employed against them. There were, however, significant differences in their treatment, as we shall see.

In 1937 a young lawyer named Rudolf Klare wrote a book, *Homosexualität und Strafrecht*, to provide the ideological underpinnings for the war on homosexuals. With Klare's book, SS officers in charge of indoctrination could explain to the often ignorant members of the folk community how their natural, healthy instincts would be affected by sexual vagrants.

Like his superior, Himmler, Klare shared a disposition to draw fine distinctions. A chart classified same-sex felonies according to the following criteria:

- Simple contemplation of desired object (abstract coitus)
- Plain touching (which might lead to hyperesthesia, erection, ejaculation, orgasm)
- Petting, embracing, kissing of the partner with results similar to above
- Pressing of (naked) penis to any part of the partner's body, such as thigh, arm, hand, etc.
- Pressing of two bodies against one another with or without friction
- Rhythmic thrusts between knees or thighs, or in armpits
- Touching of penis by partner's tongue
- Placement of penis into partner's mouth
- Pederasty or sodomy (placement of penis in anus)[10]

This catalogue was not inclusive enough for the Nazi ideologues. Later, courts decided that a lewd glance from one man to another was sufficient grounds for prosecution.

The revision of Paragraph 175 had not banned sexual acts between women. Klare sought to correct this oversight. He pleaded to make "gross indecencies" between females as punishable as those between males. Marriage and childbearing, he wrote, were the two main pillars on which Nordic racial heritage was based. Criminal law must see to it that the folk community remained pure. Fortunately, he claimed, it was alien to the German woman to indulge in lesbian activities. On the contrary, most German women showed nothing but contempt for it. Klare admitted there were problems. Lesbians, unlike some homosexual men, had not developed theories exalting a special, same-sex society; they had produced no Hans Blüher. Moreover, women could be tender with other women without arousing undue suspicion, and it would be difficult to discover, much less prosecute, lesbian acts that were carried out in private. Klare therefore regretfully accepted the fact that, for the moment, sexual contacts between women would have to go unpunished, but he hoped this would prove only temporary.[11]

Nazi jurists ignored Klare's pleas, and Himmler seems never to have made any statements about lesbians. Nevertheless, some—albeit very few—German lesbians were caught in the machinery of the secret police. Little was known of their fate until quite recently. In 1975, Ina Kukuc published an account of how some SS officers had arrested and sentenced lesbians.[12] The one victim on whom she reports most extensively was brought to court on a charge of treason—which was almost certainly false. Helene G. from Schleswig-Holstein had been working for the counterintelligence division of the Luftwaffe and sharing her residence with another woman, a lesbian. Toward the end of 1944, a young lieutenant wanted to bed Helene's girlfriend and, when rebuffed, took his revenge. The two women were denounced and arrested. Helene, indicted for military subversion, was expelled from the air force and sent to Camp Butzow. This violated regulations because Butzow was specially designated as a penal camp for recalcitrant prisoners of war. It did not matter. She and five lesbians were thrown into an empty cell block, under the command of male constables. "These are the scum of the earth," the guards are reported to have told the French and Russian POWs. "We wouldn't fuck them with a sofa leg." The prisoners were promised a rare reward: for each woman they penetrated, they would be given a bottle of schnapps. This grotesque sport was, of course, a violation of Himmler's orders concerning the purity of the German race. POWs were to be severely punished for having had, or having tried to have, intercourse with German women. But then, the entire case, like so many others, had no legal foundation and serves only to emphasize the extent to which the SS felt itself to be free of all moral and ethical restraint. In the end, the only law that was respected was the law of the jungle.

Another example of arbitrary punishment of real or presumed lesbian relationships is to be found in the memoirs of Isa Vermehren, a German intellectual who was arrested because her brother had defected to the Allies in 1944. She was dragged through Dachau, Ravensbrück, and Buchenwald. She reports that some older inmates in Ravensbrück attacked two young girls whom they suspected of having an affair. The female block warden yelled at them that lesbian love was a crime and threatened to punish them.[13] Some instances of lesbian or crypto-lesbian relationships can also be found in Fania Fénelon's fictionalized memoir, *Playing for Time* (1977).

There also exist some interviews with lesbian survivors conducted by Ilse Kokula, a Berlin social worker and journalist.[14] The women—now in their seventies—tell of their arrest and mistreatment by Gestapo officers during the early

1940s. Several of the women were taken into custody when the SS raided a lesbian bar—again, an action illegal even within the Nazi judicial code. And here, too, the courts upheld prison sentences when not even the newly minted Nazi sex laws had been violated. Nevertheless, these instances are exceptions. Most lesbians managed to survive unscathed. Fortunately, they fell outside the universe of Himmler's sexual obsessions.

Another group that emerged untouched were some of Germany's most prominent and open homosexuals in the performing and decorative arts, who obtained the protection of high Nazi officials. The most famous example is that of the actor Gustaf Gründgens, who was much admired by Göring's actress-wife, Emmy Sonneman. Despite the fact that his homosexual affairs were as notorious as those of Roehm's, Göring appointed him director of the State Theater, and Gründgens quickly became head of theatrical life in the Third Reich. In 1936, Klaus Mann wrote the novel *Mephisto*, a bitter satire of Gründgens, who had been married to Mann's sister, Erika. He wrote the book to "analyze the abject type of treacherous intellectual who prostitutes his talent for the sake of some tawdry fame and transitory wealth."[15]

On October 29, 1937, in what appears to have been a concession to Göring's rule over the arts, Himmler advised that actors and other artists could be arrested for offenses against Paragraph 175 only with his personal consent, unless the police had caught them *in flagrante*.[16]

Still, the flood of antihomosexual injunctions kept rising. On April 4, 1938, the Berlin Gestapo issued a new directive: a man convicted of gross indecency with another man *could* be transferred directly to a camp. Then, on September 27, 1939, the Office for Combating Abortion and Homosexuality was reorganized within the Federal Security Bureau to free up more agents for the headhunts.

On July 15, 1940, Himmler added an amendment to his April 1938 directive: men arrested for homosexual activities who have seduced more than one partner *must* be transferred to a camp after they have served their prison sentences. This was the usual fate for most people caught in the Gestapo net, whether they had committed a burglary, embezzled money, or happened simply to be contragenics: after prison they would be shipped to a camp. On September 4, 1941, the Ministry of Justice published an extraordinarily vague ruling that anyone who threatened the health of the folk community must be put to death.

On November 15, 1941, Himmler issued the Führer's Decree Relating to Purity in the SS and Police. Henceforth any SS or police officer engaging in indecent behavior with another man or allowing himself to be abused by him for indecent purposes was to be condemned to death. That Himmler had to promulgate such an order suggests that, despite his vigilance, homosexuality within the elite SS had not entirely ceased; indeed, Himmler conceded at one point that he had to deal with one case a month.[17] In February 1942, the Führer's purity decree was extended to *any* male engaging in homosexual activities. Finally, on May 19, 1943, after the Russians had retaken Stalingrad, after the German forces in Africa had surrendered, Himmler advised the army and navy chiefs of staff that his bureau held jurisdiction over soldiers and sailors convicted of same-sex indecencies. This seems to have been the last ruling to make Germany *homorein* (homofree).[18] The absence of further decrees should not be taken to mean that homosexuals were now left alone; the Gestapo kept arresting suspects until the Russians had encircled Berlin.

▽

The policies of persecution carried out toward non-German homosexuals in the occupied territories differed significantly from those directed against German gays. The Aryan race was to be freed of contagion; the demise of degenerate subject peoples was to be hastened. Such was the "logic" of Himmler's sexual cosmology, as we have seen. But what guidelines were actually issued? No systematic inquiry has ever been undertaken. Such a survey is beyond the scope of this book. Still, the broad outlines can be sketched. Each country conquered by Hitler had its own unique characteristics that must be taken into account. A few nations, for example, had no laws banning sexual activities between consenting male adults. Others had vague laws that were not rigorously enforced. In some countries, such as the Netherlands, the population, from the start, battled against the invaders; labor unions organized general strikes to protest the deportation of Jews. Except for a few quislings, Dutch intellectuals and artists did not cooperate with the Nazis—nor did the Germans expect them to do so. In France, things were more complex because there were two administrative zones, one of which, officially independent under Pétain, was invaded by the Nazis in November 1942. Conditions deteriorated rapidly as the occupying forces changed from "correct" amiability to the rapacious brutality inherent in SS rule. While some of the French collaborated with the victors, assisting in the arrest and deportation of Jews and other "undesirables," others organized resistance units. Officially, French homosexuals were not arrested by the occupying powers. Prominent gay artists like Jean Cocteau and Jean Marais were left unmolested; on the other hand, in 1943, the Vichy police issued an injunction for the arrest of gays on the Riviera.[19] Only homosexuals from Alsace-Lorraine were hounded systematically at first; these provinces were to be made regular components of the future Reich. Thus, the populace had to be "purified." Young men from these provinces had to serve in the German military;

refusal risked expulsion to southern France. The people of Alsace-Lorraine were subject to all German laws, including the newly revised Paragraph 175.

In Poland, Himmler was eager not only to wipe out the Jews, but also to eliminate deviants who tried to have sex with German men. In March 1942, the Gestapo issued a detailed memorandum on the possible arrest and sentencing of Polish citizens guilty of sexual misdeeds.[20] The secret memorandum was to be mailed to eleven different directorates and directors. It sought to eliminate "crimes of abortion and sexual offenses" among Polish citizens. It is written in a twisted legalese and is so over-elaborate that one can easily get lost in the din of double-talk. The following is an accurate, if condensed, translation:

> We National Socialists are fighting abortion and homosexuality only among pure Nordics in order to strengthen German health and morals. It would defeat these aims if we would help alien groups, often antagonistic toward their German hosts, by punishing abortion and homosexual acts taking place among themselves. This would, in a way, strengthen their numbers and increase their vital powers. However, the Poles present a special problem. In the new territories we have started to administer, Polish people dwell in close proximity to us Germans. Their lives and activities cannot be seen as isolated from those of the Germans. This means that degeneracy and demoralization extant among the Poles can contaminate German nationals. Such contamination is especially frequent when it comes to homosexuality, which, as we know, "is the result of seduction." Also, men who carry out abortions, even if they are concerned only with Polish nationals, present a direct danger to German peoplehood.... Therefore we deem it necessary to proceed against homosexuals and professional, that is, paid abortionists, even if these are Poles and have sexually interacted with Poles only. However, it is not

necessary to bring to court Poles who abort Polish women or have sexual intercourse with Polish men. Rather, they must be evicted and transported to an area where their activities present no danger to Germandom.

Then, after a short subdivision on Polish women who abort or kill their children themselves—no objections are raised—follows this instruction: "Concerning those Polish for-hire abortionists and other sexual criminals who have done damage to the German people but have not been sentenced to death, reports would be forwarded to the Reich Central Security Office." Five lengthy footnotes list the many legal offices that, under certain circumstances, must be informed of this decree.

The injunction regarding the treatment of "racially inferior" homosexuals who either have sex with one another or with German males throws some light on the ideology underpinning the whole fanatic campaign. What was decisive for all occupied nations was the particular station assigned to them in the blueprint of the Nazi planners. The future status of a country in Hitler's Europe determined the destiny of its minorities. Also important was the structure of the satellite government, its attitude toward minorities such as Jews, Gypsies, and homosexuals, and its ability to negotiate with its Nazi overseers. After victory, Poland would be a slave state. Its upper classes and Jews were to be wiped out. Only peasants, granted a minimal education, would be allowed to exist in order to provide their German masters with food. Thus the Nazis did not punish Polish women who aborted their fetuses, and merely evicted male Poles who had bedded their countrymen. The rules were changed, however, if a Polish male seduced a German one. One might reasonably ask how a Slavic man, by definition inferior, could ever succeed in bewitching a truly German specimen—but, then, Himmler's reasoning was, as we have seen, full of holes. He never let the contradictions of his convictions subvert the intensity with which he held them.

The Netherlands offers a considerably different picture. Here, too, it is important to understand what part in Hitler's overall scheme was assigned to the Netherlands during the war and later, after the war was won. The answer is simple: in the future Greater Germany, Holland would be a province like Hesse or Baden; the Dutch language would be relegated to a dialect. In May 1940, when the Nazis invaded the Netherlands, the Dutch royal family fled to Britain. This, one might say, opened up a judicial gap. In neighboring Belgium, where King Leopold had chosen to remain, something odd happened. Although Belgium was ruled by a German military protectorship, Leopold's civilian bureaucracy continued to function. Although here, too, many Jews suffered deportation, Hitler's deputies never gained the sovereignty they tried to achieve. The Belgians, seemingly acquiescent, carried out a good deal of subtle sabotage. Holland was more vulnerable. Since their leaders were in exile, the Dutch had to knuckle under to the rules of the German civilian authority, headed by Arthur Seyss-Inquart, an ambitious old-time Nazi lawyer who had played a key role in making Austria a legal part of Germany. Probably that is why he was chosen to oversee another part of the future Greater Germany. Seyss-Inquart lost no time. In July 1940 he issued a decree banning "illicit sexual acts between males," which was an exact replica, translated into Dutch, of the June 1935 revisions of Germany's Paragraph 175.[21] Since 1911, Dutch law had not bothered itself about sexual acts between males, unless one of the partners was under twenty-one years of age. Moreover, a prominent Dutch jurist, Jacob Schorer, had studied under Magnus

Hirschfeld in Berlin and, in 1911, had opened branches of the Scientific-Humanitarian Committee in Amsterdam and The Hague. The committee even published two issues of a magazine about homosexual problems.[22] Seyss-Inquart's injunction, so far as is known, was the only publicly published antihomosexual regulation issued against the populace of an occupied territory. The reason was simply that, in Hitler's utopia, the Netherlands were to be an integral part of Greater Germany. Special efforts were made to induce young Dutchmen to volunteer for a Dutch SS brigade, for the German armed forces, for work in war factories. It was therefore necessary to protect them from homosexual contamination. After all, Dutchmen were thought to be "true" Nordics able to father children with Nordic women.

The new antihomosexual injunctions granted Dutch homophobes and pro-Nazis ample opportunity to denounce fellow Dutchmen and thus curry favor with the new masters. Yet, unlike the particularly vehement—and successful—persecution of the Dutch Jews, that of homosexuals ran into serious difficulties. Seyss-Inquart's deputies were not pleased with the meager results of the arrests of homosexuals carried out by the various Dutch policing units. In January 1941 a high Nazi official sent an angry letter to his Dutch counterpart: What methods, he demanded, could impel the police to more vigorously pursue these sexual vagrants who, according to a prominent Dutch psychiatrist, constituted more than 1.5 percent of the adult male population? The answer that Seyss-Inquart's assistant received must have made him rather unhappy. The Dutch official replied that in order to catch the often elusive deviants, policemen needed certain qualities, such as long experience, a flair for ferreting out crimes of a sexual nature, and a pride in their profession. Such qualities, he noted regretfully, were mostly absent in members of the Netherlands police forces.[23] In general, the Dutch had shown little sympathy for their invaders. Of course, there were Dutch Nazis, but many Dutch families hid Jews, at considerable risk to themselves. And it appears that the average Hollander had little interest in turning a homosexual countryman over to the Nazis. Dutch homosexuals "passed" relatively easily and melted into the general population. Some went underground. Among the so-called Gerrit van der Veen resistance unit in Amsterdam were some well-known gays who helped pull off a famous coup: they dynamited a key Gestapo office. No figures exist to show how many Dutch homosexuals were caught; Dutch authorities told researchers after the war that the records had not been kept. But despite a dedicated effort by Himmler's police bureaus, despite a special decree outlawing same-sex acts among Dutch adults, the Nazi crusade against the homosexuals in the Netherlands must be called a failure.

▽

How were homosexuals identified? The answer is—not easily. Unlike Jews and Gypsies, whose religious or ethnic origins were routinely noted on their birth certificates, and unlike Communists, Socialists, and Social Democrats, whose politics could be determined merely by a glance through their parties' membership rolls, gays were difficult to discover. No straightforward documents or physical identification existed for homosexuals. The single exception was the central bureau of the Berlin criminal police, which in 1897 had compiled lists of about twenty to thirty thousand homosexuals throughout Germany.[24]

The tradition of keeping track of as many potential undesirables as possible and the building up of a huge documentation system gave Himmler a head start. To this aging list were added the names obtained by the first large-scale arrests after the Roehm purge. Not only members of the SA, but civilians caught in gay bars or clubs were seized, interrogated, their names noted. The Gestapo used the same tactics it applied to all enemies of the state: pressure was put on victims to denounce others. In 1934 the arresting officers still behaved somewhat guardedly; the courts had not been beaten into total submission. Nor had the old Weimar police force been everywhere replaced by Nazi fanatics. A well-connected homosexual could sometimes still find a lawyer to obtain release from jail. However, after the revision of Paragraph 175, coercion was more openly used. Names of friends and lovers were extracted under torture, and Himmler's list grew longer. Bartenders not overly sympathetic to their gay clientele would occasionally provide names. One address book led to another, one name to the next.

Fortunately, Hirschfeld's Scientific-Humanitarian Committee had destroyed its membership rosters in time. But it is not known if the larger organization, the Friendship League, headed by Radzuweit, managed to get rid of its archives early enough. Some 28,000 members paid regular yearly fees to the League.[25] Their names may well have landed on the desk of Captain Meisinger. Another means of identifying suspected homosexuals lay in the confiscated subscription lists of about thirty magazines of more or less homosexual orientation then available in larger cities.[26] Although most of these were probably purchased on newsstands, some may have been obtained by subscription. By 1938 and 1939, gay bars, clubs, and organizations had disappeared. Yet informers on all contragenics were constantly being trained. The authorities encouraged every citizen to report on all who exhibited the slightest evidence of deviance. Moreover, how was it possible for a suspect to prove that he had *not* thrown an "offensive glance" at another man? In at least one instance, a man was arrested not because he had been watching a young couple make love in a park, but because he had been seen observing the actions of the man more than those of the woman.[27] Julius Streicher, editor of *Der Stürmer*, had urged his readers to write to him about Jewish men suspected of having, or trying to establish, relations with non-Jewish women. Denunciatory letters poured in.[28] The same pattern held true for other contragenics. It was easy for anyone who wanted to get rid of a competitor to brand the rival as a homosexual. With one short anonymous note to the local Gestapo branch, the enemy of the state could be taken into protective custody or, at least, thoroughly interrogated. Later, after the war had started in earnest, the authorities divided every city into administrative blocks. Each block was supervised by a block warden, whose mission was to spy on everybody.

Still, many homosexuals managed to avoid detection by the authorities. Survival depended on either the suspension of one's sex life or its successful pursuit in furtive, secret, often anonymous encounters, conducted at considerable risk.

▽

Three special offensives were launched against homosexuals, or that used the charge of homosexuality as a pretext to rid the regime of suspected opponents. These campaigns were directed against the youth movement, the Catholic Church, and the armed forces. The first was organized by Baldur von Schirach, an aristocratic drifter, partly American by descent, who had met Hitler in the early 1920s and won his confidence. By 1931, Schirach held the reins of the Hitler Youth firmly in his hands. He was determined to dissolve the competing youth groups, to get rid of their leaders, and to push their charges into joining the Hitler Youth.

Schirach made it clear that his was a military outfit, designed to produce future, purebred National Socialist soldiers. During the Roehm purge, a number of SA youth leaders had been imprisoned, and some had been executed. Now that the SA had been morally cleansed, any suspicion that Hitler boys ever so much as looked at one another "lewdly" must be headed off. Schirach never tired of proclaiming the purity of his mini-armies. After 1933, Hitler granted him money and assistants to conscript the youngsters. Schirach gradually stormed one fortress after another; his gangs occupied the various youth orders' offices, sweeping out former key personnel. What made his task easier was the fact that the vague political concepts of most youth orders, with the exception of those of Catholic or Marxist orientation, were often close to such Nazi tenets as the worship of the farmer and the warrior, of "blood and soil," of war as ultimate sensual intoxication. Schirach's program consisted largely of strenuous military training together with interminable indoctrination classes.

Every year was given a grandiose label. Thus he dubbed 1934 the "Year of Training." He organized huge sports spectaculars, and showered medals and prizes on the winners. In addition, a teen Gestapo was established, the so-called Baby Gestapo. Selected youngsters were trained to report on cowardly behavior, lack of respect for Nazi ritual, work evaders, and homosexuals. Soon, accusations charging comrades with sexual misbehavior flooded in.

In 1941, Schirach's office issued a manual on the behavior of the young, part statistics, part indoctrinational tract, part prescription for action against violators of the sexual and behavioral code of the Hitler Youth. The need to do so suggests that not all members of the Hitler Youth were always able to conform to the code of Nordic purity and righteousness. It was entitled *Criminality and Delinquency of Youth*.

Once again, homosexuality was defined as a dangerous, contagious epidemic. The Weimar Republic was accused of standing by "while this epidemic spread everywhere, and even criminal statistics did not bother with registering it." One page illustrates the snowball effect with graphics. A photo of one "main seducer" named Hasso Engel is placed in the middle of a chart. Grouped around him are the genealogies of those whom he had seduced, those whom the seduced subsequently had seduced, and so on. Hasso was precocious: he admitted having started his activities at age eight, "a warning example of a hereditarily unsound delinquent who had helped spread this epidemic and must be viewed as a contamination risk."[29]

The book concedes that not all sexual activities between adolescents are proof of "true" or "compulsive" homosexuality. Sometimes youngsters take to mutual masturbation out of sheer curiosity. Still, it easily leads to "genuine perversion, and in the free-youth orders the leaders occupied themselves mainly with the seduction of younger males. This led their victims, as they grew older, to similar homosexual crimes. Thus, like an epidemic, these sex crimes spread further and further." It is clear that the book has borrowed from Blüher.[30] The intellectual development of the free-youth sects led logically to homosexuality. It was supplemented by the idea that " 'the Order is destiny.' It meant everything to its brother-members, including the sexual sphere. Homosexuality was part of the program. Even more, in various political and philosophical disguises it was accepted as a basic ideological creed. Thus, the unnatural became the guiding principle."

The chapter on "Homosexual Crimes of Male Juveniles" spares no effort to justify the methods used to eradicate those infected by this epidemic. Since the book was issued as a secret dossier, it candidly listed the measures to be undertaken to "combat the dangers of free-youth activities."

1. All free-youth orders and their organizations were to be exterminated, with special attention to be given to cliques.
2. Former free-youth leaders were to be expelled from the Hitler Youth. Or, as the case may be, they were not to be accepted as members.
3. All former ideologies connected with the free-youth movement were to be suppressed. All formerly accepted principles concerning leadership, organization, and education were to be prohibited.

If, despite all precautions, some former free-youth leaders had succeeded in joining the Hitler Youth, the book recommended that wherever the commanding officers of the Hitler Youth had not hit on plausible legal justifications for getting rid of infiltrators, "we have always succeeded in eliminating them by using indictments for crimes against Paragraph 175."

According to statistics compiled by the Nazis and discovered after the war's end, only 3,976 male teenagers between fourteen and eighteen years old, of the more than 25,000 juveniles arrested for crimes against Paragraph 175, were convicted between 1933 and 1940. Since the total of juveniles during this period amounted to about 2.4 million, this number is relatively small. The legal department of the Hitler Youth had researched the cases of 100,000 juveniles convicted of all sorts of illegal deeds only to discover that on the average, just forty-seven out of ten thousand crimes were of a homosexual nature. This was embarrassing; Schirach, like Himmler, was convinced that homosexuals formed a greater portion of the criminal population. Still more embarrassing proved to be a second inquiry into same-sex felonies committed between July 1939 and August 1941 *within* the newly purged Hitler Youth. Of those ousted from the organization, 293 were charged with homosexual misdeeds—nearly 15 percent of the total expelled, a rather large percentage.[31]

These figures must be treated with caution. They indicate only the number of people arrested and sentenced for homosexuality; they tell nothing of the truth of that charge. Further, they reflect only the number of arrests and convictions the Nazis decided to record. It was not unusual for people to disappear without a trace.

How far the police bureaus were willing to go in order to wipe out people judged to be enemies of the state, how they would fabricate allegations of homosexual indecencies, bribe or intimidate witnesses, and, finally, establish kangaroo courts called "People's Courts," can be seen during their campaign against the only youth formations that, around 1936, still put up some resistance. These were the various Catholic youth groups. The drive against these groups is, of course, interwoven with that against the Catholic Church, but a short sketch of that battle for the souls and bodies of Catholic youth is necessary.

In July 1933, Pope Pius XI signed a concordat with the Hitler government which guaranteed certain freedoms to clergy, monasteries, nunneries, parochial schools and hospitals, and even to Catholic laymen. But Pius XI had underestimated his foe. It took Schirach only nine days after the signing to issue a decree that no young man could belong to a clerical organization and to the Hitler Youth at the same time. A second directive stipulated that nobody could become a member of the Nazi Party who had not completed four years of service in the Hitler Youth. Since the better jobs in nearly all fields were open only to party members, this dealt another blow to those youth groups that somehow had managed to coexist with the Nazis. With Schirach's approval, juvenile gangs invaded Catholic youth centers, stole the roll books, smashed the furniture, and sometimes set fire to the buildings. By 1937, all Catholic youth fraternities were officially dissolved.

Schirach's book repeatedly berated the Catholic youth societies and the institutions that sponsored them. It zeroed in on two areas: it asserted first that monasteries had always been breeding places for homosexual activities; and second, that the parochial schools were also places of such infection. As an example, the report singled out one Catholic institution in the village of Eichstadt. Here, so the book maintained, an insider had handed a confidential memorandum to the Gestapo in 1934. The memorandum stated that "for years, the males have had sexual relations with one another. Not only mutual masturbation was prevalent, the boys indulged in other practices such as oral and anal intercourse. The police suspect that some of the teachers knew about these indecencies but did nothing to stop them. . . . No doubt the Catholic concept of sin had to do with this—the priests explained the wickedness of such activities and this aroused the students' curiosity. . . . The clergy is to blame if the young men did not seek the company of girls. . . . In all probability, the priests encouraged the gross offenses if they did not participate."

▽

With this, I have slipped into a discussion of the larger drive against the Catholic Church, which started in 1935, culminated in several trials in 1936 and 1937, and continued on a much smaller scale until 1945. The Nazis simply ignored the 1933 concordat with the Vatican. Only in 1937 did Pope Pius XI issue his encyclical "With Burning Anxiety." It is not possible here to render a complete history of the war the Nazis waged against the German Catholic Church. I must restrict myself to those skirmishes in which the Nazis employed, among other weapons, charges of homosexuality. A few representative incidents will suffice.

Like Hitler, Reichsführer SS Himmler admired the organization of the Catholic Church as much as he loathed its doctrines. Himmler often said he wanted to shape his SS troops into a well-knit elite order embodying many of the superior qualities of the Jesuits. Nevertheless, together with Goebbels, Himmler let loose a defamation campaign against the Catholic establishment which portrayed it as a hotbed of homosexual atrocities.

The Nazis had charged the Catholic Church with assisting enemies of the state to escape to foreign countries; transferring funds illegally outside the Third Reich, especially to the Vatican; committing homosexual felonies, often with minors but also with other clerics; demoralizing the armed forces through pastoral epistles; lending support to the resistance within Germany and in the occupied territories; befriending members of the forced labor battalions in German factories, both directly through distribution of food and clothing, and indirectly through counseling; spreading atrocity stories outside of Germany, mainly through the Vatican; attempting to deny all wrongdoings, hide the perpetrators, and hush up the crimes.

If one of these imputations proved to be impractical, another could be substituted. When trying to pin down a priest, the Gestapo often used combinations of charges, such as illegal money operations and homosexual misdeeds.

Paragraph 175 supplied the basis for many individual anticlerical arraignments, but the most famous witch hunt started in 1935, culminating in two show trials in 1936 and 1937. Here the authorities brought charges of gross indecencies against three groups, almost all residents of such heavily Catholic districts as Bavaria, the Rhineland, Westphalia, and the Palatinate. The first group comprised lay brothers, loosely connected and nominally supervised by the Franciscans; the second included secular clergy, priests serving in various western and southwestern dioceses; the third consisted of members of such orders as the Augustinians and the Franciscans. The battle was really three-sided: the Gestapo, seeking every shred of evidence with unremitting devotion; a frightened judiciary, split among traditional judges, wary of Nazi methods, pro-Nazi careerists, and those who were weak and wavering; and finally, the beleaguered Church. Often, defendants were not permitted to have their own lawyers; evidence was suppressed when it hampered the prosecution attorneys, or distorted or falsified when it furthered their case.

Yet it is astonishing how the clergy, from the two most prominent officials, Clemens August Cardinal von Galen, Bishop of Münster, and Konrad Cardinal von Preysing, Bishop of Berlin—to the local parish priest, put up such tenacious resistance. That the Gestapo directorates violated even their own new laws comes as no surprise. What is more startling is the extent to which they frequently blundered, and badly misjudged the effectiveness and effects of the extravagant publicity the propaganda ministry lavished on the proceedings. What they hoped to achieve was clearly stated by Heydrich in a confidential letter circulated to Gestapo headquarters in Koblenz, Aachen, Munich, and other places where the major hearings were held: to bring before the public a large number of clerics convicted of unnatural sex acts in order to discredit the Church as a haven for degenerates and enemies of the state.[32] The authorities held between fifty and a hundred hearings.

The first target the Gestapo chose was a small congregation of lay brothers in Waldbreitbach, a village near Trier in the Palatinate. These brothers, nominally supervised in a rather informal arrangement by the Franciscans, concerned themselves mainly with the care of hospitals for handicapped or retarded juveniles and adults. Many of these lay brothers had entered the congregation during Germany's worst depression and—as the clerical authorities admitted—had not been properly screened. One member, a Brother Leovigil, had been under suspicion for a while but had not yet been transferred or dismissed.[33] As the hearings started, the entire German press was ordered by Goebbels to paint the alleged felonies in vivid colors and to play up every detail of Catholic homosexual turpitude. Most papers obeyed. One or two, however, such as the influential *Frankfurter Zeitung*, managed to smuggle in a few equivocal asides. Although the battle was uneven, with all advantages on the side of the state, the Gestapo agents occasionally botched the job. In the Waldbreitbach case, the Nazi agent in charge had called one of the feebleminded patients as a witness while several of the arraigned lay brothers were seated in the first row of the courtroom. The patient was asked by the prosecutor whether among those present he could identify any person who had attempted to seduce him into deviant sexual activities. The patient nodded and then pointed to the presiding judge. The court adjourned in disarray.

It goes without saying that both Paragraph 175 and Paragraph 174, prohibiting sexual contact between older men and minors, were made retroactive. Thus, the prosecutor had indicted as a homosexual felon a lay brother nurse who, four years before, had put his arm around a male patient.

In the summer of 1936, Hitler ordered a halt. The Olympic Games had opened in Berlin; hundreds of foreign guests were expected to visit the Third Reich for the first time. The newspapers, which for weeks had been brandishing such headlines as "Sex in the Sacristy," now turned to the joys of sport. Just as "Jews Not Wanted" signs were removed from public benches, just as gay bars were reopened and Himmler himself issued circular letters enjoining the police not to bother gay foreigners, so too were the Catholic trials suspended—without explanation. The uneasy peace was soon shattered. In March 1937, Pope Pius XI issued his encyclical "With Burning Anxiety," deploring the unjust persecution of German Catholics and condemning the authorities for violating the concordat. Within a day, the publication of the text was prohibited. Any mention of its existence was declared an act of treason. Gestapo agents monitored sermons in as many churches as they could; the issuance of ministerial letters was proscribed—and the trials, all at once, were resumed.

Previously there had only been attempts to involve secular clergy and the monastic orders. Now the authorities went all out. In two major cities, Cologne and Aachen, Gestapo agents confiscated the registries of the General Vicariat. But things did not go smoothly. The trials were too hastily organized and, in the event, the conservative members of the judiciary proved more resistant to Gestapo pressures than the government had anticipated. After twelve weeks Hitler ordered a postponement—again for political reasons: he seems to have realized that the campaign had begun to backfire. He was reluctant to antagonize vast segments of the population with further anticlerical trials. Moreover, the Gestapo, despite heroic efforts, had not been able to carry out mass arrests of homosexually active clerics. Goebbels's strident propaganda had boomeranged. It is also possible that Mussolini, whom Hitler needed as an ally in his war schemes, had persuaded him to leave the Catholic Church alone for the time being. The Vatican was not only a power of enormous, history-proven resilience, but served as a conduit to the world press. At this moment, in 1937, Hitler still hoped to vanquish France and Eastern Europe while keeping Britain and America out of the war. It would not do to alarm Catholics in the West unduly.

During the twelve weeks of the 1937 trials, however, Goebbels had tried to destroy what he called "the ulcer on the healthy body of Germany." The propaganda had reached its climax in a Goebbels speech delivered in May 1937, carried over nationwide radio, reprinted in most newspapers, and repeated in Sunday editorials. The speech was cluttered with such remarks as "the sacristy has become a bordello, while the monasteries are breeding places of vile homosexuality." Monks must never be allowed to educate children, and parents were exhorted to pull their children out of parochial schools. Goebbels—a lapsed Catholic—repeatedly condemned the organization of the Catholic Church as such, especially "the unnatural life of single men confined to monasteries, which promoted the spread of this unnatural vice." He accused the ecclesiastical authorities of knowing what went on but claiming ignorance as reason for their inaction. That clerical institutions were seedbeds of anti-German propaganda, of perfidious atrocity tales, was no surprise, according to Goebbels, since homosexuals had been traitors throughout history.

Thousands of Catholic sex criminals planned to corrupt German children, he shouted. The crimes uncovered by the police were only a fraction of those taking place behind so-called sacred doors. In addition, the Church was waging a ruthless campaign against the new state and its Führer. Goebbels cited the liquidation of Roehm as an example of the high ethical standards of the party.

The party faithful wildly applauded him, but Hitler, it appears, was having second thoughts. Now was not the most opportune moment to continue the anti-Catholic campaign. The hearings were called off.

This did not mean that the entire anti-Catholic campaign

had been canceled. From 1933 until 1941, Catholic institutions were under siege. By 1936 and 1937, not a single Catholic youth organization remained active. By then, inmates of about thirty-five monasteries had been expelled. In 1941, Goebbels closed down all Catholic newspapers and magazines.[34] Between 1937 and 1945, more than four thousand clerics died in concentration camps through torture, pseudo-medical experiments, or simply lack of food.[35] Non-German clergymen arrested in occupied territories, accused of having assisted the resistance, were either shot or shipped to Dachau, the special camp for the clergy. Nevertheless, the 1936–37 show trials, staged with an awesome expenditure of rhetoric, venom, and print, had yielded a startlingly small harvest. Of the total of three thousand lay brothers, only 170 were sentenced; of a total of 21,000 secular clergymen, only fifty-seven went to jail; of a total of 4,000 members of monastic orders, the judges found only seven (!) guilty of crimes against Paragraph 175.[36] If Goebbels had expected his media blitzkrieg against the Church to spur mass defections, the available statistics prove him wrong. Between 1933 and 1943 (there are no figures available for 1939), less than half of one percent of Germany's 22.4 million Catholics left the Church.[37] Despite Himmler's repeated declarations ("There can be no peace between the National Socialist state and the Church. The demand for total power by the Catholic clergy is opposed to the legitimate demand for total power by our state."), the Catholic population remained almost entirely immune to his pleas.[38]

In July 1937, at the height of the media broadside against allegedly homosexual clerics, a pilgrimage took place at the Rhenish city of Aachen, as it had for seven hundred years. One bishop wanted to postpone it; he believed pilgrims might stay away out of fear. The presses, he argued, that had printed the Pope's encyclical had been sequestered; no posters could be exhibited; what remained of the Catholic press was under orders from Berlin not to mention the planned event. Still, between 750,000 and 800,000 pilgrims went through the streets of Aachen and the police were unable to stop the crowds.

The Aachen example is only one of many similar happenings.[39] Throughout the twelve years of the Third Reich, certain parishes continued to celebrate important holy days. A few monasteries and nunneries bravely hid baptized and non-baptized Jews. Bishops like von Preysing and von Galen never lost the allegiance of their parishioners. To be sure, the Nazi state abolished the Catholic youth groups, shut down Catholic institutions, and persecuted and killed several thousand clerics. But the offensive to defame the Catholic Church by smearing clergymen as treasonous homosexuals definitely miscarried. The hoped-for massive flight from the Church did not take place. The Nazi machine utterly failed to shake the faith of millions of German Catholics.

▽

As we have seen, the Roehm purge proved Hitler could get away with murder. It also proved that the SS, under Himmler, was a more pliable and effective force than Roehm's unruly SA. Roehm's removal had reassured the old officer corps who had feared Roehm's plans to dismantle the *Reichswehr* and replace it with an army of his own. After the purge the generals assumed they had reasserted their proper place within the state without having to bloody their hands; Hitler had done the dirty work. They approved of using Roehm's homosexuality as a pretext for getting rid of him. These mostly right-wing soldiers, many from noble families, wavered in their attitudes toward the Nazi dictatorship. By instinct and training, they tended to regard Hitler, Himmler, Goebbels, and the rest with contempt, as lower-class upstarts. Nevertheless, they hoped that Hitler would provide them with more money, soldiers, weapons, and power while respecting their traditional independence. The murder of Roehm seemed to suggest that Hitler was prepared to strike against the extremists within his own party, and to pursue a course of moderation and cooperation. Nothing was further from the truth. What the generals had not foreseen was that, as Alan Bullock has noted, "within ten years of Roehm's murder the SS would have succeeded where the SA failed in establishing a party army in rivalry with the generals' army. . . ."[40] Moreover, Hitler continued to harbor an enmity toward the old military establishment; he feared them as potential conspirators and rivals, and retained a twisted remnant of the front-line soldier's contempt for his superiors. "The General Staff," Hitler would remark, "is the only Masonic Order that I haven't yet dissolved." And he declared that "those gentlemen with the purple stripes down their trousers sometimes seem to me even more revolting than the Jews."[41] He was determined to break their independence and curb their pride. Once again, charges of homosexuality would provide the perfect pretext.

The following discussion of the cashiering of Werner von Blomberg, first minister of defense, later general marshal of the armed forces, and of Baron Werner von Fritsch, commander-in-chief of the armed forces, is perhaps tangential to a chronicle of homosexuals under the Third Reich. Nevertheless, if I am reluctant to consign it to a footnote, it is because such a discussion demonstrates Hitler's use of charges of sexual misconduct, some possibly factual, others clearly spurious, to force the resignations of men like von Blomberg and von Fritsch, who had become difficult and obstinate, and because the trial of von Fritsch irreparably undermined the independence of the military commanders who, until 1938, had successfully resisted the encroachments of the SS and the Gestapo.

The 1938 trial of von Fritsch on charges of homosexual indecencies was based on documents collected by Göring, Himmler, and Heydrich. To understand their animus it should be remembered that von Blomberg was so strongly convinced that Hitler would bring stability and grandeur to the army that in August 1934 he had arranged for the officers of the army to swear a personal oath of loyalty to Hitler. During the Roehm massacre, von Blomberg had done nothing to protest the murder of his two colleagues, General Kurt von Schleicher and General Kurt von Bredow. Von Fritsch, however, had demanded an explanation from Göring, then head of the Prussian police. Göring alerted the two most sinister power brokers on Hitler's staff, Himmler and Heydrich, but neither could offer an explanation that satisfied von Fritsch. This, one might say, formed the nucleus of hatred that the Göring-Himmler-Heydrich faction harbored against von Fritsch.

That Hitler himself joined the team is due to the events of the Hossbach Conference of November 1937. Hitler had gathered the heads of all the armed services and lectured them for several hours on his plans for the conquest of Europe. Von Fritsch protested that the army was in no way ready. Von Blomberg vacillated but finally overcame his scruples and started preparing for "Operation Green," the code name for the campaign against Czechoslovakia. During the conference, the usually cool von Fritsch lost his temper and argued energetically against Göring. It did not endear him to Göring.

The unimaginative timidity of his generals convinced Hitler that he had to dismantle the army high command. He had to get rid of von Blomberg, von Fritsch, and the other traditionalists. Göring, too, realized that with the exception of the upper echelons of the Catholic Church, the armed forces were the only source of institutional power the Nazis had not yet subdued. Göring also hoped to be appointed successor to either von Fritsch or von Blomberg. He fanned the fires against von Blomberg, and luck was on his side: von Blomberg had married a girl "with a past."

Von Blomberg, a widower in his sixties with two grown children, had met a woman named Eva Gruhn, whose mother had once run a massage parlor. Though Göring had discovered that Eva had once posed for several nude photos, some of which bordered on the pornographic, he did not immediately inform von Blomberg. Von Blomberg married Eva in a simple ceremony; the witnesses were Göring and Hitler. Shortly afterward, Göring showed von Blomberg the police blotter containing the photos of his new wife. To avoid public disgrace, von Blomberg, broken and humiliated, tendered his resignation and took Eva on a honeymoon to Italy. Hitler did not hand over von Blomberg's job to Göring, but instead appointed himself chief of the Supreme Command of the Army, a post he invented.

Now the more resilient von Fritsch had to be tackled. Baron Werner von Fritsch, at first glance, conveys the image of the exemplary Prussian officer, complete with clipped speech and monocle. In fact, this brilliant military tactician was a shy, deeply religious introvert. He had a pronounced sense of justice, and frequently interfered to soften the punishment of soldiers caught violating minor army regulations. His sense of personal responsibility, his total devotion to the army, won him the admiration of officers and enlisted men alike. He had only one hobby: he loved to ride horses whenever his duties permitted it. He had never married and had few known relationships with women. Such conduct was not viewed with suspicion; it corresponded to a tradition of the Prussian army, some of whose most brilliant generals had been lifelong bachelors.

Von Fritsch was also immune to the charm the Führer occasionally lavished on those he needed, and tended to stay aloof from the new Nazi court. Solitary, straightforward, and pious, he was no match for the plots of his adversaries. Although he never trusted the Nazi leaders, he only caught on to the true character of Hitler and his aides when it was too late.

Even while the von Blomberg crisis took its course, the Göring-Himmler-Heydrich machine was searching for material to incriminate von Fritsch. It is not certain who first unearthed a dossier containing information dating back to 1933. It recorded the confessions of Otto Schmidt, a twenty-nine-year-old thief with a long record of fraud and blackmail. Captain Meisinger, the newly appointed head of the Gestapo's Security Office for Combating Abortion and Homosexuality, listened with interest as Schmidt claimed that in the winter of 1933 he had seen an elderly gentleman in a brown coat with a fur collar and carrying a cane picking up a well-known hustler. The two men had disappeared into a dark alley, where Schmidt said he saw them commit homosexual acts. After the two separated, Schmidt followed the gentleman and began to blackmail him. Schmidt could not squeeze much money out of his prey; the gentleman soon collapsed and hired a nurse who guarded him faithfully. Schmidt swore that the man he had blackmailed was General Werner von Fritsch. Whether Meisinger knew from the start that the gentleman Schmidt allegedly had watched was actually Captain Achim von Frisch, an ailing retiree, remains open to speculation. Probably he found out after a few weeks of inquiry. Still, during an interrogation in 1936, when he showed Schmidt some photos of General Werner von Fritsch, Schmidt assured him this was the man he had blackmailed. Meisinger was delighted. He notified Himmler and Heydrich.

Hitler, given the documents, seems to have felt that the time was not ripe for a break with von Fritsch. Hitler needed the army: he had just finished his illegal march into the Rhineland. Although he wished to keep the story quiet, Hitler confided the matter to Göring. Now, nearly two years later, Göring, having succeeded in removing von Blomberg, saw a way to undo von Fritsch. At the end of 1937, Schmidt was again grilled, this time in jail. He was eventually set free on condition that he work as a "sexual deviants informer."

A fellow blackmailer and the hustler were also interrogated. It became obvious—even to the Gestapo—that the gentleman had indeed been Captain von Frisch, not General von Fritsch. This awkward fact should have made it impossible even for an operator like Göring to uphold the fiction that the Gestapo had not known about the identity of Schmidt's victim. But it didn't. In January 1938, von Fritsch was summoned to speak to Hitler. He not only found himself facing the Führer but also Göring and Schmidt, the blackmailer, who called out: "That's him." Von Fritsch said only: "I don't know this person." His denial was not enough.

Von Fritsch's first trial took place in March 1938, but was aborted just as the blackmailer began to be cross-examined. Hitler had decided to march into Austria. When the trial resumed a few weeks later, von Fritsch's counsel had prepared several traps for Schmidt. The Gestapo was also unable to browbeat the hustler into identifying von Fritsch. Finally, old Captain Achim von Frisch, although obviously beaten in prison, admitted everything.

The court acquitted von Fritsch of all charges. It did not

matter. The armed forces had suffered a devastating blow to its morale, from which it was never to recover. Now that von Fritsch was "rehabilitated," Hitler mailed him a letter that is a masterpiece of double-talk. Hitler observed that he, like the general, had suffered much slander. Hitler promised to make public the general's vindication before the German people. He never did. Instead, he appointed von Fritsch to the colonelcy of his old regiment—a meaningless gesture. Von Fritsch was killed during the war in Poland in September 1939.

Schmidt was sent to the concentration camp at Sachsenhausen for nearly four years, then liquidated on Göring's orders. Some of the bunglers in the Gestapo were transferred. The fate of the hustler is unknown; no records have come to light. Probably he ended up in a camp, with a black (asocial) or a pink (homosexual) triangle sewn on his sleeve.[42]

▽

To understand what happened to those homosexuals in the armed forces who did not "pass"—that is, those who were caught and convicted—three factors must be taken into account. First, after July 1935, as draft-age gays began to grasp the ferocity of the new antihomosexual laws, many decided to volunteer for the navy, army, or air force. Neither General Keitel of the army, nor Admirals Raeder or Doenitz of the navy, nor even Marshal Göring of the air force shared the homophobic obsessions of Himmler. Second, after the Roehm purge had eliminated the homosexual SA elite, no halfway intelligent gay was likely to join the homophobic SS. Third, none of the armed forces were inclined favorably toward homosexuality. Statistics from 1940 show that the military courts were busy with sexual offenders as more and more young men joined or were drafted. Simultaneously, indictments of male civilians for the same felonies stayed the same or dropped slightly. In 1941, about 3,700 civilians were sentenced for same-sex activities. During the same year, the number of men indicted for the same crime within the armed forces amounted to just over 1,100.

Between 1940 and 1943, nearly 5,000 German military men were indicted for homosexual misdeeds, of which 205 held the rank of officer and 1,434 that of noncommissioned officer.[43] Homosexuals in the higher ranks seem to have been more adept than enlisted men at dodging the snares of Paragraph 175. The armed forces struggled to keep their own long-established legal procedures intact. Until 1942, the military courts distinguished between "libidinal felons," meaning offenders who were by nature homosexual or could not resist an urge to commit occasional same-sex misdeeds, and essentially heterosexual victims of incidental aberrant feelings, who had been either seduced or had transgressed because they were overstimulated and had found no other outlet. Service personnel in the first category were to be put in a military jail or in a penal combat battalion.[44]

In 1942, Hitler declared that the armed forces were too lenient in their treatment of sexual deviants. There was probably more behind this than Hitler's pleasure in badgering the military. Himmler, who a year earlier had prescribed the death penalty for any SS member guilty of homosexual actions, had probably pressured Hitler to get the armed forces to conform. After all, an SS man caught with a sailor could be executed, while the sailor might get away with one or two years in jail. A psychiatrist, Otto Wuth, was appointed to alert military jurists to the dangers of all types of homosexuality. Wuth, a firm believer in Himmler's scriptures, disapproved of the distinction between full-time libidinal felons and part-time victims. He labeled every male indulging in any type of same-sex activities a "compulsive psychopath," and sought to prove that most homosexuals had previous criminal records of one sort or another. Should men convicted of homosexual felonies be dismissed from the armed forces? Wuth thought not. He proposed to put them instead into penal combat battalions where they had to face direct enemy fire. Wuth argued that if genuine psychopaths were discharged from the fighting forces, heterosexual malingerers might pretend to be libidinal felons and use this ruse to get out of the service. For repeat offenders, Wuth recommended demotion in rank for minor violations, and strict prison sentences for major crimes; all criminals were to wear a visible badge denoting their status.

Wuth, it appears, was not able to win over the legal chiefs of the military. There followed prolonged periods of wrangling between the various Himmler directorates and the armed forces. In 1943 a draft was worked out that established three categories: (1) libidinal felons who were incorrigible; (2) men who had committed only one or two homosexual crimes, probably when seduced; and (3) defendants whose inclinations were dubious. This time around, the first category, the libidinal felons, faced sharper penalties. They would be convicted and handed over to the "proper authorities," meaning the Gestapo, and they could be condemned to death. The second group should also be severely punished, but could be rehabilitated. The third group must be put into penal combat battalions, but if observation suggested they had reformed, they could rejoin their former units. The psychiatric and legal experts could not agree on whether a "successful" visit to a military bordello should be taken as sufficient proof that the offender had been reformed and was, so to speak, heterosexually reborn. Neither these nor later, stricter directives were put into effect because the worsening plight of all armed forces after 1943 meant that every able-bodied man was essential.

Another Hitler memorandum restored some power to a special military court, originally organized to rule over the militia but now covering the entire realm of military juris-diction. The court's president was Paul von Hase, a foe of Nazi ideology, as was his counsel, Army Court Martial Judge Karl Sack, the jurist who had been instrumental in unmasking the Gestapo intrigue against von Fritsch. This court heard cases of desertion, treason, corruption, and crimes against Paragraph 175. It is reasonable, even in the absence of sur-viving evidence, to assume that these two oppositionists did their utmost to soften or delay punishments meted out to servicemen accused—rightly or wrongly—of treason (which included self-mutilation), desertion, or homosexual felonies.[45]

Still, the military was not overly lenient toward same-sex offenders. It meted out justice according to the old laws es-tablished by the Prussian army before 1870. There are only a few examples for which the records have been preserved. In 1940 a special naval tribunal was convened to hear the case of a sailor described only as Emil B. Emil and a com-panion named E. had been drinking beer aboard a coast guard cutter; Emil had kissed E. several times. The court decided that six months in jail was "an appropriate and just punish-ment." Another naval tribunal was convened in August 1942 to decide the case of an engine-room machinist named B. He was accused of having made indecent proposals to several sailors on his minesweeper. Two sailors insisted they had rejected his advances; another confessed that he had indulged twice in mutual masturbation with B., but only at B.'s urging. B. was ordered to serve in a special penal combat camp for two years and was deprived of his civil rights. His petitions for parole and reentry into his old job on the minesweeper were rejected because the court concluded that he was a "li-bidinal felon."[46]

The armed forces had also to grapple with the behavior of non-German fighting men recruited after 1942. These for-eign volunteers—among them Turks, Azerbaijanis, Cossacks,

Armenians, Turkomans, Arabs, Belgians, and Frenchmen—had often grown up in cultures whose traditions permitted occasional homosexual acts, especially when young men had no access to women. Neither the German army nor navy seems to have asked the Gestapo's advice on how to handle them. To all appearances, the armed forces tribunals tended to treat non-Germanic personnel with moderation. In February 1944, for example, a naval court convened in the northern German town of Glückstadt to try three French-speaking Arabs. It seems that Dhu, Deb, and Beaug had satisfied each other's sexual needs quite openly at various places, mainly in the showers. One episode in particular shocked the court. While a marine captain had delivered an illustrated lecture about the wartime duties of the true German fighting man, defendant Dhu, protected by the backs of the sailors sitting in front of him, went down on his knees and satisfied his companion Deb. Two German sailors had watched and reported the crime. Verdict: seven months in jail for Dhu, five months for Deb, and two months for the less active Beaug, who was only involved in the shower incidents.[47] If these non-Germanics had been members of a forced-labor battalion in some German city and had been apprehended by the Gestapo, they would have been either executed on the spot or sent to a concentration camp. There they would have been worked to death or shot "while trying to escape."

If the military did not follow Gestapo practices in their treatment of crimes against Paragraph 175, it was not because it considered homosexuality a natural variant like left-handedness. To declare a kiss between two drunken sailors an offense deserving six months in jail does not exactly indicate preferred treatment for homosexual offenders. After the Gestapo entrapment of von Fritsch, however, every legal employee was wary of Gestapo efforts to curtail and to destroy the independence of the armed forces judiciary. It was, quite simply, the conservatism of the military establishment that defied Himmler. The experts in the various departments might accept a guideline here, a directive there, but in principle they resisted outsiders, and the Gestapo directorates were definitely felt to be intruders. Himmler, for instance, never succeeded for long in placing informers on navy vessels. They were always detected.

▽

No exact figures can yet be given of those who suffered in the campaign of persecution against homosexuals. However meticulous the Nazis were in their mania for keeping records, they were also eager to conceal the extent of their savagery. Those documents that survived the war are often incomplete and untrustworthy. Nevertheless, there is material that bears on the question from which we can infer the criteria necessary for any reasonable evaluation of its scope.

First, the number of male homosexuals in the German population of 1933–45, for which it is impossible to give a precise figure. On the basis of his 1909 survey, conducted only in Berlin among 6,611 factory workers and students, Magnus Hirschfeld concluded that there were about 1.2 million gays, or about 2.2 percent of the male population.[48] Earlier, in 1897, the Berlin police had compiled a list of between 20,000 and 30,000 known or suspected homosexuals throughout the country.[49] In 1928, German sociologist Robert Michels also put the number of homosexually inclined men at 1.2 million.[50] He seems only to have echoed Hirschfeld's estimate. Himmler, too, seems to have embraced this figure, although in at least one instance he placed the number of homosexuals at 2 million.[51] There was, of course, no way to know. Nevertheless, in the light of later sociological research (Kinsey et al.), such a figure was perhaps not significantly inaccurate.

Second, the number of those—both civilian and military—convicted for violations of Paragraph 175 can be considered. Here we must rely on the often conflicting records of the various Nazi police organs. The Gestapo, for example, listed nearly 37,500 men sentenced for homosexuality between 1933 and the first half of 1940.[52] The Federal Security Office for Combating Abortion and Homosexuality also compiled statistics of the number of homosexuals sentenced from 1936 to 1939, the peak years of Himmler's campaign against the gays. Its total of nearly 43,000 is considerably greater than the Gestapo figure of almost 30,000 for the same period.[53] For the war years 1941–44 the most reliable estimate is of about 12,000 homosexual men sentenced.[54] Overall, we may reasonably estimate the number of males convicted of homosexuality from 1933 to 1944 at between 50,000 and 63,000, of which nearly 4,000 were juveniles. (Also recorded were the arrests of six lesbians—a bewildering statistic, since sex between women was not against the law.)

Despite the paucity of reliable statistics, it seems reasonable to conclude that a considerable number—perhaps even a majority—of the tougher and more circumspect, resourceful, and just plain lucky homosexuals survived the Third Reich undetected. Himmler never ceased his efforts to ferret them out, though. But unlike other contragenics like the Jews, Gypsies, the Jehovah's Witnesses, or political opponents, homosexuals were usually difficult to detect. Still, even for those who managed to survive, their days and nights were filled with fear. It was impossible to trust anyone, especially strangers. Even a casual contact might prove to be an informer. Moreover, from 1935 on, every gay German man knew that if he was caught he risked being shipped to a concentration camp. There, disease, degradation, and almost certain death awaited him.

5

IN
CAMP

BEFORE DESCRIBING WHAT HAPPENED TO those homosexuals who were caught in Himmler's net and sent to concentration camps, I must confess that it is hard to maintain here the necessary disinterest required for proper historical investigation. Several of the difficulties besetting anyone trying to grasp the enormity of the horror of the Third Reich have been outlined in the Introduction, and they do not have to be named again. Still, I must sound a fair and personal warning: to analyze the documents from the camps—official directives, police dossiers, hastily scribbled entrance-and-departure lists, the "Death Books," often mangled and yellowed by time into illegibility—demands a formidable degree of dispassion.

When I spent time at the International Tracing Service in Arolsen, West Germany, its huge rooms piled to the ceiling with papers rescued from the camps—the records not yet completely catalogued—I often had to stop. Since it is impossible for any single person to review even a fraction of the material, I decided to concentrate mostly on the camp at Buchenwald, near Weimar, in what is today East Germany. Unlike many other camps, its files are comparatively intact, including those on pseudo-medical experiments administered to homosexuals by Carl Vaernet, the Danish hormone specialist. Several years earlier, a team of young German researchers under the direction of Rüdiger Lautmann reviewed most of what was available from the thirteen or fourteen institutions that had incarcerated homosexuals. Lautmann and his researchers opened up a territory nobody had surveyed or mapped before. His pioneering study, the first statistical and sociological analysis of what happened to homosexuals in Nazi camps, based not only on the Arolsen documents, but also on the recollections of non-homosexual prisoners, was published in Germany in 1977.[1] Nevertheless, Lautmann is the first to admit that his researchers were unable to obtain complete data. The Nazis never kept orderly books. There were also advantages to be had by compiling misleading statistics. In addition, collateral police blotters in East German and Russian centers were not and, as of this writing, are not accessible.

All statistics must be regarded with caution. We do not know, for example, how many gays were detained in a specific camp during a specific month. No irrefutable figures are available. The Nazi penal bureaucracy was concerned with no more than a prisoner's name, age, and reason for detention. Professional or marital status, place of residence, and arresting agency were not always noted.[2] Some camps kept thorough records only during periods of comparative quiet; others lacked competent clerks who knew how to fill out official forms or how to spell a difficult name. And toward the end of the war, the SS burned countless documents.[3]

Homosexuals constituted a very small minority, perhaps one of the smallest; only the categories of "emigrants," "race defilers," and "armed forces transfers" contained fewer men. For example, in Natzweiler-Struthof, a camp in Alsace-Lorraine, from April 1942 to June 1944, the number of homosexuals varied between 20 and 50.[4] In Mauthausen, from February 1944 to July 1944, the camp's books list the names of between 50 and 60 gay prisoners.[5] In Buchenwald, from

January 1943 to March 1945, the tables show between 60 and slightly more than 150 gay inmates.[6] For Dachau, Lautmann found 150 homosexual inmates for the period of March 1938 through September 1938.[7] These are partial statistics, with many months and even years missing. How many homosexuals were actually held in the camps remains uncertain, perhaps unknowable. One might estimate that from 1933 on, the various institutions detained at all times several hundred homosexuals. Later this increased to about one thousand. Altogether, somewhere between 5,000 and 15,000 homosexuals perished behind barbed-wire fences.[8]

As I combed through the Arolsen files, I realized that just as the various camp registrars were not able to keep track of the prisoners' names, especially those with names unfamiliar to the German clerks—in Eastern Europe the name Schwarz could be spelled in more than eighty ways—the bookkeepers, too, left out vital information. In Buchenwald, for instance, on a certain day there were noted down not sixty-one homosexuals as listed the previous day, but only fifty-eight. It is not clear whether the missing three died, were remanded to one of the Dora-Mittelbau labor units, or were sent to an altogether different camp. If, on a day soon after, there appear three additional numbers—no names—for the Buchenwald homosexual contingent, it is not possible to say whether these are the same three men omitted from the group of sixty-one listed before, whether they had been shipped to Buchenwald as first offenders, or whether they had been transferred from another institution. The same uncertainties still afflict researchers seeking precise data on the fate of other contragenics, especially the Slavs. For many millions of Russian prisoners of war, the Nazis did not bother with detailed lists at all—they were to be eliminated too rapidly to bother recording their names. Nevertheless, maniacally obsessive archivists pressed on with their grisly task. In 1945, shortly before the surrender, while Allied guns could be heard clearly booming close to Buchenwald, some of them kept on scribbling entries for homosexual prisoners—all such numbers now being illegible.[9]

Another essential source of information—the reminiscences of those fortunate enough to survive—runs very thin when it comes to homosexuals. Not many were that lucky. Most memoirs are the work of former Jewish or antifascist prisoners. Except for Rudolf Hoess, no prominent executive of the Nazi penal system wrote his recollections. When Lautmann publicly invited those still living to come forward to be interviewed, only a small number accepted his offer. Those few who did insisted on anonymity. Since then, the slightly improved political climate in West Germany has encouraged others to testify—that is, to allow scholars and journalists to question them about a time that most would rather forget. It must be remembered that until 1969, sexual acts between consenting adult males were still considered a crime under West German law. The few former pink-triangle survivors who had reentered civilian life had usually concocted "cover stories"—for example, some claimed to have been arrested as anti-Nazi resisters. A few had married; some had children and grandchildren; none wanted the past to reemerge and threaten their present lives. Over the years, I have been able to interview only a handful of survivors willing to share their experiences with me. Likewise, only a few were willing to send me written testimonies. I have also drawn extensively on Lautmann's work. What follows is only a beginning and cannot be considered the definitive chronicle of homosexuals kept behind the barbed-wire fences of the Third Reich.

▽

The first camp, Dachau, near Munich, was opened on March 30, 1933, on Himmler's orders. Set up in haste to relieve the prisons, which were overcrowded after the Reichstag fire, the camp was poorly organized. The SA arrested, and sometimes discharged, people at random. The earliest prisoners included antifascists, Catholics, homosexuals, and Jews. The commandant, Major Hilman Wäckerle, attempted to maintain some order; "violent insubordination" and "incitement to disobedience" were punishable by death. Still, he could not keep his constables in check. Himmler, angered by the adverse publicity generated by the murder of several prisoners, dismissed Wäckerle, who was subsequently charged by the Bavarian criminal prosecutor's office.[10]

In June 1933, Himmler appointed Theodor Eicke, the man who, more than anyone else, shaped the character not only of Dachau but of later camps. He organized brutality courses for the SS novices, worked out a graded system of confinements, and succeeded in welding the newly born Order of the Death's Head into a fanatical gang of bullies, imbued with hatred toward the charges they regarded as subhumans. Eicke's favorite slogan, frequently shouted by the guards at newcomers, was, "There are enough German oak trees to hang anybody who dares to defy us."[11] It was Eicke who transformed Dachau from a disorderly open-air jail into a place of carefully calibrated punishment and deprivation schedules. It was Eicke who provided the model for all later institutions. Men trained under him often ended up as high officers in the larger camps. And it was Eicke who brought the revolver into Ernst Roehm's prison cell and, when Roehm refused the proffered suicide, shot him on Hitler's orders, thus bringing to a climax the Night of the Long Knives. Whether Eicke's governing techniques stemmed from his experiences as police informer, terrorist, and SS officer, or whether they simply mirrored the mind of a butcher born to the task—a bully who enjoyed tyrannizing others—remains difficult to decide. What is incontestable is that it was his policies that shaped the repressive contours of all camps and made them into the indispensable and diabolical instruments of Hitler's and Himmler's rule by terror.

Basically, Eicke worked out two sets of rules, one for camp personnel, one for inmates. Of the code for guards, only certain sections were put on paper; much of it was passed on through indoctrination sessions. Foremost, he insisted on unconditional obedience. Every order by a superior officer had to be carried out. Frequently he emphasized "that every prisoner be treated with fanatical hatred as an enemy of the state."[12] Eicke developed a set of procedures that would breed in the guards a conviction that they were not only carrying out legitimate orders but punishing dangerous subversives. He began a "Brutality Training Academy" whose graduates ruled over almost all later penal institutions—first those in the West, later in the extermination mills in the East. The earlier camps, located within German, Austrian, Dutch, French, and Belgian borders, did not dispose of inmates by mechanized crematoria. They cannot properly be labeled extermination camps, although thousands perished in them.

Men like Rudolf Hoess, later supreme ruler of Sachsenhausen and Auschwitz, were educated in the older camps and then graduated to the death factories, purposely placed in the East, away from the eyes of the German population.

For the regulation of the inmates, Eicke's manual for "The Maintenance of Discipline and Order" remained the standard text for the camps.[13] It granted the commandant the power to punish prisoners as he saw fit. Eicke legalized various procedures through which the inmates were humiliated and broken, a process vitally necessary if a small—albeit well-armed—group of SS troopers was to reign over much larger numbers of prisoners.

Himmler, recognizing Eicke's talent for running Dachau

more efficiently and ruthlessly than his predecessor, asked him, in April 1934, to think about reorganizing all existing camps: their number had grown so fast that Himmler deemed centralization essential. Himmler appointed Eicke to serve directly under him. In October 1934, Eicke was transferred to Berlin to ready the headquarters for the newly centralized *Kazets* (concentration camps). Although he ultimately moved his headquarters—fittingly, one might say—into Sachsenhausen, he continued to work closely with Himmler. Soon Eicke closed down numerous smaller camps, shipping their inmates to the larger establishments. Some of the old camps lasted longer than planned, however, because they had to absorb the unforeseen overflow, among them Flossenbürg, in Bavaria, and Stutthof, near Danzig, where large numbers of homosexuals were interned.

By 1937 the indefatigable master builder had set up four basic units: Dachau, Sachsenhausen (near Berlin), Buchenwald (near Weimar), and, after Austria had rejoined the Fatherland, Mauthausen (near Linz). In time, every one of these gave birth to numerous satellite camps, some serving newly built war factories. Each camp was patterned after Dachau, which stands as a monument to Eicke's gift for organized tyranny. Only the exigencies of the war, the feuds among rival Nazi directorates, threatened to overwhelm Eicke's troopers and cause dangerous cracks in the carefully constructed control apparatus.

In his guidebook on discipline and order, his training drills for the misfits and malcontents who made up his armies, Eicke created a nightmarish world of barbarism and doom, so far removed from the experience of most Western nations that what went on inside the camps was at first not believed. If Himmler was initially ordered to organize the extermination of large minorities, such as Jews and antifascists, if he later added the crusades against the smaller groups of contragenics such as Gypsies and homosexuals, it was Eicke who provided the needed confinement structures that soon dotted three-quarters of Europe.

The camps, thanks to Himmler, existed outside any legal restrictions. They presented a new type of penal colony where anybody resisting the established order could be quickly silenced. How the camps functioned, from exhaustive day to exhaustive day, has been told by so many excellent observers and historians that there is no need for detailed analysis here.[14]

Nor is it necessary to render in minute detail the chain of command as it prevailed in most institutions—from the commandant at the top, whom few of the prisoners ever saw, to the SS block sergeant, of whom they saw too much. It is sufficient to note that in between ruled various middlemen and numerous administrative assistants and adjutants to the commandant, representing special departments. The pyramid of power was patterned by Eicke after that of prisons and the armed forces, and as in these institutions, some areas of authority were ambiguous; guerrilla skirmishes between departments frequently erupted. Such rivalries sometimes made it possible for prisoners to survive. Even more crucial was the composition of the "self-government" forced on prisoners by their SS overseers. These "prison aristocrats" wielded enormous influence and could save their confederates' lives, assign an adversary to an infamous work detachment, or get rid of a hated guard or an inmate suspected of being an informer. On the other hand, such power brokers were in a constant bind. Some of the rank-and-file prisoners naturally saw them as tools of the enemy, while the camp administration, for its part, held them responsible for everything happening within their area of control, from an escape plot to minor disciplinary infractions. In short, the SS rulers used inmates against inmates. This ancient technique promoted strife among prisoners, something the authorities needed and cherished. Even so, differences were rife among the prisoners: class background, social status, racial type, religious creed, sexual preference, and, later—as non-German prisoners were herded in—national origin.

The entire process of dehumanization on entering the camp—the stripping, in some cases the shaving of all, even the pubic, hair, the loss of name and personhood, caused profound trauma. The jolt was accompanied not only by the enduring sensation of powerlessness; the victim, under daily assault in one way or the other, also began to realize that nothing he had achieved, done, or owned counted here. It has been said that in the inferno all are equal.[15] But for one group the shock of incarceration was not as destructive as for the others. To habitual criminals, the trauma was less intense; they had spent years in jails developing a repertoire of survival techniques.

Some of the criminal prisoners, identifiable by the green triangles they were forced to wear, had learned through long years in prison to abide by a special code based on group solidarity: one does not squeal on a buddy, one looks after one's mates, one respects "honor among thieves." This group of seasoned penal graduates did not include the so-called asocials, tagged by black triangles, often those who had run away from labor camps or were chronically unemployable. They were considered stupid, unable to communicate, lacking the courage to stand up for a brother. The SS despised them— the color of their triangles was an insult to their own black uniforms.

After the initial baptism of mortification, newcomers had to learn to cope with their utter defenselessness. All were treated like criminals, all had to do spine-cracking labor, and, what was worse, all were forever at the mercy of both the SS and the *Kapos*, who were prisoners, usually camp elders, appointed by the commandant, charged with ensuring obedience and discipline in the barracks. Education, wealth, achievement—none of these mattered. On the contrary, the guards and their *Kapo* deputies favored farmers, laborers, lumberjacks, and craftsmen; they had nothing but contempt for former white-collar clerks, merchants, teachers, lawyers. They rejected foreigners, especially Slavs, Jews, and Gypsies, and they loathed homosexuals, clergymen, and artists—except, perhaps, musicians, who were sometimes recruited for an orchestra to perform on social occasions, such as the Führer's birthday, SS socials, and hangings.[16]

Newcomers who failed to adapt fell after a time into a state of acute apathy. They did not wash, shave, or mend their clothes. They never participated in the most essential inmate activity: the bartering of goods, miserable as these might be. Such men began gradually to resemble the living dead. If a newcomer, determined not to succumb, fell in with an old-timer, usually someone with a similar ethnic, political, or work background, willing to teach him what not to do and the little he should do, he might gradually and painfully learn to adjust.

The civilian penitentiaries of Europe had not been established to eliminate their inmates but rather simply to mete out punishment, to keep criminals away from society, and, perhaps, to reform them. The Nazi camps had a far different objective. They were planned to neutralize and isolate enemies of the state, to subdue, and, if needed, get rid of resisters and entire peoples and groups deemed to be subhuman.[17] To the public, Himmler touted the camps as "beneficial reeducation centers" but by 1942 nobody believed this any longer. Indeed, editorials in *Das Schwarze Korps* or the *Völkischer Beo-*

*bachter* had occasionally been rather explicit: yes, the camps were attempting to reeducate the purely misguided, yet they must show no mercy toward intractable saboteurs or racial and sexual misfits.

From the beginning, Himmler and Eicke had constructed their penal colonies to spread a sense of terror over the population at large. They succeeded beyond all expectations. The word *Kazet* radiated the same numbing fear as the word "Gestapo." By 1941 the camps had assumed two additional functions. They served as "shelters" for the forced-labor battalions in the war-related factories that German businessmen had erected nearby.[18] Only slave labor in the Nazi camps kept the German economy afloat. But this expanding labor force exacerbated the never-ending tug-of-war between what one might call the "pragmatists" and the "fundamentalists." One group, made up of planners and industrialists such as Albert Speer, needed captive workers to produce planes, tanks, guns, chemicals, and so forth, and tried to prevent the other group, the fundamentalists, from exterminating these workers. The pragmatists also frowned on the other function that certain camps had assumed as centers for experimental tests on humans. Here, SS physicians carried out pseudo-medical experiments on inmates without their consent and, it should be added, without proper scientific supervision. None of these tests ever brought results of any worth either to medicine or to war technology.[19]

▽

What was the fate of homosexuals in the netherworld of the camps? How did a homosexual newcomer fit into the institutional mechanism the SS had set up to dominate the inmates, and how did he fit into the counter-mechanism the prisoners had developed to survive? How did homosexual prisoners hold their own in the internal feuds between criminals and antifascists?

After a homosexual arrived in camp, he underwent the first experience of all newcomers: he was seized by a profound trauma. He was battered, kicked, slapped, and reviled. According to at least one witness, homosexuals and Jews were not only given the worst beatings, but their pubic hair was shorn; others lost only their head hair.[20]

A clergyman, remanded to Dachau in September 1941, describes the process well: "The SS man asked everybody on what charges he had been sentenced. One man was there on account of crimes against Paragraph 175. He was cuffed, forced to tell in detail what he had done and how. Then they fell upon him, cuffing and kicking."[21] Another victim recalls his first day in Sachsenhausen: "When my name was called, I stepped forward, gave my name, and mentioned Paragraph 175. With the words 'You filthy queer, get over there, you butt fucker,' I received several kicks . . . then was transferred to an SS sergeant in charge of my block. The first thing I got from him was a violent blow on my face that threw me to the ground . . . he brought his knees up hard into my groin so that I doubled over with pain . . . he grinned at me and said: 'That was your entrance fee, you filthy Viennese swine . . .' "[22]

Another witness testifies about his reception at Camp Natzweiler: "I can swear an oath that because of my pink triangle I was separated from other inmates. An SS sergeant together with a *Kapo* mistreated me in the most brutal manner . . . three times their fists hit my face, especially my nose, so that I fell on the floor three times; when I managed to get up again, they continued battering and hitting me . . . I then staggered back to my barracks, covered with blood."[23]

These degradation rituals were applied to crush all novices.

That, as some survivors have maintained, the pink triangles were always larger than those of other colors, has not been proven.[24] Equally uncertain is whether there was ever any order to sequester homosexuals in special barracks or to distribute them among the regular barracks population. In Dachau, Flossenbürg, and Sachsenhausen they were kept apart for a while. Rudolf Hoess, one of Eicke's prize students, a Dachau official, then commandant of Sachsenhausen and Auschwitz, explained in his memoirs that he ordered homosexuals isolated to make it easier to control them.[25] Hoess also developed the "salvation through work" theory, which he tried out on homosexuals in Sachsenhausen and Auschwitz. It was intended to make the depraved deviants work so hard that they nearly collapsed from exhaustion. This, it was hoped, would "straighten them out." Hoess admitted that it did not always work out this way, but he still kept them separated and assigned them to the cement works, from which it was nearly impossible to emerge alive.

Hoess's directives to keep the homosexuals strictly controlled, apart from all other prisoners, was followed for a while in several camps. Of Flossenbürg, one survivor writes: "Our block was occupied by homosexuals, with about 250 men in each wing. We could sleep only in our nightshirts and had to keep our hands outside the blankets." This was to prevent them from masturbating. "The windows had several layers of ice on them. Anyone found in bed with his underclothes on, or his hands under the blankets—there were several checks every night—was taken outside and had several buckets of water poured over him before being left standing in the cold for a good hour. Only a few people survived this treatment. The least result was bronchitis, and it was rare for any homosexual taken into the sick bay to come out alive."[26] In other institutions, the gays shared quarters with Gypsies, asocials, or foreigners. Occasionally, homosexuals were distributed throughout various barracks and were treated no worse than other prisoners.[27]

What put the homosexuals into a low—if not the lowest—category of prisoner were several factors, some easy to formulate, others more elusive. Hoess, for example, insisted on sequestering the gays. Sealed off in their barracks, they could not fraternize with the antifascist underground, which, Hoess knew, occupied key camp positions. Like Himmler, Hoess seems to have been convinced that most homosexuals were intellectually above average, and thus they might serve as useful allies to the dangerous antifascist power block within the camp. Hoess also believed that homosexuality was an illness that might spread to other inmates or even to the guards. Himmler shared this conviction and, to counter the danger, installed bordellos in many penal colonies. In Sachsenhausen and Auschwitz, Hoess ordered homosexuals to visit the bordellos—perhaps thereby they would be cured and become useful camp laborers.[28]

There appears to have been an additional, deep-rooted folkloric dogma at work that doomed efforts by gays to associate with one another or with their fellow sufferers. In his reminiscences, Hoess observed that "even if they were in poor physical shape, they always had to indulge their vice."[29] It wasn't only Hoess and other SS rulers who presumed that homosexuals always had sex on their minds and were forever bent on seducing heterosexuals. The inmates themselves also tended to regard gays as men for whom nothing was more important than their genitalia. After all, that was why they were jailed, that was what distinguished them from all other prisoners. In the camps, with no women present, even the political prisoners worried that the situation offered the gays too many opportunities to approach sex-starved males. Such contact, in turn, was likely to lead to private relationships, perhaps with *Kapos* or even guards, which might endanger the solidarity of the antifascist coalition. Thus, when gay inmates tried to join a clandestine camp committee, they were rejected. Both Nazi overseers and their prisoners took it for granted that the men with the pink triangles were somehow biologically programmed to seek nothing but sexual satisfaction. Homophobia flourished everywhere, making it nearly impossible for gays to join any effort by prisoners to improve conditions in the barracks. They were suspect as a class. Whatever assistance they might offer was thought to mask a sexual motive.

This widely accepted dogma had long been a staple of German folklore. It was taken as gospel not only by ordinary workers but also by lawmakers, educators, and politicians. From the start, the Nazi regime shrewdly exploited the antihomosexual sentiments of large segments of Germany's populace, much as it had played on the anti-Semitic attitudes of most classes. Nevertheless, while Himmler had branded homosexuals as enemies of the state, as he had labeled Jews, Communists, and other contragenics, this honor did not necessarily mean that non-gay prisoners were particularly willing to accept homosexuals as equal victims.

There were additional factors complicating the lives of gay prisoners. First, a few SS guards were homosexual. Although they risked everything, they made some younger inmates, usually Poles or Russians, their "dolly boys" (*Pielpel*). They would also occasionally compete with *Kapos* for these teenagers. They even drew lots to determine who should go to whom. Naturally, it enraged the other inmates to watch as these youngsters received extra food rations and were exempted from tough work assignments in exchange for sexual favors.[30] There were also some SS guards who took special pleasure in occasionally masturbating while torturing prisoners.[31] For such acts, the gay inmates were, so to speak, held accountable by the non-gay inmates: homosexual guards, however hostile, were seen by non-gay prisoners as belonging to the homosexual underclass. Thus, homosexual prisoners were often tainted by the crimes of homosexual guards— even though they themselves were often the victims.[32]

Cooperation among camp homosexuals was rare. Unlike the hard-core criminals, the antifascists, and the Gypsies, the gays came from such widely disparate backgrounds that group solidarity was hard to achieve. As Raimund Schnabel has observed in his study of Dachau: "Among the homosexuals were exceptional people whose deviance could be called tragic; on the other hand [there were] also cheap hustlers and blackmailers. The prisoners with the pink triangle never lived long. They were exterminated by the SS quickly and systematically."[33] Eugen Kogon, who survived six years in Buchenwald as a political prisoner, went on to write the still-classic account of the camp experience, *The Theory and Practice of Hell*. Kogon gives more attention to the fate of contragenic minorities than do most other writers. He confirms what Schnabel discovered about Dachau, that the plight of homosexuals was made especially terrible.

This group had a very heterogeneous composition. It included individuals of real value, in addition to large numbers of criminals and especially blackmailers. This made the position of the group as a whole very precarious. . . . Homosexual practices were actually very widespread in the camps. The prisoners, however, ostracized only those whom the SS marked with the pink triangle. The fate of the homosexuals in the concentration camps can only be described as ghastly. They were often segregated in special barracks and work details. Such segregation offered ample opportunity to unscrupulous elements in positions of power to engage in extortion and maltreatment. Until the fall of 1938 the homosexuals at Buchenwald were divided up among the barracks occupied by political prisoners, where they led a rather inconspicuous life. In October 1938, they were transferred to the penal company in a body and had to slave in the quarry. This consigned them to the lowest caste in camp during the most difficult years. In shipments to extermination camps, such as Nordhausen, Natzweiler, and Gross-Rosen, they furnished the highest proportionate share, for the camp had an understandable tendency to slough off all elements considered least valuable or worthless. If anything could save them at all, it was to enter into sordid relationships within the camp, but this was as likely to endanger their lives as to save them. Theirs was an insoluble predicament and virtually all of them perished.[34]

Lautmann's team, examining the dossiers of 1,572 homosexual inmates, corroborates Kogon's assessment. Moreover, Lautmann found very few gays who acted as *Kapos*. Without a *Kapo*, prisoners were unable to strike profitable life-saving deals with camp officials and guards.[35]

Lautmann's analysis of the occupational backgrounds of homosexuals shows that while 77 percent of the political prisoners and 81 percent of the Jehovah's Witnesses were employed as manual laborers, only 56 percent of the homosexuals did such work. About 44 percent of the gays held office jobs of some kind, whereas only 23 percent of the political prisoners and 19 percent of the Jehovah's Witnesses were clerical workers.[36] The contempt of blue-collar prisoners for men who had once held desk jobs might also have helped to isolate the homosexuals from the bulk of the camp's inmates.

In the life of every prisoner, connections with the outside world played a vital part. Many survivors remember bitterly how the SS constables, together with corrupt *Kapos*, stole packages or rifled them, and how they withheld mail at whim or as punishment. Still, a few parcels and letters managed to slip through. To the jailers, the incoming mail of an inmate meant that he had contacts, possibly with officials who might exert pressure or pay money to work out a transfer or even a discharge. Most homosexuals, however, were cut off from contacts with the outside world. Very few families seem to have been willing to stand by sons, brothers, husbands, or other relatives convicted of crimes against Paragraph 175. Few gay friends would dare to establish communications when such a gesture might endanger their own precarious existence. In the climate of terror that the Nazis had created, even direct relatives, close friends, or former lovers hesitated to contact homosexual prisoners. Some homosexuals in camp, anxious to avoid entangling others, sought intentionally never to initiate contact with the outside.[37]

What counted in the never-ending struggle for dominance between politicals and criminals were positions of power and the tight organizational bonds of toughened men determined to resist the SS at almost any price. The small minority of homosexuals, utterly disunited, usually apolitical, and thought to be abnormally passive, were particularly vulnerable to abuse. Thus, if a quota had to be filled for one of the more crushing labor details, such as the dreaded cement works, an antifascist Kapo was likely to choose criminals, Jehovah's Witnesses, asocials, and homosexuals before turning to his political comrades.

Hardened criminals, when running a camp such as Flossenbürg, would occasionally give a single homosexual a chance. A handsome young homosexual might improve his lot by becoming a dolly boy. One Austrian survivor recounts how he was saved at Flossenbürg:

> We were led to our block by an SS guard, and transferred there to the sergeant in charge . . . a group of eight to ten Kapos gath-

ered round us and looked us up and down. I was already wise enough to know exactly why [they] . . . were admiring us in this way. They were on the lookout for a possible lover among the new arrivals. Because I still did not have a full beard, even though nearly twenty-three, so looked younger than my years, and because I had filled out a bit again thanks to the supplementary rations from my Sachsenhausen *Kapo*, I was obviously very much at the center of these *Kapos'* considerations. I could tell as much from their unconcealed discussions. The situation in which the five of us found ourselves seemed to me very much like a slave-boy market in ancient Rome. . . . When the sergeant had departed, and the block senior had to assign us new arrivals our beds, he immediately came up to me and said: "Hey you, kid, do you want to come with me?"

"Yes, certainly," I said right away, knowing very well what he meant. My immediate acceptance somehow made an impression on him. He said: "You're a clever kid, I like that," and patted me on the shoulder. . . . The senior whose lover I became was a professional criminal from Hamburg, very highly regarded in his milieu as a safecracker. He was much feared by the prisoners for his ruthlessness, and even by his *Kapo* colleagues, but he was generous and considerate to me. Only half a year later he became camp senior, and remained so until the Americans liberated the camp. Even later on, when I was no longer his lover, his eye having fallen on a young Pole, he kept a protecting hand over me. He saved my life more than ten times over, and I am still very grateful to him for this today, more than twenty-five years later.[38]

Such behavior is no surprise. This is the pattern of penal institutions and their inmates everywhere. But while such an arrangement might improve the prospects of an individual, it could never do anything to advance the status of homosexual prisoners as a group. On the contrary, it helped to isolate the young "favorites," thus arousing the fury of those less well fed, and exposing the dolly boys to the suspicion that they were informers.[39] It was very difficult for a dolly boy who enjoyed the friendship of a green *Kapo* or an SS officer to join a camp's clandestine opposition—he had, so to speak, been bought by the other side, and had bartered his birthright as an inmate for bread from the foe.

One additional note. The two most knowledgeable historians of the camps, Italian chemist Primo Levi (a survivor of Auschwitz) and Kogon maintain that just as the majority of women stopped menstruating after four to six months in Eicke's penal chambers, so too did men gradually lose their sexual urges; they were weakened by the grueling work, the starvation diet, and the lack of medical care. Even the stronger prisoners came to loathe their emaciated bodies, infected with parasites and covered with dirt.[40] For the majority of prisoners, homosexual activity was, at best, tacitly tolerated as "locational sex," a hygienic relief measure—if it did not put others at a disadvantage. This was true so long as the older partner was able to dispense favors without getting caught and the dolly boys did not gossip and stayed out of trouble. None of the participants in these locational sex activities had been arrested as violators of Paragraph 175; they wore green, red, and black insignia in various combinations. In contrast, men with the pink triangle were stigmatized from the start and had to bear the brunt of the centuries-old hostility toward homosexuals.

L.W., a Protestant theology graduate student at the time of his arrest, has observed that the supervisor of his Sachsenhausen penal labor battalion referred to the pink triangle wearers as "menwomen" (*Mannweiber*). These sissies, he declared, deserved the worst, and he proudly reported that the labor in the Sachsenhausen cement works finished almost all of them. L.W. also repeats the testimony of other survivors: in most penal institutions where he had been held, gays and

Jews were considered the lowest, most expendable group.[41] Another survivor remembers that the guards lashed out with special fury against those who showed "effeminate" traits. In one case, this witness had to watch helplessly while a guard battered the penis and testicles of a young dancer. The witness himself, incidentally, was released because of family connections to Himmler, who, declaring him a "Nordic, manly specimen," had him discharged when he promised to "mend his ways."[42]

Two of the worst assignments the camps forced on homosexual inmates were the special labor details in the quarries of Flossenbürg, Buchenwald, Sachsenhausen, Mauthausen, or Dora-Mittelbau, and the medical experiments carried out in various institutions. To understand what these assignments meant necessitates knowing some essential facts of camp life. At least three-quarters of an inmate's day was spent on some work detail. The prisoners had to build the first camps themselves. Most of the work was truly needed—if they wanted a barracks made secure from rain and cold, they had to do a creditable job. But because the available supplies and tools often proved to be of poor quality, much of what was done collapsed and had to be done over and over again. However wearying these tasks proved to be, they were resented less than those designed primarily to punish the detainees—senseless exertions, such as building a wall in the morning and tearing it down in the afternoon. These cruel practices not only gave pleasure to the overseers—it gave them an opportunity to mock their charges—but they emphasized the limitless power held by the SS. The abyss between the powerful and the powerless grew infinitely when both were aware that the tasks demanded were utterly meaningless.

Later, after industrial enterprises grew up near the camps, conditions should have improved—after all, you need a halfway healthy laborer to get work done that is not only exhaustive but sometimes demands precision. Yet, while a few specialists managed to slip into less strenuous jobs, the conditions in many of the forced-labor factories were not better than in the regular camps. Certain assignments had the reputation of being death warrants. One of the most notorious was Dora-Mittelbau, a maze of underground factories near Buchenwald that produced V-2 rockets. Its tunnels—dark, moist, and without proper latrines—had narrow bunks stacked on four tiers in which workers had to sleep. The stones often dripped water; plaster and cement dust ruined the lungs, rapidly causing tuberculosis. The percentage of homosexuals ordered to Dora-Mittelbau was larger than that of any other group.[43] Hoess proudly reported how, in Sachsenhausen, he had assigned the homosexuals to the cement works for its "educational" value. Such work would "cure them of their vices." He conceded, though, that the work was "hard."[44] The recollection of L. D. von Classen-Neudegg differs markedly from that of Hoess.

It happened in June 1942. In Camp Sachsenhausen, there started one of those special operations designed to get rid of a few hundred people. This time, they worked out the final solution for the homosexuals; they would be put into a special liquidation command where forced labor and starvation would bring about a slow, painful end. . . . After roll call . . . an order was suddenly given: "All inmates with pink triangles will remain standing at attention." We stood on the desolate square . . . our throats dry from fear. . . . Then the guardhouse door of the command tower opened and an SS officer and some of his lackeys strode toward us. Our *Kapo* barked: "Three hundred criminal deviants present as ordered." . . . We learned that we were to be segregated in a penal command and the next morning would be transferred as a unit to the cement works. . . . We shuddered because these bone mills were more dreaded than any other work detail. . . . "You don't have to look so dumb, you butt fuckers," said the officer. "There you'll learn to do honest work with your hands and afterward you will sleep a healthy sleep. You are a biological mistake of the Creator. That's why you must be bent straight. . . ." Guarded by staff sergeants with machine guns, we had to sprint in lines of five until we arrived. . . . They kept beating us with rifle butts and bullwhips. . . . Forced to drag along twenty corpses, the rest of us encrusted with blood, we entered the cement quarry. Then the martyrdom started. . . . Within two months, the special operation had lost two-thirds. . . . To shoot someone "trying to escape" was a profitable business for the guards. For everyone killed, they received five marks and three days' special furlough. . . . Whips were used more frequently each morning, when we were forced into the pits. . . . "Only fifty are still alive," whispered the man next to me. . . . When I weighed not much more than eighty-five pounds, one of the sergeants told me one morning: "Well, that's it. You want to go to the other side? It won't hurt. I'm a crack shot."[45]

These assignments left the inmates totally at the mercy of the SS. Here the guards could give full vent to their loathing of the "butt fuckers," far away from the camps and barracks where *Kapos* and other middlemen could occasionally exert a moderating influence.[46] From the few sources available, it appears that the percentage of homosexuals shipped to the quarries of Flossenbürg, Sachsenhausen, Buchenwald, and Mauthausen was larger than that of any other group.[47]

In one of the institutions for which few records have survived, Natzweiler-Struthof, a camp in Alsace-Lorraine,[48] a gay physician recalls that

While we were working, my partner, a barber, and I were continually kicked and beaten by both the SS guards and the *Kapos*. One evening, when we had to parade in the nude for delousing, our block leader took pity on us and tried to make at least the *Kapo* stop the torture. He could not do anything about the SS brutalities. Then we two with the pink triangles were assigned to different details—the barber to the sick bay and I—who by now was convinced I was the only scapegoat left alive in the camp—to a unit near Metz. There I obtained a position in the registry. In addition to my regular job, I had to work at night, between midnight and 2:00 A.M.

For this, the prisoner was rewarded with some leftover food that saved his life.

He ends his story on a note familiar to all who have talked to survivors: "Please don't ask me for more incidents. During the last two nights, all these nightmarish scenes from Natzweiler kept haunting me again. It makes me ill."[49]

Perhaps the most feared assignments were to a detachment marked "Medical Experiments."[50] Kogon has concluded that, again, the number of homosexuals used for these pseudomedical undertakings was disproportionately large.[51] Consider the hormone experiments administered in Buchenwald by the Danish endocrinologist Carl Vaernet with the German surgeon Gerhard Schiedlausky. These were only a few of the many that took place there.[52] I have singled out those by Vaernet because he used homosexual inmates exclusively, and because the sources in Arolsen were sufficient to draw conclusions. The hormone tests, however, can stand as a model for virtually all of those tests carried out by the Nazis on their human guinea pigs. These experiments brought illness and death to the subjects and had no scientific value. Often, physicians and laboratory technicians did not know how to proceed; files and samples were incomplete or misplaced; medicine could not be checked for purity; and there was no control group. In the case at hand, Allied bombers repeatedly destroyed containers carrying blood, urine, and other specimens in transit from Buchenwald to Vaernet's laboratory in Prague.

In December 1943 the Buchenwald inmate roster lists 169 homosexuals; in March 1945, the last entry, four months before defeat, reveals their number to have dwindled to eighty-nine.[53] The Buchenwald statistics have been comparatively well preserved for 1943. They group the prisoners into such categories as hard-core criminals, asocials, antifascists, Jehovah's Witnesses, homosexuals, "racial defilers," and convicted former armed forces members. Vaernet's hormone tests took place in 1944, a year for which only scant files have been salvaged. Like so many similar atrocities in the Third Reich, the tests were frequently encoded.[54] The hormone tests were coded but plainly labeled "Medical Experiments on Homosexuals." The extant dossier consists of two parts: first, notes on the progress or failure of the program; second, the correspondence between Vaernet in Prague and Schiedlausky, the Buchenwald surgeon.[55] The first section, labeled "Medical Experiments No. 5," is dated July 29, 1944. It notes that "five genuine homosexuals should be selected so that Dr. Vaernet could try out his theory." Vaernet's theory was probably based on the premise that homosexuals could become heterosexuals by hormone treatments, a field in which Vaernet had specialized. If successful, such treatments would aid Himmler's unending efforts to produce more offspring, in conjunction with his directives to send homosexuals to bordellos for "conversion."

From the start, complications beset the two physicians. Subalterns did not seem capable of following orders. Although the documents mention the names of only five men selected at the start of 1944, a later entry notes the names of ten gay subjects. Another gives the names and numbers of seven gays selected for castration and hormonal "rebirth," but their names are only partially identical with the five chosen originally. In short, the sources, as is so often the case, are incomplete and frequently filled with contradictions. The letters between Prague and Buchenwald complain about incompetent handling all around, about missing names, slipshod identification—in at least one instance the prisoners' numbers were mailed without their accompanying names—and loss of good urine. The camp itself did not have the laboratory facilities to measure the hormone levels of the subjects or to analyze blood, sputum, and urine. Vaernet's method was brutally simple: castrate several homosexuals, inject them with huge doses of male hormones, then wait to see whether they would begin to exhibit signs of interest in the opposite sex.

Schiedlausky laments the fact that during the long trip to Prague the urine samples would change chemically to such an extent as to be useless. It is not clear how the doctors overcame this problem, but in September 1944, by special permission of Himmler, Vaernet traveled to Buchenwald. Eight prisoners were chosen for castration. The documents do not detail their fate. Instead, they speak of new complications: for instance, there had been confusion as to which subject's blood sample was in which container. The actual operations seem to have been delayed for other reasons: Allied bombers were attacking targets between Prague and Buchenwald—though not Buchenwald itself. Thus, Vaernet, who seems to have gone back to Prague, could not visit again. Finally, on October 1, 1944, Vaernet managed to get to Buchenwald, intent on checking the cholesterol and calcium levels in the subjects' blood before and after castration.

Since surviving entries are spotty, if not nearly illegible, one can only conclude that on October 1, 1944, a group of seven homosexuals was operated on, and a second group, consisting of eleven more, on October 10. Additional tests may have been administered, because Vaernet visited Buchenwald again in December. The evaluation process seems to have hit many snags. Again and again, Vaernet criticizes the sloppy labeling of the samples arriving in Prague. Some subjects became ill; some, so it seems, must have died, because new names appear on the rosters of those actually castrated. Vaernet carefully filled out order forms for chloroform, bandages, and new medical instruments, and handed out instruction sheets explaining how Buchenwald physicians should continue the castration-hormone tests without him. No final report has survived that notes the results of the experiments on the castrated men.

Vaernet was forced to stop his tests because of the danger of a yellow fever epidemic in the camp. The epidemic was not a result of infection from outside sources, such as prisoners of war from the East, as frequently happened in other institutions. The Buchenwald outbreak followed experiments with the microorganism responsible for yellow fever, which had gotten out of hand. Although Buchenwald seems to have provided better isolation wards than most camps, many prisoners—and some guards—died. By then Vaernet had probably returned to Prague, but his name appears again in the files for Neuengamme, a camp near Hamburg, where he attempted to repeat his castration-hormone tests. The Neuengamme documents do not state whether he actually finished them.

From the available records it cannot be determined whether homosexuals were also used for other pseudo-medical experiments, administered not only in Buchenwald but in camps like Dachau, Sachsenhausen, Ravensbrück, and Auschwitz. Dachau specialized in tests involving malaria, high-altitude simulation, and underwater tanks; Buchenwald in yellow fever and sulfur drugs; Auschwitz in the sterilization of women. Most experiments recruited larger numbers of subjects than Vaernet did.[56]

▽

It now seems appropriate to draw a balance sheet. From available police and Gestapo statistics, from numerous testimonies, including those by SS officers, from surveys, interviews, and recollections—of which I have given a few representative examples—five basic facts seem to explain why most homosexual detainees were destroyed in the camps.

1. The homosexuals constituted one of the smaller minorities. Unlike antifascists, Jews, and foreign nationals who sometimes succeeded in setting up active inmate organizations, gays offered no challenge to the SS personnel.

2. The homosexuals were a decidedly heterogeneous group, and therefore hard to rally. Their members ranged from professionals and artists to hustlers and laborers. For political reasons, some men had been stigmatized with a pink triangle, although they had never committed crimes against Paragraph 175. In all, the gays offered the reverse pattern of those tightly bonded national groups who, in several places, fought for and gained minor food and work benefits.

3. Inside the camps, the barracks were run either by criminals or antifascists. Each of these factions, having once gained the power positions in the key offices, favored its own members in all vital areas of camp existence, especially food distribution, labor assignments, and sick-bay referrals. Thus, few Gypsies, homosexuals, clergymen, Jehovah's Witnesses, asocials, "race defilers," or armed forces deserters were placed in the privileged positions that of-

fered some measure of relief from the daily trials. If an inmate could not slip into any of these jobs, his chances for getting out alive were extremely low. In addition, gays were often shipped to high-mortality tasks in factories and quarries.

4. Neither the hard-core criminals nor the antifascists were interested in cooperating with the homosexuals. To be sure, a green *Kapo* might pick an attractive young gay inmate as a favorite, but gays as a group did not profit from such an arrangement. The inmates themselves reflected the rejection that homosexuals had faced in Germany long before Himmler and Eicke had built penal colonies. On their side, the SS overseers were drilled to treat all prisoners as dangerous contragenics and to apply unremitting violence as the only appropriate method for keeping inmates under control. To them, homosexuals were despicable degenerates, and therefore they could and did indulge in manifold humiliation rituals.

5. Outside assistance was scant. Close relatives often would not lend support because they were ashamed that "one of the family" had been convicted for crimes against Paragraph 175. Former associates, friends, or lovers were even more reluctant—for good reasons. Thus the homosexual prisoners were virtually cut off from the world outside.

Whatever statistics we possess tend to substantiate these five points. The death rate can only be tabulated for those prisoners for whom records have been preserved. Those we possess show that in 1945, when the camps were liberated, the mortality rate of the homosexuals was higher than that of the other units investigated.[57]

Considering the large numbers of other prisoners, homosexuals played a minor role in the SS blueprints, just as they constituted a minor part of the inmate organizations. That at the war's end, in 1945, so few were able and ready to come out and testify cannot be explained alone by the fact that so few survived. The world into which they found themselves liberated was still officially hostile. According to German law, homosexual ex-prisoners were to be treated as criminals. East Germany voided the Nazi version of Paragraph 175 only in 1967; West Germany followed in 1969, adding minor alterations in 1973. Moreover, some American and British jurists of the liberation armies, on learning that an inmate had been jailed and then put into camp for homosexual activities, ruled that, judicially, a camp did not constitute a prison. If, therefore, someone had been sentenced to eight years in prison, had spent five of these in jail and three in a camp, he still had to finish three years in jail after liberation. In at least one instance, a homosexual camp detainee was given a stern lecture by an American colonel, informing him that the United States also considered what he had done criminally offensive.[58] For homosexuals, the Third Reich did not fully end with its defeat. None of the lucky few who came out alive was granted any compensation when the new postwar West German government, bowing to American pressure, set up a cumbersome but functioning legal bureaucracy to grant restitution to political, Jewish, and other selected ex-inmates. Moreover, gay survivors often did not return to a loving family or a group of sympathetic peers during the first months of readjustment. Families frequently refused to take back a homosexual ex-inmate. And former gay friends were usually displaced or dead. Although they were no longer compelled to wear the stigmatic pink triangle, they felt marked for life. And like so many victims of the Third Reich, most gays never recovered emotionally from the Nazi boomtowns of hell.[59]

# CONCLUSION

The persecution and attempted extermination of homosexuals represents but one part of the exhaustive crusade the Nazis launched to purge Germany of contragenics of all kinds and to create an Aryan elite that would dominate Europe and, finally, the world. Today, hindsight enables historians more clearly to assess the successes and failures of the Nazi regime's policies. But the distance of time and professional "objectivity" has by no means resolved the riddle of the Third Reïch. The crimes committed, and the crimes planned, were so unspeakably monstrous that the human mind fails to apprehend their full dimensions. What happened is now known; the question of why it happened remains unanswered.

A number of historians have interpreted the Nazis' war as a crusade, kindled not by greed for territorial and material gains but by a mission: to create an exclusively Aryan utopia. If millions had to be sacrificed for this lofty goal, it did not matter. Other historians consider World War II a replay of World War I. Both interpretations are partly correct. Hitler waged several wars, and Himmler waged several wars; occasionally their aims overlapped. The generals, whose obedience was assured after the von Fritsch debacle in 1938, tried to carry out Hitler's often amateurish orders in a professional way. After 1943, a few recognized his folly and occasionally thwarted his directives. Hitler's aims were clear: he was as eager to conquer Europe as he was to annihilate the Jews.

# Conclusion

Toward the end, with one part of his mind registering the fact that final military victory might elude him—although until the last nights in the bunker he would not confront this—he decided at least to win that other war, the one against the Jews.[1]

Himmler, for his part, was overtaxed. First, he had to carry out orders for the elimination of Jews, Poles, antifascists, and other "dangerous" groups. Second, he untiringly pursued his own efforts to strike out against other contragenics such as Gypsies, Jehovah's Witnesses, and homosexuals. From a practical and strategic point of view, this campaign was not worth the huge policing effort it needed to succeed. But, then, few of his goals could be called reasonable or practical. While the Allies held Germany encircled, Himmler still wasted energy and personnel in pressuring the armed forces to more vigorously prosecute sexually deviant soldiers and sailors.

Himmler's and Eicke's innovation—the concentration camps—must be understood as the evil icons of our century. The Nazis' totalitarian apparatus could not tolerate nonconformity of any kind, and all deviants were to be eliminated. The German military machine, however, was engaged in a conventional war of territorial conquest. As the net closed tighter around the Nazis, every able-bodied male was needed—at the front or in the war factories under Albert Speer. These two goals kept colliding: here castigation and slavery, there attempts to run an efficient economic machine. In vain Speer tried to obtain better conditions for his forced-labor battalions: they remained ill-fed, ill-housed, ill-clothed, and unable to fulfill work quotas. Whether Speer knew more about conditions in the camps than he admitted is debatable. Police authorities were continually meddling with the running of camp enterprises. They arrested inmate-laborers for trifling infractions. Throughout their tenure, Hoess and other commandants were caught in a double bind. They continually received contradictory orders—for example, to provide manpower for a new munitions depot, and simultaneously to apply stricter punitive measures against recalcitrant prisoners. Even notorious commandants such as Franz Stangl of Treblinka or Josef Kramer of Belsen could not increase war-related production in the camps while the prisoners who manned them were brutalized or eliminated.

By 1944, less ideologically blinded Nazis began to realize that what Hitler had brought forth was, indeed, a modern version of hell. The fact that some officials became aware of the need to cover up their crimes can be seen from the frenetic efforts, starting as early as mid 1942, to erase all proof. Records were burned and witnesses eliminated—which, of course, produced other witnesses. These exertions failed for several reasons. First, crimes of such enormity cannot be kept hidden. Even when Hitler cautiously began the euthanasia program in 1939, involving a limited number of native misfits and cripples, it could not be kept concealed. The villagers soon knew what the black smoke rising from the new "asylums" meant. Although many of the new penal colonies were purposely built amid the vast plains and marshes of the East, the mass transports and the mass killings—and the smell of the smoke—could not be kept secret. Second, from early on, the antifascists and some of the better organized Jewish prisoners started copying and hiding important files and records, sometimes burying them in the grounds or bricking them into the buildings they were constructing. Of course, most buildings did not last, and the hastily scribbled lists mostly disintegrated. But enough telltale evidence escaped oblivion. After 1943, Allied headquarters also knew of these infernos in the East, although the Allies preferred to deemphasize their true nature.[2] And, naturally, not all camp employees could be counted on never to talk out of camp. Quite a few paid for their indiscretions and were arrested for "spreading subversive rumors"—but the damage was done. If the Nazis tried to create "holes of oblivion," they failed on a vast scale.[3]

The Nazi penal machinery, as I have indicated, was both illogical and inefficient. It sacrificed the practical needs for manpower and materiel to an ideological rationale that undermined the effort to win the war. The enormity of both the penal bureaucracy and the crimes committed by it and its chiefs compounded that inefficiency in both the short run and the long run, by destroying the war-winning capacity of Germany and by devastating the country's national image for generations to come.

That homosexuals, by a series of laws, were treated as subhumans does not seem in retrospect particularly illogical or even unexpected. After all, their classification as heretical deviants boasted a long lineage. From the viewpoint of Nazi logic, the extermination policy concerning homosexuals had a kind of ideological justification. Himmler's concept of a National Sexual Budget classified homosexuals as "propagation blanks" and diagnosed them as a health hazard because they spread a so-called homosexual infection. Eicke's police needed no such ideological rationale: homosexuals were simply regarded with the hatred characteristic of ancient homophobic superstitions.

In the course of European history, a vast number of bulls and mandates, pamphlets and tracts lumped together Jews, homosexuals, and other heretics, and linked them to witches, sexual deviants, and traitors. In the thirteenth century, for example, the Fourth Lateran Council of 1215 forbade Jews from holding public office; they were directed to wear special garments to distinguish them from Christians. Perhaps it was here that the practice of scapegoating by coded badges began, a technique that, some seven hundred years later, the Nazis would use to identify contragenics. It seems that if the Inquisition called a man a heretic, it meant that he was a practicing homosexual, and vice versa.[4] And in England, from the thirteenth century on, as the Jews were driven out, a new code condemned to death arsonists, sorcerers, heretics, those who slept with the wives of their feudal lords, and those who had intercourse with Jews, animals, or their own gender.[5] Again and again, authorities charged their opponents, both real and imagined, with religious (and later political) and sexual malpractices. From the thirteenth century to the twentieth, the hold of these anti-Semitic and homophobic mythologies has never been broken among large parts of the population of Western Europe.

Given this rich tradition of hatred in Western civilization, a fundamental question arises as to whether certain features of Hitler's reign of terror were an eruption of evil unique to twentieth-century Germany. Over this issue historians and sociologists have quarreled violently and inconclusively. For some, Hitler and his followers represent a gang of perverted if not demented paranoiacs; for others, the Third Reich is judged to be the legitimate heir to the militarist-imperialist traditions of Germany. Neither explanation satisfies. Perhaps Richard Rubenstein was closer to the heart of the matter when he suggested that it was wrong to "isolate Nazism and its supreme expression, bureaucratic mass murder and the bureaucratically administered society of total domination, from the mainstream of Western culture."[6] The Third Reich forever destroyed the myth of inexorable human progress. In less than one hundred years after most Western nations had finally abolished slavery, Hitler and Himmler brought it back. This time the slaves were not a special ethnic group, exploited solely for economic purposes, but rather contragenics of all kinds who were pushed into the forced-labor battalions in the camps and the factories surrounding them. While the Gulag that dots Russia's northern tundra was not designed to exterminate its inmates, it enslaves them and must be classified as a close relative of Hitler's bone mills. One is tempted to say that the twentieth century has mistreated minorities in a more brutal fashion than many preceding periods. And it is precisely technological progress that has made possible ever more refined techniques of brutalization, torture, and obliteration.[7]

Thus the fate of the gays under the Third Reich may serve as a touchstone for all those victims swept away by the hurricane of hatred. To this day, the extent and impact of this catastrophe has not been fully understood. At the end of hostilities, when Allied soldiers first entered the concentration camps, they did not really comprehend what they saw. And despite the overwhelming flood of information about the Nazis' infernal machine, we still have not understood what it may foreshadow. In many ways, the specters of the Third Reich still haunt us—not because a few elderly Nazis may be hiding in South America and not because groups of younger neo-Nazis demand attention with recycled swastika ideologies and emblems. The specters begin to come to life whenever fanatical fundamentalists of any sect—religious or secular—take over a nation and call for a holy war against its most vulnerable and vilified minorities.

# E P I L O G U E

When the war ended in 1945, my job was in jeopardy. For nearly four years I had worked as a translator-scriptwriter-broadcaster for the U.S. Office of War Information. Our team of three took mimeographed releases from OWI headquarters in Washington, sometimes serviceable, sometimes bizarre, most of the time marvelously inappropriate, and fashioned brief anti-Nazi newscasts to be transmitted by European "black stations" set up by the British. To this day I cannot say whether our propaganda ever reached its target—people in Europe would be severely punished if they were caught tuning into these pernicious foreign broadcasts. Now the OWI was gradually being dismantled. But the loss of a job bothered me far less than what I was beginning to learn in great detail about the concentration camps.

Shortly after I reached America in 1938, I had established contact with a German-Jewish weekly called *Aufbau* ("Reconstruction"). I contributed articles on film, literature, and theater. *Aufbau* was one of the first papers in New York to publish documentation on the camps, on the destruction of the Jewish communities. It printed eyewitness accounts by those who had lived through Dachau, Buchenwald, Auschwitz, and others. Like most emigrés, I did not really believe them at the time. Only later, as more facts were disclosed in American and Swiss publications, did I begin to accept the unacceptable. I knew my father had not survived; it took years until my sister in Holland could find me, or, rather, until I could find her. And at night, when sleep evaded me, my brain conjured up Eric Langer, the one true friend of my Frankfurt years, who had joined the German navy in 1935 and of whom I had had no news for more than ten years. The day after Germany's surrender I began writing Hilda, his mother, at their old address in Cronberg, near Frankfurt— but invariably the letters came back marked "Addressee moved. No forwarding address." Again and again I flipped through the tattered pages of my Frankfurt address book, picking out names and places. But my missives went unanswered.

That Ferdi, another companion of my school years, never responded I could have anticipated. Ferdi, erratic, sexually compulsive, politically promiscuous, and altogether reckless, had for years lived in furnished rooms and changed them frequently. And of course no relatives of mine were still living in my hometown. In short, I was cut off. Only by revisiting Frankfurt might I find Eric, or at least discover somebody who knew of him and his mother. But while one part of me urged me to go back, leaving everything in America behind, the other part shouted the opposite: after what had happened in Germany, it was impossible to return. In some way or another, every adult beyond a certain age had collaborated, it seemed, with the barbarians. Only the very young could be trusted, and they could not provide the clues I needed.

One voice told me to leave behind, at least for a while, the first satisfying job I had obtained since the OWI broadcasting unit was disbanded. I had been hired on three days' notice as an adjunct lecturer in German language and literature at the City College in New York. Against all expectations, I took to my work. After a few semesters I had even learned the intricate procedures of academic etiquette, or, rather, I had learned which rules to observe and which to bend. Yet I felt so insecure that I did not dare take other than summer vacations. When I discussed my predicament with a checkered group of German-speaking emigrés who assembled every Saturday evening at the comfortable ramshackle apartment of a Viennese woman known as Countess Valeska—no one knew her real name—I received no advice, but a lot of heat. Several members castigated me for even thinking about setting foot on German soil; others, equally fervent, declared their intention of going home to help build a new strong German democracy.

Not until much later did I stop vacillating. I do not recall my first positive step, but I am certain it came from a chance meeting with a man from Frankfurt, who, after being arrested, had been shipped to Neuengamme and then, around 1943 or 1944, had been transferred to a penal brigade in Russia—an outfit from which few ever returned. This man, whom I will call Willy, was now employed as a butler by a wealthy American businessman. If Willy told me he was in his forties, I had to believe him, just as I had to believe his odyssey, which defied probability. He was of medium height, with gray eyes, sandy hair turning white, an exquisitely lined face, and a voice that suppressed all emotion. His hands kept moving as if animated by a hidden motor. The only reason Willy agreed to meet with me was that I, too, had grown up in Frankfurt where he and his current lover were born, and because he hoped I might be able to tell him about some friends of the past with whom he had lost touch. Unfortunately, I could not tell him anything. When Willy was arrested in 1942 he had been a pharmacology student. The Gestapo had discovered some of his letters at the home of his lover, an older pharmacist. His lover, Willy assumed, had been arrested and executed immediately—he never confronted him in a trial and did not know why he himself had been spared. As he recalled, the letters were not especially compromising, but then, his lover had been a practicing Catholic who had not always kept his opinions to himself.

Willy would not provide more particulars about his arrest or his later stay at Neuengamme, near Hamburg. At first the jailers roughed him up, but then left him alone—he was the youngest in jail. In Neuengamme he worked endless hours on outdoors detail, often up to his waist in fetid marsh water. Like most of the men with the pink triangle, he was beaten by the guards and he witnessed the deaths of several fellow prisoners. Then a *Kapo* picked him as his "friend" and managed to place him in sick bay because of his knowledge of pharmacology. There Willy had access to food and was comparatively safe from the beatings the guards gave all those with either yellow or pink triangles.

In 1943–44 the tide of the war turned against Hitler. As more soldiers and workers were needed, Himmler promised to free those who would either agree to be castrated and work in war-essential factories or volunteer for frontline duty. By that time Willy's protector had been transferred, and Willy felt more insecure than ever. Together with a colleague he "volunteered" for frontline service and was shipped east to join the Dirlewanger Brigade. Captain Oskar Dirlewanger, a certified ex-criminal, operated antipartisan units behind the German front in Russia and the Ukraine. In Willy's opinion it was worse than the work in the marshes. Dirlewanger distrusted everybody and often had his own soldiers shot.

"At first Dirlewanger did not know I had worn a pink patch," Willy said. "Since I am a Catholic, he may have thought I had been arrested for not following the anticlerical Nazi line. Again I was fortunate because I had been assigned to a first-aid corporal who was fed up with the entire operation. He did not tell on me. I don't know who did. In any case, one night I was ordered to get up with two others. We had to pin huge pink triangles on the shirtsleeves and pants of the summer uniforms they issued us. Then they marched us to a clearing in the forest. It was below freezing." The soldiers tied their victims to some trees, cursed them, and then rushed back to their quarters. Willy thinks he lost consciousness after about one hour. A group of Russian soldiers from a reconnaissance patrol cut them free and brought them to their divisional headquarters. They did not know the meaning of the pink patches and at first believed all three to be dead. However, a Russian-Armenian physician brought Willy back to life and taught him enough Russian so he could help out in the hospital. Willy did not know how the physician, named Aram, managed to keep him from either being shot or put into a prisoner-of-war camp. Perhaps Willy's pharmacological skills were needed.

After Willy had regained some strength, Aram managed to secure an assignment at a hospital near the Black Sea. Once again, how Aram succeeded in taking him along, Willy could not tell. By that time the war was nearing its end. Aram, who had family ties in both Turkey and America, apparently had planned an escape from Russia beforehand. In 1945, Aram and Willy crossed the border into Turkey, where Aram's cousin took them in. Later another relative, living in Massachusetts, arranged entry into the United States. Aram and Willy lived in New York only a short while before Aram died. Willy quit the pharmacy college where he had enrolled and eventually obtained his present job as a butler.

Our meeting had lasted more than an hour. Willy seemed exhausted and did not want to talk any longer. Again and again, I had to promise not to reveal his identity. When I pressed him for more information—how Aram had succeeded in keeping the Russian authorities from taking Willy away, how Aram had managed to get transferred to a Black Sea hospital unit so far behind the front—he shook his head. I did not have the nerve to push any harder, and asked for a second interview. Though I gave him my address and phone number when he left, he did not give me his. After a few weeks he dropped me a curt note. No more meetings. He wanted to forget the past, not to relive it.

During the interview I kept thinking of what might have happened to Eric—might he have been as lucky as Willy? Still, I could not decide on a voyage to Europe. Then, in the early fifties, an air-mail letter arrived from Switzerland: my old companion and sponsor Justus, now a practicing physician in Basel, had somehow traced my broadcasting efforts and written to OWI for my present address. Of course, I must visit him and his family in Basel right away so we could catch up on more than a decade of world and personal history. Justus asked if I still entertained that project to investigate what happened to the gays under the swastika. If so, I must visit not only him, but a new institute that had started collecting data on all the camps and inmates: those who had died, those who had gotten out, the guards, the clerks, the administrators, even the officials who had issued the orders— in short, everything deadly in the Third Reich penal machinery. Justus knew the director. During the war, both had worked for the Swiss Red Cross. While Justus had returned to his practice, his colleague, Dr. Albert de Cocatrix, had accepted a position as chief of the International Tracing Service (ITS), located in the tiny southern German village of Arolsen. Justus would drop a note to the director. But first I must hurry to Basel. His letter gave me the push I needed. How could I refuse such a chance? In Arolsen I might be able to unearth some of the facts about the gays caught by Himmler, perhaps check the camp registries, and even find out something about people I had known.

I made preparations to go to Europe by ship the following June. I sent a detailed, sentimental note to Justus accepting his offer as intermediary between me and the institute. Then I sent a letter to Dr. Cocatrix, asking him to grant me access to the ITS. Soon his answer arrived, quite positive and encouraging. Even more, Mr. Eric Henschel, a member of his staff, had put together a preliminary list of folders from which pertinent information might be culled. On an extra sheet Mr. Henschel had enclosed an invitation to come to him with any problem, and he added a suggestion that the Pension Estonia nearby would offer adequate shelter and halfway decent meals.

For some reason, Justus could not be in Basel until the end of July, and although my trip now followed a bizarre sort of itinerary, I decided to tackle Arolsen first, then travel south to Switzerland and celebrate my reunion with Justus in Basel, my second hometown. At the Pension Estonia I found a note: Dr. Cocatrix would see me the next morning at ten. Over the main entrance to the three-story building complex was a stone tablet in German, French, and English: "This building has been erected to house the archives of horror which testify to the extermination, torture and slavery inflicted by the National Socialist dictatorship. These archives will help to furnish relief for their victims and their families. May they serve as a warning to future generations that never again must such horror afflict humanity."

I spent long weeks in these archives, which did more than "testify to the extermination, torture and slavery" inflicted by the Third Reich, but preserved, sifted, and organized the testimony so it could never be denied. Although Eric Henschel and his assistant guided me gently through the various mazes, I never lost my sense of trauma. Here in a central index the fate of roughly 39 million people was put on record. Here the certificates of incarceration filled all the folders on one side of the room housing Buchenwald, while on the other side stretched endless rows of other Buchenwald files—inmate registry entries; work assignment rosters; personal effects cards; plain prisoner lists, usually by numbers, sometimes by names; transfer and location sheets; medical work abilities records; and last, but most revealing, the death books. On neighboring shelves in the Buchenwald room, in which I usually worked, lay equally thick folders on the *Kapos*, the camp guards, the SS administrative personnel, amounting to hundreds and hundreds of names. The Arolsen collectors had also acquired nearly complete lists of the various decrees, injunctions, directives, regulations, and sub-regulations that the Himmler bureaus had issued, plus a good part of the officially secret correspondence between the remote killers in Berlin and those who executed their orders on the spot.

One wing of the ITS complex housed only the documents on the camps; in another wing there was an equally overpowering array of documents concerning displaced persons (DPs), many of whom had been forced laborers. At the time of my visit these homeless men and women were still sheltered in temporary barracks all over Germany and the formerly occupied countries. Many had vanished, many did not want to be repatriated. Daily, the ITS received hundreds of inquiries asking the whereabouts of DPs. Of course, requests about former camp inmates also reached Arolsen by the hundreds. It was difficult to assess, Henschel remarked, which of these tasks was the more strenuous.

Although it was painful, I had accepted the fact that someone like me, working alone, with limited time and no assistance, could never dream of doing justice to the wealth of evidence on the fate of the gays under Hitler. The Buchenwald collection was relatively complete. Others were not. In truth, only a fragment of what happened had been catalogued, and new material was constantly emerging. To give just one example: while I was working at the institute, a Polish agency mailed a list of several new satellite camps, never accredited before. This meant new lists of the missing, new statistics, new death books—in short, new additions to the central index.

It is probable that there will never be a complete catalogue for the Third Reich.

To examine the death books perturbed me for a long time. Not only were the sheets beginning to turn yellow and disintegrate, but often the clerk had applied an exceedingly fine handwriting to such characteristic notations as: "Inmate 4-175, born Frankfurt-Main, 1911, barracks 12-S, green and pink triangles, deceased (TB) April 8, 1944." If the Arolsen employees over the years had managed a semblance of equilibrium, I needed to fight to stay cool, not to get emotionally entangled. It was not easy. For instance, through Henschel I had learned to decipher the entries on the various medical experiments in Buchenwald, where all guinea pigs were humans. Here, as if the perpetrators had been aware that their activities must never be made public, Himmler's doctors had encoded all reports, even the correspondence between the outside governmental bureaus and the physicians in the camps. Without assistance I would never have been able to check the experiments on gays in Buchenwald. Equally encoded were such special notations as "*auf der Flucht erschossen*" (ADFE), "shot while trying to escape." This was usually scribbled in the margin of a prisoners' death book.

Life at Arolsen was wearisome. During the day I was busy scanning lists, entries, rosters in the company of the dead or missing. My evenings were spent alone, typing notes or walking through the tiny village, which ignored me. The prevailing beery coziness of the inns repelled me, and I imagined all these redfaced men with their paunches had been in the SS. After many weeks, again through Justus, I received another dispatch from the past. Harold, though some fifteen years older, had been an occasional companion of mine in Frankfurt, and had gone underground in 1935. Now he was living in Offenbach, a Frankfurt suburb. No, he wrote, he did not play piano or organ any longer; he was running a garage and owned

a small house, nothing special but with enough room for me
—come right away, he urged, be my guest. He was so happy
to have reestablished contact. Could I phone him immediately?

Like Justus's first letter from Europe, Harold's letter touched
a raw spot. Quite often, as I searched the death books, sometimes with magnifying glass and flashlight, I had the vision
of hitting upon the name "Langer, Eric." I never did, but I
dreaded it. By the time Harold's invitation arrived, I had made
some progress. With the continual help of Henschel, I had
examined a substantial number of the Buchenwald entries,
and filled voluminous notebooks. I phoned Harold—first I
would travel to Justus in Basel and unwind, then I would
visit Harold and face Frankfurt.

My meeting with Justus and his family yielded sheer con-
tentment and restored my mind, although I was saddened to
hear that Miss Gaby and other friends had died. I still felt
comfortable in Basel, sterling middle-class, old-fashioned,
Calvinistic, and untouched by Hitler's gruesome follies. One
night I sauntered past my nemesis, the Department for Aliens,
stared at the forbidding temple of xenophobia, and invented
several elaborate curses. Justus had not remained in neutral
Switzerland during the war. As a Red Cross physician he had
inspected prisoner-of-war camps in Germany, Belgium, and
England, but, to his dismay, not in Eastern Europe or America. After browsing through the illegal photographs he had
taken there, I encouraged him to put his experiences on paper;
instead, he spurred me on to follow up my own project: "Now
go organize those findings, digest them, write them down,
and get this thing finished, because few others will or can get
involved in this. And go home and look for Eric. . . ."

As I sat down in the compartment of the Basel-Frankfurt
express, it suddenly struck me that on the same track more
than twenty years ago I had hurried away from Frankfurt to
Basel. Now the train seemed to be welcoming me back as it

clicked and clacked through southern Germany: "Lucky you. You came through. Lucky you . . ." I had become an American, and nothing in a Frankfurt reborn or revisited could frighten me or shake me, I thought.

I was wrong. Knowing that what was your childhood has been pulverized is one thing. Seeing what has risen in its place is another. On the one hand, that enormous cathedral of industry, the central Frankfurt railroad station, appeared as awesome as it had two decades before. But when I stumbled outside to look for a cab, new glittering buildings greeted me, along with old-timers such as the Hotel Emerald, which still boasted a Victorian green turret, now half splintered. Most bomb scars had been patched up, so that I realized I would not have to walk through those charred stone wrecks I had seen in the newsreels. Now, in the fifties, the ruins had been torn down or plastered over with new façades.

In Offenbach nothing looked familiar. After cruising around aimlessly, the driver—a sullen refugee from East Germany—discovered Harold's Garage. At the entrance stood a heavyset, white-haired man peering from behind thick glasses. Harold, the mentor of my late adolescence, could not hold back his tears. Often during the time I stayed with him at his apartment above the garage, he fought with tears and he always worried that his co-workers might catch him. During the next few days I learned to wait for Harold to start talking. I never asked about the two fingers missing from his right hand—he would never be a church organist again. The Gestapo had shipped him to Camp Flossenbürg for "acts inimical to the state." What he had done was to vouch for Ferdi when Ferdi was in jail and to smuggle another member of our old network, a Jewish boy called Curt, in his car to Holland. In the end Curt made it to Scotland, but the Gestapo caught Harold on his return to Germany. Only with an effort could I reconcile this brokenhearted man with the Harold I had known, a man whose vitality had never flagged. Fortunately he had been classified as a political felon and tagged with the red patch, not the pink one reserved for sexual deviants. When, one day in 1944, Ferdi was transferred into the same Flossenbürg barracks, Harold was afraid Ferdi might give him away—Ferdi had been stigmatized with the pink triangle. But Ferdi did not last long after a few weeks of forced labor in the notorious Flossenbürg quarry, whereas Harold's gift for anything mechanical endeared him to the *Kapos*, who needed experts to repair the crumbling camp machinery. In addition, Harold had joined the leftist underground group, which, by 1944 and 1945, had won grudging respect from the guards. All this he poured out to me night after night.

From the start, I had asked about Eric. In a local library, Harold and I unearthed some charred 1942 telephone books of Cronberg. No listing for Langer. I waded through mountains of other phone books listing Frankfurt proper and the surrounding townships. Then, about a week after my arrival, Harold's brother, a priest named Father Thomas, who had been thrown into Dachau, came to visit. Thomas, a huge, quiet man, possessed a serenity that enveloped you like a consoling current. He phoned a brother clergyman in Cronberg. Yes, Eric Langer had last been stationed on the battleship *Prinz Jürgen* near Drontheim in Norway. So far he had not come back. Hilda, he thought, had taken up residence in a home for the aged. Within a day or so he would be able to tell me which one. I fought my urge to take the train to Cronberg and go to the local police headquarters, or just wander around and ask. But Harold restrained me. Cronberg was no longer the idyllic village of my childhood, but a sprawling suburb favored by the rich who had moved there to escape the bombing of Frankfurt.

I ventured north into Frankfurt to visit Reuterweg, where I had spent my childhood. To my surprise, streetcar Number

6 still traveled from Offenbach to my station, Grüneburgweg. That the streetcar was sleeker than the one that had taken me to school did not matter—I was too busy staring at the garishly reborn city. The old-fashioned street signs had been literally reproduced, like false antiques, but not a single block brought the sting of remembrance. When I got off, I found Reuterweg, but not my house. The entire tract had been redesigned, divided into tall concrete apartment squares with Lilliputian balconies hanging uselessly on the front. Number 66, where I had grown up, had been swallowed by a communal "60–75" at the entrance of the housing project. Perhaps I should have been shocked, but instead I was filled with a fog of indifference. I was almost tranquil when I came back to Harold, who presented me with a chocolate cake covered with whipped cream. He asked me to please tell him about my "lives and loves" in America, and begged me not to worry about Eric.

My mood grew increasingly dark. Of course I tried not to show it to Harold, who kept serving me rich meals and was so ecstatic to have someone with whom he could re-create the good old days that he neglected his business. But when I told him about my project, he shook his head. Nobody would believe me, and besides, how could I do it in English? All these Nazi words "will lose their ugliness in English," he said. Also, Americans were too happy-go-lucky to accept my discoveries, especially since most Americans he had met firmly believed that evil people were usually atheists, alcoholics, Communists, child molesters, homosexuals, or possibly all five. I did not argue with him but agreed to accompany him to Winnie's, a new bar in Frankfurt, an "Onkelchen bar," that is, a place where older gays liked to spend their evenings. Perhaps I would find another camp ex-inmate willing to talk.

Winnie's turned out to be a glum pub near the railroad station, whose bartender greeted Harold and me exuberantly, switching from German to English in my honor. This time Harold championed my cause, inquiring whether "Big Herbert" was still around. The barkeep, one of the new breed of German athletes who tried to look authentically Southern Californian, promised to "deliver" Herbert. He did deliver—but Herbert, a corpulent, taciturn man in his late sixties, would talk only under certain conditions: first, he and I should be alone; second, if I took notes, all names had to be omitted; third, no patron of Winnie's must be told. To make him feel more secure, I typed an agreement and signed it. This seemed to satisfy Herbert, but his voice—high-pitched and flat—often wavered as he told me his story at a nearby restaurant, jumping from one year to the next and scrambling the events. In the end, I pieced together the following.

Herbert had been a baker's apprentice when he met Franz, a Jewish medical student, around 1934. Because the university had banned all "non-Aryans," Franz was forced to emigrate. He went to England, planning for Herbert to follow as soon as he was settled. By that time the new anti-gay laws were in force. Herbert's father, an ardent admirer of Hitler, found Herbert out, called him a traitor and a "warm brother" (a nickname for gays in Germany), and forced Herbert to leave home. Papa really taught his boy a lesson in patriotism: the baker for whom Herbert worked was dutifully enlightened, and he, too, threw Herbert out. Since Franz did not have the means to bring Herbert to England—and how would Herbert get those needed papers?—Herbert took a job with an older gay baker, stayed with friends, and led a quiet life. In 1941 he was arrested for "deviant sexual activities" and put into jail. The trial was a mockery; he was forced to sign a confession and then was sent to Buchenwald.

At this point Herbert's thin voice gave out. He told me how Nazi physicians had experimented with various drugs on prisoners. For hours Herbert vomited after certain injections; in addition he was exposed to poison gas; and there were further experiments that he would not—or could not—recall. In 1943, Himmler introduced a new ruse. Pink-triangle wearers willing to be castrated could leave the camp to work in war-essential factories. This happened to Herbert, who considered himself fortunate: he was released readily, while other castrated gays were sent to a deadly penal brigade on the Eastern Front. When, together with other prisoners, Herbert was shipped to a munitions factory near Frankfurt, his train was attacked by Allied aircraft. The prisoners welcomed the bombings—they proved that the defeatist rumors about Allied air superiority had been right, that Germany might be beaten. This gave them the added strength to survive the inhuman labor conditions, lack of food, and atrocious living quarters. In 1945, at the war's end, while the factory supervisors fled in panic, Herbert hiked back to Frankfurt. In the suburb of Bockenheim he encountered an old friend with whom he stayed.

I never met the man with whom Herbert was then living. Herbert was suspicious of anyone trying to come close; he worried that someone might drop an anonymous note to the baker for whom he was now working. Of course, he admitted he should not hang out at Winnie's, but so many of the old crowd had died and he needed new friends. I encouraged him to speak about other gay inmates at Buchenwald—to his surprise, I knew something about the experiments—but during our last talk he faltered and could not go on.

Then, suddenly, he became angry. He blamed the Allies for not having bombed the camps or for having done too little, too late. In many camps, he pointed out, the SS quarters and war factories were located outside the barbed-wire fence enclosing the inmates. "They could have spot-bombed the SS villas, commissaries, dog kennels, without hitting us! Why did they wait until 1944? Yes, I know, during the big raid on Buchenwald a few inmates got killed. But we didn't mind because SS guys got hit, too, and the electric fence and a number of factories were blown up. And you know what? Those SS big shots with their villas and the guards with their whips, they got scared. All of a sudden they realized that Goebbels had been lying and that Germany was losing the war. Do you know what happened? They made deals with the prisoners' committees. Yes, the Allies could have bombed many camps and they should have done it systematically. The military chiefs knew all about them."

I just sat there speechless, startled by the unexpected outburst, and could not find an answer. Herbert did not expect one; he rose awkwardly and lumbered away.

I returned to Harold's. Father Thomas had left a note for me: "Hilda Langer, now at Villa Taunus, Cronberg. Good luck!" I did not even wait to phone. I took a local train and nearly missed Cronberg; nothing suggested that this had once been farming country. It was thickly settled with luxury food shops and imposing mansions, some of which still revealed bomb scars, reminding me more of acne than of war injuries. Villa Taunus turned out to be a gingerbread house with a shattered roof. Inside, a stern woman in a nurse's outfit informed me that Hilda was on the second floor, but she had to phone first. After a while I was permitted to proceed. My heart began to beat rapidly. When I embraced Hilda—she was so tiny I felt like a giant—I knew all at once what I had feared and somehow guessed all along: Eric was dead. At first, neither of us could speak. I held her hand. Finally, glancing at a row of photographs of her husband and Eric, she poured out her heart to me.

During the last months of the war, Eric, stationed on the battleship *Prinz Jürgen*, off Norway, had gotten in trouble again. On leave near Drontheim, he and some mates had listened in the back room of an inn to an English broadcast claiming that Germany had been beaten. Since Eric had a record as a nonconformist, the navy handed him over to a higher authority, the Gestapo. All of this Hilda had learned from a surviving friend of Eric's who had mailed her a letter after the war—though he did not tell her where and when Eric had been executed. In December 1945, a terse communication from the secretary of the German navy informed Hilda that her son had died on duty during a bombing of the *Prinz Jürgen*. More Hilda did not know or want to say. She had spoken without emotion and I had to hold back mine. Although my childhood stammer had returned in full force, I begged her to tell me whether I could do something for her. She shook her head. For the moment she seemed to have retreated from reality as her eyes wandered to the photographs. Into our silence a bell rang—I had forgotten that in the homes for the elderly, dinner was served early. By that time I was unable to hold back my tears. Then Hilda came back to me, drew open a drawer, and handed me two framed photos: one, of Eric and me, aged about twelve or thirteen, taken when we were playing in the Cronberg farm yard; the other taken at least five years later, with Eric protectively looming over me. I had ventured a dumb smile, but Eric, who had put two fingers on my right shoulder, stared out of the photograph with an intensity that burned a hole in my heart.

Promising Hilda to come back soon, I rushed away, feeling drained and dull. I had made a vow that Frankfurt would not intimidate me, but I had not been able to keep it. All at once, I did not want to stay in this feverishly prosperous city. "To be frank, I had guessed it," Harold said when I told him about my visit. "We all figured Eric never made it back from Norway. He simply could not knuckle under to the Nazi bullies or to those in the navy. But you had to find out for yourself." When I confessed that I wanted to go home as soon as possible, he just nodded.

Harold and two of his workers took me to the railroad station. Now, at the last moment, these teenagers asked how it was that I, apparently an American, could speak German so fluently, even with the local accent. What could I tell them? A blitz-synopsis of the Third Reich; a summary of what Hitler had inflicted not only on the Jews but upon the Germans themselves; an explanation of why thousands were forced to get out and why Frankfurt had lost something irretrievable, despite skyscrapers rising up and whipped cream flowing. The trip to the station was too short to spell out any of this, yet even if it had taken two hours I would have failed, because the teenagers had not been told what really happened after 1933. I mumbled something about relatives having come from Frankfurt, and let it go at that.

As proper adult males, Harold and I avoided any display of emotion when it was time for me to board my train. During the long journey I could neither eat nor sleep. Only when I settled down on the ship bound for America did I begin to relax. By a series of lucky accidents I had been spared, saved from the erupting volcano that had obliterated the country of my birth, my hometown, and many of those close to me. I needed to repress some aspects of the nightmare but never to forget certain others. I would never be able to put Eric out of my mind. His image would always be with me. As I conjured up his likeness, he seemed to be pushing me forward, as he had always done. Forget about your stuttering, he would say. Your being afraid of it just brings it about. If he were here he would tell me to stop stuttering around, organize what I have learned, and put together a chronicle that would throw light on this neglected corner of history. I did not know then that it would involve so much muscle, nerve, and sinew, or that it would take so many years.

# APPENDIX 1
## TEXT OF
## PARAGRAPH 175

Text of Paragraph 175, with amendments as issued on June 28, 1935.

**175:**

1. A male who indulges in criminally indecent activities with another male or who allows himself to participate in such activities will be punished with jail.
2. If one of the participants is under the age of twenty-one, and if the crime has not been grave, the court may dispense with the jail sentence.

**175(a):** A jail sentence of up to ten years or, if mitigating circumstances can be established, a jail sentence of no less than three years will be imposed on

1. any male who by force or by threat of violence and danger to life and limb compels another man to indulge in criminally indecent activities, or allows himself to participate in such activities;
2. any male who forces another male to indulge with him in criminally indecent activities by using the subordinate position of the other man, whether it be at work or elsewhere, or who allows himself to participate in such activities;
3. any male who indulges professionally and for profit in criminally indecent activities with other males, or allows himself to be used for such activities or who offers himself for same.

**175(b):** Criminally indecent activities by males with animals are to be punished by jail; in addition, the court may deprive the subject of his civil rights.

# APPENDIX 2
# CHRONOLOGY

1871: Kaiser Wilhelm I of Germany proclaims the Second Reich. Paragraph 175 of the Prussian Penal Code is adopted for the entire Reich. It makes sexual acts between males punishable. In practice, German courts usually prosecute only homosexual behavior that resembles "coital acts."

1897: Dr. Magnus Hirschfeld establishes the Scientific-Humanitarian Committee.

1899: Hirschfeld issues the first volume of the *Yearbook for Intersexual Variants*, which he edits until 1923. This scholarly journal publishes essays on the medical, legal, historical, and anthropological aspects of homosexuality, together with pertinent bibliographies. These bibliographies demonstrate that homosexual research advances considerably: in one year alone, more than three hundred publications on homosexuality are issued in Germany. The committee also presents a petition to the Reichstag for abolishing the punitive Paragraph 175. These efforts continue until 1929. Major scientists, writers, and artists who sign the petition at one time or another include Richard von Krafft-Ebing, Martin Buber, Alfred Döblin, Albert Einstein, George Grosz, Gerhard Hauptmann, Hermann Hesse, Engelbert Humperdinck, Karl Jaspers, Käthe Kollwitz, Max Liebermann, Thomas Mann, Rainer Maria Rilke, Max Scheler, Arthur Schnitzler, Felix Weingartner, Heinrich Zille, August Bebel, Karl Kautsky, and Harry Graf Kessler.

1903: Hirschfeld's Scientific-Humanitarian Committee distributes more than 6,000 questionnaires concerning personal sexual preferences to Berlin students and factory workers. It is the first investigation of this kind ever tried in Europe. One result is that 2.2 percent of the male population responds that it has had homosexual experiences.

1908: Effort by opponents of the women's emancipation movement to outlaw lesbian acts fails.

1919: First gay film in Germany, *Different from the Others (Anders als die Anderen)*, starring Conrad Veidt, directed by Richard Oswald.

1920: Hirschfeld, a homosexual, a Jew, and a liberal, is attacked while lecturing in Munich; a second assault there in 1921 results in a fractured skull; in 1923 in Vienna, a young man opens fire and wounds some members of the audience.

1921: Adolf Hitler merges various small right-wing groups into the National Socialist Workers' Party. The first SA units are established as private bodyguards. Ernst Roehm, an openly homosexual professional army captain, becomes the second SA leader, but resigns after he loses a suit against a hustler who had robbed him.

1923–24: Trial of homosexual mass murderer Fritz Haarmann creates a shock wave in Germany, pits the Communists against the Social Democrats, and hurts the German homosexual emancipation movement profoundly.

1928: The National Socialists issue their views on homosexuality when answering a questionnaire sent to all political groups: "It is not necessary that you and I live, but it is necessary that the German people live. And it can only live if it maintains its masculinity. It can only maintain its masculinity if it exercises discipline. . . . Free love and deviance are undisciplined. Therefore, we reject you. . . .

Anyone who thinks of homosexual love is our enemy."

1929: The American stock market crashes. German and Austrian banks collapse. Efforts to abolish Paragraph 175 nearly succeed, but the reform is postponed indefinitely because of the economic crisis. On August 2 a Nazi Party rally in Nuremberg draws approximately 150,000 participants. A year later Ernst Roehm is recalled and made head of the SA. The Nazis quickly grow to about two million members.

## 1933

January 30: Hitler is appointed chancellor.

February 23: Pornography banned, and homosexual-rights groups are proscribed.

February 27: The Reichstag burns down.

February 28: A presidential decree gives Hitler emergency powers. Civil rights are eliminated. The reign of terror begins. Some SA concentration camps are established near Berlin. A law is passed against "Communist acts of violence."

February 29: Marinus van der Lubbe, the Dutchman who allegedly set the Reichstag afire, is dubbed a homosexual, and can now be executed legally.

March 5: The last elections with more than one party on the ballot are held; the Nazis gain 44 percent of the vote. Actions begin against the Jews.

March 9: Heinrich Himmler is made chief of the Munich police.

March 13: Joseph Goebbels is appointed Minister of Propaganda. The process of "co-option" begins: political, social, and private life must be in line with Nazi ideology.

March 21: Special courts are established for prosecution of political enemies.

March 22: Dachau, the first major concentration camp, is built, originally for 5,000 inmates.

March 24: The Reichstag passes the Enabling Law, eliminating the Weimar constitution.

April 1: Nationwide boycott of Jewish businesses and professional people. All pamphlets issued by the Jehovah's Witnesses are banned.

April 7: New public-employee laws are the first to exclude non-Aryans.

April 26: The Gestapo is founded.

May 2: Leaders of labor unions are arrested; their headquarters are occupied by the Nazis.

May 6: Magnus Hirschfeld's Institute of Sexual Research is vandalized, and its valuable book and photo collection is set afire.

May 10: Books "inimical to the state" are burned throughout Germany.

June 4: So-called "matrimonial credits" are arranged: parents are to receive 125 marks for each child.

June 27: SA squads storm Jehovah's Witnesses buildings in Magdeburg: Bibles and books worth two million marks are burned.

June 30: Additional laws are passed to remove Jews and non-Nazis from the legal professions and the civil service.

July 14: The Nazi Party is declared the only legal party. The denaturalization of "non-Germanics" means loss of German citizenship for many Eastern European Jews. Laws for the "protection of hereditary health" are enacted (also called "laws for the prevention of racially inferior offspring"). A euthanasia program is developed, and is carried out six years later.

July 20: In Rome an agreement is signed between the new regime and the Vatican.

September 22: The Reich Chamber of Culture is established, under Goebbels. Jews and other "enemies of the state" are excluded.

# Chronology

November 12: The first general election under the one-party state is held: 93 percent of the electorate votes for Hitler.

December 1: A law for "security of state and party" is passed.
*Throughout 1933, approximately 40,000 Germans are arrested.*

## 1934

March: Soviet Russia passes legislation making homosexual acts punishable by law.

April 20: Himmler is made acting chief of the Gestapo.

June 28: "The Night of the Long Knives." SA chief Ernst Roehm's associates are murdered, together with three hundred men not connected with his organization. Roehm is executed two days later. Hitler issues a stern directive that homosexuals are to be expelled from the ranks.

July 3: The Ministry of Justice declares the Roehm purge "to be entirely within the law." Hirschfeld's successor, Kurt Hiller, is shipped to Oranienburg, a concentration camp near Berlin. He survives the war.

July 20: The SS is established as an independent organization under Himmler.

August 2: President Paul von Hindenburg dies.

August 17: A law is passed against "fomenting subversion among the armed forces."

August 19: Hitler asks the German people to approve his new powers; more than 90 percent do so in a vote.

October–November: The first large wave of arrests of homosexuals occurs throughout Germany.

October 24: A secret letter is sent by the Gestapo to police departments throughout the country, ordering them to submit lists of all men known to be, or to have been, homosexually active.

October 26: A special department on abortion and homosexuality is set up in the Berlin Gestapo under SS Captain Joseph Meisinger.

November 20: Himmler is appointed head of the entire Gestapo organization.

December 20: A law against "insidious slander" is passed, under which any criticism of the regime, even as a joke, is considered criminal blasphemy.

*Throughout 1934, approximately 70,000 Germans are arrested.*

## 1935

March 16: All able-bodied men between the ages of eighteen and forty are drafted for military service.

April: Jehovah's Witnesses are banned from all civil-service jobs and are arrested throughout Germany.

May 21: Only men with proven "Aryan ancestry" can serve in the armed forces.

May 22: The SS magazine *Das Schwarze Korps* demands the death penalty for homosexual men.

June 28: New laws are passed concerning Paragraph 175. The SS courts use the law and the new amendments to widen the scope of persecution. They come to regard as felonious almost any conceivable contact, however tenuous, between males.

July: The courts issue several landmark decisions. Any action is punishable as a crime if the "inborn healthy instincts of the German people" demand it. Furthermore, any action can now be punished without a judge's referring to a specific criminal statute. The basic precepts of Western judicial procedure are thus abolished.

September 14: The Nuremberg laws are enacted as "laws for protection of German blood and honor." Jews are deprived of civil rights and citizenship. Intermarriage is prohibited. Sexual contacts between Jews and non-Jews are considered crimes of "racial desecration." So-called People's Courts are established to try cases of racial treason.

October 28: A directive is issued to promote "biological marriage," under which women are encouraged to
produce illegitimate children.

December 12: The "Spring of Life" organization is established
to supply homes and care for unmarried mothers
and their children. SS men are to act as studs for
childless women.

*Throughout 1935, approximately 85,000 Germans are arrested.*

## 1936

February 10: Gestapo actions are declared not legally reviewable.

March 7: The German army reoccupies the Rhineland.

March 29: The SS is increased to 3,500 men.

June: Women are forbidden to act as attorneys and judges.
The Institute for Racial Hygiene and Population
Biology is founded. The institute deals with asocial
groups such as Gypsies.

June 17: Himmler is appointed chief of German police. He
now rules all SS and police forces.

July: The first group of Gypsies is sent to Dachau.

August 1: The Olympic Games open in Berlin. Anti-Semitic
signs are removed and gay bars are reopened.

August 28: Mass arrests of Jehovah's Witnesses take place in
key cities. Most of them are taken to concentration
camps.

September 13: An SS ordinance requires every SS man to produce
four children—if not with his wife, then with another woman.

October: Systematic campaign begins against Catholic priests,
dignitaries, monks, and schools. They are charged
with transferring money illegally, hiding non-
Aryans, and engaging in homosexual activities.

October 10: Himmler says that homosexuals must be eliminated as a danger to the German race.

October 25: Italy and Germany sign an alliance pact.

October 26: The Federal Security Office for Combating Abortion and Homosexuality is established.

November 25: A pact is signed by Japan and Germany; the Japanese are declared "honorary Aryans."

December 10: Courts rule that "illicit sexual acts" do not have to be acts; intent is what counts. Originally meant for relationships between Jews and non-Jews, the ruling also applies to cases of "homosexual debauchery."

*Throughout 1936, approximately 90,000 Germans are arrested.*

### 1937

February 17: Himmler gives a secret speech before SS leaders in which he says all homosexuals must be eliminated. SS men caught in homosexual acts should be put in concentration camps and then "shot while trying to escape."

March: Pope Pius XI issues an encyclical denouncing the Nazi regime's persecution of Catholic clergymen and institutions, a violation of the 1933 agreement.

May: A decree allows unmarried mothers to change their names and those of their illegitimate children.

May 28: In a nationwide radio broadcast, Goebbels says that all Catholic institutions are breeding grounds for homosexual activities.

July 1: Martin Niemoeller, pastor of the Protestant Confessional Free Church, is arrested.

Summer: The Ministry of Justice issues an ordinance stating that beating of prisoners is permissible for "purposes of intense interrogation," but it must be limited to twenty-five blows. Hitler orders a stop to anti-Catholic trials.

October 29: Himmler issues a special memorandum to the effect that actors and other artists can be arrested for homosexual offenses only with his own special permission.

November 5: At the Hossbach Conference, Hitler reveals his plans for the conquest of Europe to the General Staff.

December 14:  A confidential ordinance for preventive anticrime legislation is initiated, under which people suspected of being "enemies of the state" can be arrested without any specifically cited reason. They need only be defined as "anti-community-minded." The same legal concept, previously applied to Jews and homosexuals, is now applicable to all Germans.

### 1938

January 5–6:  Gestapo powers are enlarged. Anybody endangering state security can be taken into protective custody.

January:  Chief of Staff General Werner von Fritsch goes on trial for trumped-up homosexual activities.

January 25:  General Werner von Blomberg is blackmailed into retiring after allegations concerning his wife's sexual history are leaked. Hitler assumes the newly created rank of Chief of the Supreme Command of the Army.

January 30:  The court finds von Fritsch innocent of all charges.

February 3:  Von Fritsch resigns.

March 13:  Hitler annexes Austria.

April 4:  Himmler issues a directive that men convicted of homosexual crimes can be transferred directly to concentration camps. He will revise the directive in 1940, declaring that they *must* be transferred.

April 20:  Jews must register their possessions.

June 14–15:  Jewish businesses must be registered and marked as such. All Jews with police records are arrested.

July 6:  An international conference is held in Evian, France, on the problem of Jewish refugees from Germany and Austria. No country, including the United States, wants them.

July 25:  Jewish physicians lose permission to practice.

August 17:  Jews must change their first names to Sarah and Israel by January 1939.

# Chronology

September 15: Chamberlain visits Munich and yields Czechoslovakia. In return, Hitler promises peace.

November 7: Hershel Grynszpan, a displaced Jewish youth, kills the third secretary of the German embassy, Ernst vom Rath, in Paris.

November 12: "Crystal Night." Mobs throughout Germany smash and burn Jewish stores and synagogues. Thousands of Jews are arrested. German Jews are fined one billion marks.

November 15: Jewish children are expelled from German schools.

December: All Gypsies must register with the police.

December 13: Compulsory "Aryanization," i.e., theft, of all Jewish enterprises begins.

*By official count, 170,000 Germans are in various concentration camps.*

## 1939

January 1: The Yearbook of the Reich Central Security Bureau publishes criminal statistics: the names of approximately 33,000 German homosexuals are on record.

January 30: Hitler announces a policy of extermination of European Jews in case of war.

March: All Germans between the ages of ten and eighteen are to be conscripted into the Hitler Youth.

March 15: Bohemia and Moravia become German protectorates.

April: Jehovah's Witnesses are arrested throughout Germany. Only those who renounce their faith are freed.

April 10: A secret Gestapo report reveals that 302,535 German political prisoners are held in concentration camps.

May 21: Women with four or more children are to be awarded a "Mother Crest."

June: Two thousand Gypsies from Austria are sent to various camps.

June 5: Illegitimate children of German mothers can be furnished with documents testifying to their "Aryan" ancestry. This enables them to attend school.

July 21: Adolf Eichmann is made director of the Jewish "emigration office" in Prague.

August 23: The German-Russian nonaggression pact is signed.

September 1: Hitler decrees that "those who are, as far as it is humanly possible to judge, incurably sick . . . may be granted a merciful death." Mass killings of "unneeded consumers" begins: approximately 70,000 in asylums, 3,000 children in reform schools, up to 20,000 in camps, and all Jewish inmates in institutions. Germany invades Poland.

September 3: Britain and France declare war on Germany.

September 5: A new decree against "enemies of the people" as "dangerous deviants" is issued.

September 9: The first group of Austrian homosexuals is shipped to a newly established camp, Mauthausen, near Linz. A decree of the Ministry of the Interior establishes medically supervised brothels for German troops in occupied territories.

September 17: Russian troops enter eastern Poland.

September 23: German Jews are forbidden to own radios.

October 12: The first deportation of Jews begins from Austria, Moravia, and Bohemia to Poland.

October 21: Reinhard Heydrich organizes the elimination of the Gypsies.

October 28: Himmler issues an ordinance encouraging married SS men to have illegitimate children if their wives do not produce the desired number of offspring.

November 23: Jews in occupied Poland must wear a yellow Star of David.

November 25: Foreign workers are to be severely punished for sabotage in industry or the armed forces, or if they have sexual relations with German women. The latter is called "racial desecration."

## 1940

February 10: First deportation of German Jews to Poland.
April 9: Invasion of Denmark and Norway.
April 30: The first enclosed ghetto is organized in Lodz.
May 10: Germany occupies Belgium, Luxembourg, and the Netherlands.
May 15–18: Gypsies are moved from Germany to the east.
May 30: Hitler issues an unwritten secret order to Hans Frank, chief civilian officer of occupied Poland, that the Polish leadership is to be annihilated completely.
June 22: France capitulates.
July 15: Himmler issues a directive that men arrested for homosexual activities who have seduced more than one partner must be transferred into a camp after serving a prison sentence.
August 13: The Battle of Britain begins.
August 15: Eichmann presents a plan for resettling Jews in Madagascar. The plan is never implemented.
October 22: Further deportation of Jews begins, from southern Germany and Alsace-Lorraine to Auschwitz.
November 15: The Warsaw Ghetto is sealed off.
December: The first mass murder of Jews occurs at Treblinka.

## 1941

February–
April: Seventy-two thousand Jews are transported into the Warsaw Ghetto.
March 7: A new decree states that German Jews can be used for forced labor in Germany.
May 14: Three thousand six hundred Parisian Jews are arrested by French police forces. Premier Henri Pétain pledges collaboration with the Nazis.
June 22: Germany attacks the Soviet Union. A new wave of arrests of all groups occurs throughout Germany.
September 4: New decrees are issued against "deviant criminals": they must be put to death if "they threaten

the health of the German people." This applies to homosexuals, among others.

September 8: A confidential Gestapo directive orders that henceforth Russian prisoners of war are to be shot.

September 23: The first tests for gassing of prisoners are conducted in Auschwitz.

October–November: Austrian and Czech Gypsies are shipped to the Lodz Ghetto.

November–December: Firing squads start shooting German Jews in the East.

November 15: Himmler issues a decree relating to "purity" in the SS and police: any SS officer or policeman caught "engaging in indecent behavior with another man or allowing himself to be abused by him for indecent purposes will be condemned to death and executed."

December 7: The Japanese attack Pearl Harbor.

December 8: Japan declares war on the United States and Great Britain.

December 11: Germany declares war on the United States.

## 1942

January: "The Subhuman" is published by the German government and translated into several languages. Over three million copies are distributed. The brochure contrasts the heroic-handsome features of "Nordic Aryans" with those of "subhumans" such as blacks, Slavs, Jews, and so forth.

January 20: The Wannsee Conference begins, its purpose being to decide the fate of European Jews: the "Final Solution" to the "Jewish problem" is developed. Himmler and Heydrich are to supervise the roundup and transport of Jews to eastern camps, where they will be exterminated.

February 1–10: An amendment to the 1941 law extends the death penalty to any German male engaging in sexual activity with another male.

March 21: Heydrich decrees that only German homosexuals are to be arrested; those of other nationalities are to be deported from Germany.

March 28: The first transport of French Jews to Auschwitz begins.

June 4: Heydrich, as SS governor in Prague, is assassinated by the Czech underground. In retaliation, the Germans destroy the town of Lidice six days later.

June 23: The first systematic gassings begin in Auschwitz.

July 12: Warsaw Ghetto inmates are transported to concentration camps.

July 15: The first prisoners are brought from the Netherlands to Auschwitz.

August 1: A Gestapo ordinance states that German camp inmates can be whipped only by Germans.

August 23: The siege of Stalingrad begins.

August 26– Seven thousand Jews are arrested in unoccupied
28: France.

October 4: All Jews still in regional camps are ordered to Auschwitz.

November 7: The Allies land in North Africa.

November 11: Germany invades unoccupied France.

November 22: The Soviet Union starts a counteroffensive.

November 25: The first deportation of Norwegian Jews to Auschwitz begins.

### 1943

January 14: At the Casablanca Conference, Roosevelt, Churchill, and Stalin announce terms for the "unconditional surrender" of Germany.

February: A roundup of remaining Gypsies occurs throughout Germany.

February 18: German students in Munich rebel against Nazi policies; Sophie and Hans Schell are executed.

March: Himmler orders Dutch Gypsies transported to Auschwitz.

April 19: Warsaw ghetto uprising begins.

May 9–13: German forces in Africa surrender.

May 19: The Gestapo tries to establish jurisdiction over army and navy personnel convicted of homosexual activities. Military leaders have often ignored the orders concerning homosexual behavior.

June 11: Himmler orders liquidation of all Polish ghettoes.

July 9–11: The Allies land in Sicily.

August 2: Inmates rebel in Treblinka.

September 8: Italy surrenders to the Allies.

October 18: Jews are deported from German-occupied Rome.

## 1944

January 3: Russian troops reach the Polish border.

January 16: Eisenhower assumes command of Allied forces.

February 10: Ernst Kaltenbrunner decrees that foreign workers who have had sexual relations with German women are to be executed.

March 20: Hitler, outraged by his wavering Hungarian ally, occupies that country.

April–June: The Nazis transport 476,000 Jews from Hungary to Auschwitz.

June 6: The Allies invade Normandy.

July 20: Klaus von Stauffenberg attempts to assassinate Hitler. The Führer survives. Himmler's squads execute all real and suspected conspirators.

July 24: Soviet troops liberate Maidanek concentration camp in Poland.

August 1: Poles in Warsaw rise up against the Germans. Soviet troops across the river make no moves.

August 23: Drancy, a concentration camp in France, is liberated by Allied troops.

August 25: De Gaulle enters Paris.

September: Last transports from the Netherlands and France to Auschwitz begin.

October 7: Various attempts are undertaken by prisoners to break out of Auschwitz.

November 3: Russian troops reach Budapest.

# Chronology

November 8–    Eichmann transports 38,000 Jews from Budapest
16:    to Buchenwald, Ravensbrück, and other camps.

November 26:    Himmler orders the Auschwitz crematoria destroyed because of approaching Soviet troops.

## 1945

January 17:    Soviet troops enter Warsaw after the Nazis have crushed Polish resistance. Hungarian Jews are liberated by Soviet troops.

January 26:    Auschwitz is liberated by the Russians. Approximately 15,000 inmates, mostly Jews, are rescued.

April 13:    Vienna is occupied by Soviet troops.

April 15:    Bergen-Belsen, in northern Germany, is liberated by the British. Approximately 40,000 prisoners are freed.

April 20:    American troops enter Nuremberg.

April 23:    Mauthausen, near Linz, is taken over by the International Red Cross.

April 28:    Dachau is liberated by American troops.

April 28:    Mussolini is executed by Italian partisans.

April 30:    Hitler commits suicide in his Berlin bunker. American troops liberate about 30,000 inmates from several German camps.

May 2:    Berlin capitulates to Soviet troops. Theresienstadt is taken over by the International Red Cross.

May 7:    General Alfred Jodl signs Germany's unconditional surrender at Reims, France.

May 23:    Himmler commits suicide.

November 20:    The Nuremberg trials begin.

# NOTES

## INTRODUCTION

1  Shirer, *The Rise and Fall of the Third Reich*, 79–80.

## CHAPTER 1  BEFORE THE STORM

1  On the collapse of the Weimar Republic, see Friedrich, *Before the Deluge*; Bullock, *Hitler*; Craig, *Germany 1866–1945*; and Fest, *Hitler*. On the origins of Germany's homosexual-rights movement, see the seminal study by James D. Steakley, *The Homosexual Emancipation Movement in Germany*. I am indebted to Steakley's work for much of this chapter's historical information.
2  Craig, *Germany*, 450.
3  As quoted in Friedrich, *Before the Deluge*, 153.
4  Geissler, "Homosexuellen-Gesetzgebung," 64, 77.
5  Weinberg, *World in the Balance*, 73–74.
6  Smith and Peterson, *Himmler Geheimreden*, 93–94.
7  For a comprehensive picture of Berlin's lesbian subculture, see Bollé, *Eldorado*.
8  Allport, *The Nature of Prejudice*.
9  Haffner, *Anmerkungen zu Hitler*.
10  Hirschfeld, *Homosexualität*, 1005.
11  Bleibtreu-Ehrenberg, *Tabu Homosexualität*, 301.
12  Steakley, *The Homosexual Emancipation Movement*, 12.
13  Quoted by Bleibtreu-Ehrenberg, "Die Entartungs-Theorie: Homosexualität als 'Moralischer Wahnsinn,' " in Lautmann, *Gesellschaft und Homosexualität*, 88.
14  Steakley, *The Homosexual Emancipation Movement*, 9.
15  As quoted in Bleibtreu-Ehrenberg, *Tabu Homosexualität*, 337.
16  Steakley, *The Homosexual Emancipation Movement*, 10.

17   Ibid., 12.
18   Ibid., 10.
19   As quoted in Bleibtreu-Ehrenberg, *Tabu Homosexualität*, 321.
20   Steakley, *The Homosexual Emancipation Movement*, 5.
21   See Bebel's speech as quoted in English in Lauritsen and Thorstad, *The Early Homosexual Rights Movement*, 13–14.
22   Eissler, "Sexualpolitik," 22, 26.
23   Manchester, *The Arms of Krupp*, 221–32, and Steakley, *The Homosexual Emancipation Movement*, 32.
24   Eissler, "Sexualpolitik," 36.
25   In 1894, Alfred Dreyfus, a Jewish captain in the French army, was accused of selling military secrets to the Germans. He was convicted, publicly degraded, and sent to the Devil's Island penal colony. After Émile Zola published "J'accuse" (1898), proving Dreyfus's innocence, a new trial was held. But only in 1906, after the authorities finally admitted that important papers had been forged, was Dreyfus cleared. Interestingly, Bebel does not mention the Oscar Wilde trial of 1895, which received as much press attention as did the Dreyfus affair.
26   August Bebel, *Die Frau und der Sozialismus* (Berlin: Dietz Verlag, 1974), 238.
27   Eduard Bernstein, "Die Beurtheilung des widernormalen Geschlechtsverkehrs," *Die Neue Zeit* 13, no. 2 (Stuttgart: 1895), 228–33.
28   Ibid., 233; see also Eissler, "Sexualpolitik," throughout.
29   In *Der Geschlechtstrieb* (Berlin: Buchhandlung Vorwärts, 1908), Bernstein characterizes homosexuality as "another form of perverted sexual drive." This is part of a polemic disputing Hirschfeld's assertion that homosexual appetites were as common as those of heterosexuals.
30   Steakley, *The Homosexual Emancipation Movement*, 2–3.
31   Engels to Marx, letter of June 22, 1869, in Karl Marx and Friedrich Engels, *Werke* 32 (Berlin: Dietz Verlag, 1965): 324–25. Translation by author.
32   Steakley, *The Homosexual Emancipation Movement*, 72.
33   Lauritsen and Thorstad, *Early Homosexual Rights*, 68–70.
34   As quoted in Steakley, *The Homosexual Emancipation Movement*, 83.
35   Ibid., 33.
36   Ibid., 27.

37 Ibid.
38 Ibid., 25–26.
39 Ibid., 60.
40 Ibid., 43–48.
41 Ibid., 88.
42 Ibid., 87–88.
43 In none of the works by such important historians of the period as Bullock, Craig, and Friedrich is any mention made of the Haarmann murders. This is an astonishing omission.
44 Steakley, *The Homosexual Emancipation Movement*, 5.
45 Eissler, "Sexualpolitik," 136–37.
46 Ibid., 139.
47 Ibid.
48 Ibid., 140. It should be noted that during the last months of the Weimar Republic the Communists voted with the Nazis on decisive questions, thus contributing to Hitler's victory. They insisted that Hitler could not last long and that a Communist Germany would follow in a few months.
49 Translated by the author. See Fritz Lang's first sound film, *M*, which opens with children dancing in a circle singing this verse.
50 Harthauser, "Massenmord an Homosexuellen," 13.
51 Alfred Rosenberg, *Völkischer Beobachter*, August 2, 1930, 13.
52 As quoted in Steakley, *The Homosexual Emancipation Movement*, 84.
53 Mosse, *Nationalism and Sexuality*, 164. See also Bleuel, *Sex and Society*, 5, 222.
54 Steakley, *The Homosexual Emancipation Movement*, 103–5.

### CHAPTER 2 THE ROEHM AFFAIR

1 Bracher, *The German Dictatorship*, 356.
2 Gallo, *The Night of the Long Knives*, 229, 240.
3 Many of Roehm's remarks have been reported secondhand; transcripts frequently do not exist, and where they do, they vary greatly according to the bias of the transcriber. See Gallo, *The Night of the Long Knives*, 229. For another version, see Höhne, *Der Orden unter dem Totenkopf*, vol. 1, 127.
4 Roehm, *Geschichte eines Hochverräters*.
5 Toland, *Adolf Hitler*, 250.
6 Bleuel, *Sex and Society*, 99.

7  Roehm, *Geschichte eines Hochverräters*, 267.
8  Ibid., 269.
9  For Roehm's letters from Bolivia, See Wilde, "Der Roehm Putsch," in *Damals* (Spring 1959). Also see Höhne, *Der Orden unter dem Totenkopf*, vol. 1, 73–74, and Herbert Heinersdorf, "Akten zum Fall Roehm," in *Mitteilungen des Wissenschaftlich-humanitären Kommittees* 32 (January–March 1932).
10  Höhne, *Der Orden*, vol. 1, 71.
11  Strasser and Stern, *Flight from Terror*, 189–90.
12  As quoted in Fest, *The Face of the Third Reich*, 144, and Bleuel, *Sex and Society*, 97–98.
13  Bleuel, *Sex and Society*, 100.
14  Gallo, *The Night of the Long Knives*, 77.
15  Bullock, *Hitler*, 307–8.
16  Fest, *Hitler*, 451–52.
17  Gallo, *The Night of the Long Knives*, 121.
18  Bleuel, *Sex and Society*, 219.
19  Bracher, *The German Dictatorship*, 302–03.
20  As quoted in Fest, *Hitler*, 469.

## CHAPTER 3 THE GRAND INQUISITOR

1  Fest, *The Face of the Third Reich*, 112.
2  Heiber, *Reichsführer!* 7–35.
3  Carl J. Burckhardt, *Meine Danziger Mission 1937–1939* (Munich: Deutscher Taschenbuch Verlag, 1962), 123.
4  As translated and quoted in Fest, *The Face of the Third Reich*, 115.
5  Bracher, *The German Dictatorship*, 303.
6  Smith, *Heinrich Himmler*, 83.
7  Fest, *The Face of the Third Reich*, 167–68.
8  Kersten, *Kersten Memoirs*, 300.
9  Before being executed in Poland, Hoess wrote his memoirs, *Kommandant in Auschwitz*, one of the primary SS documents ranking homosexuals with Jews and Gypsies as "subhumans."
10  Hallgarten, *Als die Schatten Fielen*, 35.
11  Ibid., 117–18.
12  This is open to dispute: Mussolini's black-shirted troopers started marching around 1921, and the Nazis borrowed a large number of the Italian fascists' props, including salutes, insignias, and slogans.

# Notes

13 Smith and Peterson, *Himmler Geheimreden*, 93–104.

14 Ibid., 222.

15 Smith, *Heinrich Himmler*, 149–51.

16 Ibid., 31, 104.

17 Ibid., 100.

18 Kersten, *Kersten Memoirs*, 122–24.

19 Delarue, *The Gestapo*, 129. See also Aronson, *Reinhard Heydrich*, 55–59 and 201–3.

20 Peter Loewenberg, "The Unsuccessful Childhood of Heinrich Himmler," *Historical Review* 3 (June 1971): 612–41. Loewenberg's characterization of Himmler as an "anal type" seems to me to be an unnecessary overinterpretation.

21 Smith, *Heinrich Himmler*, 43, 143.

22 Ibid., 86.

23 Boswell, *Christianity*, 316–18.

24 Seidler, *Prostitution*, 135.

25 Smith, *Heinrich Himmler*, 86–87, 115.

26 Heiber, *Reichsführer!* 302.

27 Smith and Peterson, *Himmler Geheimreden*, 94–101.

28 Kersten, *Kersten Memoirs*, 50–64.

29 Bleuel, *Sex and Society*, 221.

30 Kersten, *Kersten Memoirs*, 56–64.

31 Smith and Peterson, *Himmler Geheimreden*, 90–91.

32 Ibid., 115–23.

33 Ibid.

34 Kersten, *Kersten Memoirs*. See especially the preface by Hugh Trevor-Roper.

35 Besgen, *Der Stille Befehl*, 25.

36 Kersten, *Kersten Memoirs*. See also Besgen, *Der Stille Befehl*, 1–66.

37 Ibid., 20. See also Besgen, *Der Stille Befehl*, 14, 66–7.

38 Ibid., 11, n. 3. Nikolas Burckhardt, letter to author. See also Carl Ludwig, *An den Bundesrate: Die Flüchtingspolitik der Schweiz seit 1933-Gegenwart.*

39 We will never know how much Himmler was aware that thousands loathed him as a cold-blooded, long-distance killer. He had managed to drape around himself the mantle of a powerful mythological figure from the *Nibelungenlied*. He identified with Hagen, the sinister villain who slays the Nordic hero Siegfried. In 1937, Himmler commissioned a writer named Edmund Kiss to publish a tribute to Hagen in a magazine called *Germanien*. (Himmler

served on its board of directors.) Kiss eulogized Hagen, writing that one "must praise the courage of murder without pity if the honor of the state is at stake . . . sometimes a man must be judge and executioner . . . not because he is bloodthirsty but for the honor of the community. . . ." What remains puzzling is this: Hagen is of mixed blood. His father is the dwarf Alberich, definitely a non-Germanic gnome. By Third Reich standards, Hagen is a racial mixture, a "Mischling," not of "pure blood." Himmler's apparent identification with Hagen deserves further investigation. See Edmund Kiss, "Germanienkunde und ihr Tieferer Sinn"; also Joseph Ackermann, *Heinrich Himmler als Ideologe*, 143–44.

40   Smith and Peterson, *Himmler Geheimreden*, 282, n. 56.
41   Kersten, *Kersten Memoirs*, 70–71.
42   Besgen, *Der Stille Befehl*, 110.
43   Kersten, *Kersten Memoirs*, 164–66.
44   Schnabel, *Die Frommen*, 116.
45   Kersten, *Kersten Memoirs*, 82.
46   Ibid., 74–82.
47   Ibid., 56–64.
48   Ibid., 57.
49   Lautmann, *Gesellschaft und Homosexualität*, 329.
50   Hillel and Henry, *Lebensborn E.V.*, 145; also Besgen, *Der Stille Befehl*, 117.
51   Kersten, *Kersten Memoirs*, 58; also Heiber, *Reichsführer!* 272, 302.
52   Kersten, *Kersten Memoirs*, 63.
53   Seidler, *Prostitution*, 193–229.
54   Bleuel, *Sex and Society*, 57.
55   Tripp, *The Homosexual Matrix*, 100–6. For the prevalence of such attitudes in Germany today, see Lautmann, "Wie man Aussenseiter Draussen Hält," *Kritische Justiz* 12 (August 1979): 28.
56   Bleuel, *Sex and Society*, 216–17.
57   Geissler, "Die Homosexuellen Gesetzgebung," 77; also Louis Crompton, "What Do You Say to Someone Who Claims that Homosexuality Caused the Downfall of Greece and Rome?" *Christopher Street* (March 1978): 49–52.
58   Fromm, *The Anatomy of Human Destructiveness*, 355.
59   Fest, *The Face of the Third Reich*, 121.
60   Seidler, *Prostitution*, 228–31.
61   Heiber, *Reichsführer!* 271–72.

# Notes

## CHAPTER 4 PERSECUTION

1 Kurt Hiller, *Leben Gegen die Zeit*, published in two volumes (1969 and 1973), as quoted in Stümke and Finkler, *Rosa Winkel*, 167–74.
2 Lautmann, *Gesellschaft und Homosexualität*, 328.
3 Erhard Vismar, "Perversion und Verfolgung unter dem deutschen Faschismus," in Lautmann, *Gesellschaft und Homosexualität*, 318.
4 Geissler, "Homosexuellen-Gesetzgebung," 18–20.
5 Harthauser, "Massenmord an Homosexuellen," 20; also Geissler, "Homosexuellen-Gesetzgebung," 11.
6 Wilde, *Das Schicksal*, 36; also Steakley, *The Homosexual Emancipation Movement*, 112, and Bleuel, *Sex and Society*, 221, who attributes this statement to Karl August Eckhardt, a Berlin University law professor.
7 Lautmann, *Gesellschaft und Homosexualität*, 318; also letter from Simon Wiesenthal to the author, May 29, 1981.
8 Geissler, "Homosexuellen-Gesetzgebung," 14.
9 Wilde, *Das Schicksal*, 53–55; also Bleibtreu-Ehrenberg, *Tabu Homosexualität*, 319–22.
10 Wilde, *Das Schicksal*, 17. Translation by the author.
11 Klare, *Homosexualität und Strafecht*, 121–23; also quoted in Schilling, *Schwule und Faschismus*, 166.
12 As quoted in Schilling, *Schwule und Faschismus*, 173.
13 Vermehren, *Reise Durch*, 49.
14 See Ilse Kokula's authoritative account of lesbians in modern Germany in Bollé, *Eldorado*, 149–61.
15 As quoted in publisher's note in Mann, *Mephisto*, i.
16 Lautmann, *Gesellschaft und Homosexualität*, 322.
17 Ibid., 324.
18 Geissler, "Homosexuellen-Gesetzgebung," throughout.
19 The Vichy auxiliary police had a reputation for being more Nazi-like than the Nazis. See Leslie, *The Liberation of the Riviera*, 62.
20 International Tracing Service, General Folders, no. 319. See also Lautmann, *Gesellschaft und Homosexualität*, 329.
21 Reproduced in *Sek* 4, April 1974.
22 Jan Rogier, "75 Jahre Emanzipation in den Niederlanden," in Rolf Italiaander, ed., *Weder Krankheit noch Verbrechen* (Hamburg: Gala Verlag, 1969), 183–93.
23 Robert Tielman in *De Groene Amsterdammer* (March 22, 1978).

24 Hirschfeld, *Homosexualität*, 1002.
25 Eissler, "Sexualpolitik," 33.
26 Steakley, *The Homosexual Emancipation Movement*, 28.
27 Wilde, *Das Schicksal*, 18.
28 Hahn, *Lieber Stürmer!*, throughout.
29 Baldur von Schirach, et al., *Kriminalität und Gefährdung der Jugend. Lageberichte bis zum Stand vom 1. Januar 1941*, Hrsg. vom Jugendführer des Deutschen Reiches, bearbeitet von W. Knopp (Berlin, n.d.). Translations by the author.
30 See also Geissler, "Homosexuellen-Gesetzgebung," 55.
31 Seidler, *Prostitution*, throughout.
32 Hockerts, *Sittlichkeitsprozesse*, 13, 76–77nn.
33 Rose, *Mönche vor Gericht*, 151.
34 Jochen von Lang, *The Secretary* (New York: Random House, 1979), 187.
35 Kempner, *Priester vor Hitlers Tribunalen*, 160; and Schnabel, *Die Frommen*, 29–178.
36 Lautmann, *Gesellschaft und Homosexualität*, 321.
37 Hockerts *Sittlichkeitsprozesse*, 161–190.
38 Ibid., 133.
39 Ibid., 205–6.
40 Bullock, *Hitler*, 307–8.
41 As quoted in *TLS: Essays and Reviews from The Times Literary Supplement 1963* (London: Oxford University Press, 1964), 197.
42 Deutsch, *Hitler and His Generals*, 406–9.
43 Seidler, *Prostitution*, 206.
44 Ibid., 213. Here is a breakdown according to a secret memorandum of the legal department of the German armed forces:

INDICTMENTS FOR CRIMES AGAINST PARAGRAPH 175
IN THE ARMED FORCES

| Year | Total Indictments | Officers | NCOs | Enlisted Men |
|---|---|---|---|---|
| 1940 | 1,134 | 36 | 273 | 825 |
| 1941 | 1,134 | 50 | 443 | 641 |
| 1942 | 1,588 | 63 | 436 | 1,089 |
| 1943 (incomplete) | 1,111 | 56 | 282 | 773 |
| TOTAL | 4,967 | 205 | 1,434 | 3,328 |

45 Ibid., 212–20. Also, Seidler argues persuasively that more German soldiers attempted self-mutilation in World War II than in World War I, 233–73.
46 Ibid., 207–10.
47 Ibid., 210–11.
48 Steakley, *The Homosexual Emancipation Movement*, 83.
49 Hirschfeld, *Homosexualität*.
50 Bleuel, *Sex and Society*, 220.
51 Smith and Peterson, *Himmler Geheimreden*, 94–101.
52 As cited in Geissler, "Homosexuellen-Gesetzgebung," 10. The official Gestapo statistics for conviction of homosexuals are broken down by year:

| Year | Homosexual Men Sentenced |
|---|---|
| 1931 | 665 |
| 1932 | 801 |
| 1933 | 853 |
| 1934 | 948 |
| 1935 | 2,106 |
| 1936 | 5,320 |
| 1937 | 8,271 |
| 1938 | 8,562 |
| 1939 | 7,614 |
| 1940 (first half) | 3,816 |
| | TOTAL 38,956 |

53 Ibid., 25. An unpublished report of the Federal Security Office for Combating Abortion and Homosexuality contains statistics for the number of homosexual men sentenced for the years 1936–39:

| Year | Homosexual Men Sentenced |
|---|---|
| 1936 | 9,081 |
| 1937 | 12,760 |
| 1938 | 10,628 |
| 1939 | 10,450 |
| | TOTAL 42,919 |

54  Stümke and Finkler, *Rosa Winkel*, 267. Much of the statistical material is in archives in East Berlin, and has not yet been made available to historians. The breakdown for the war years of 1941–44 is as follows:

| Year | Homosexual Men Sentenced |
|------|--------------------------|
| 1941 | 3,735 |
| 1942 | 3,963 |
| 1943 | 2,218* |
| 1944 | 2,000† |

TOTAL 11,916

*This figure doubles the statistic for the first half of 1943.
†This figure is purely conjectural.

## CHAPTER 5 IN CAMP

1  Lautmann, *Gesellschaft und Homosexualität*, 325–65.
2  Ibid., 332.
3  Johe, *Neuengamme*, 24; Kogon, *Der SS Staat*, throughout; and Poller, *Medical Block Buchenwald*, throughout.
4  ITS, Arolsen, book 7, folders 417 and 418.
5  ITS, Arolsen, book 7, folders 432, 439, and 440.
6  ITS, Arolsen, book 7, folder 172. The camp documents are relatively complete for Buchenwald, where there are more week-by-week rosters of homosexual inmates.
7  Rüdiger Lautmann, *Journal of Homosexuality* 6, nos. 1–2 (fall/winter 1980–81): 145–46.
8  Lautmann, *Gesellschaft und Homosexualität*, 333.
9  ITS, Arolsen, book 7, folder 172.
10  See Sydnor, *Soldiers of Destruction*, especially the first six chapters.
11  Schnabel, *Die Frommen*, 32.
12  Sydnor, *Soldiers of Destruction*, 11–18.
13  Jeremy Noakes and Geoffrey Pridham, eds., *Documents on Nazism 1919–1945* (New York: Viking, 1974), 284–86.
14  The following books are essential: Davidowicz, *The War Against the Jews 1933–1945*; Des Pres, *The Survivor*; Gilbert, *The Hol-*

ocaust; Hilberg, *The Destruction of the European Jews*; Kogon, *Der SS Staat*; and Levi, *Questo è un uomo.*

15  Kogon, *Der SS Staat,* 366–79.
16  Fénelon, *Playing for Time.*
17  See various passages in Hitler's *Mein Kampf,* as quoted by Stümke and Finkler in *Rosa Winkel,* 67–118.
18  Kogon, *Der SS Staat,* 227–80; Johe, *Neuengamme,* 24–31; and Borkin, *The Crime and Punishment of IG Farben.*
19  Kogon, *Der SS Staat,* 182–202.
20  Letter to the author from former inmate L.W., May 1980.
21  Lautmann, *Gesellschaft und Homosexualität,* 333.
22  Heger, *Die Männer mit dem Rosa Winkel,* 33.
23  Harthauser, "Massenmord an Homosexuellen," 30.
24  Lautmann, *Gesellschaft und Homosexualität,* 334. Also Heger, *The Men with the Pink Triangle,* 32.
25  Hoess, *Kommandant in Auschwitz,* 80–82.
26  Heger, *Die Männer mit dem Rosa Winkel,* 36.
27  Kogon, *Der SS Staat,* 270–2.
28  Hoess, *Kommandant in Auschwitz,* 80–81. Letter to the author from L.W.: After faking successful intercourse with a woman in the camp brothel, he was told, "Now you are a real German man." Heger also reports such "conversion therapy."
29  Ibid., 80.
30  Heger, *Die Männer mit dem Rosa Winkel,* 57. See also the posthumously published memoirs of Aimé Spitz, as quoted in *Gay Journal* (June-July 1980): 18. An Alsatian who spent three years in Natzweiler-Struthof concentration camp as a member of the French resistance, he never let his comrades or captors know that he was a homosexual. His analysis of the fate of the gays confirms the conclusions of other witnesses.
31  Heger, *Die Männer mit dem Rosa Winkel,* 69.
32  See the report on Neusustrum concentration camp by Harry Pauly in Stümke and Finkler, *Rosa Winkel,* 298.
33  Schnabel, *Die Frommen,* 53.
34  Kogon, *The Theory and Practice of Hell,* 44.
35  Lautmann, *Gesellschaft und Homosexualität,* 357.
36  Ibid., 342.
37  Recollection of an anonymous French homosexual, arrested in Mulhouse in May 1941, detained and tortured in Schirmeck concentration camp, released for forced labor service in Germany.

Notes from the French edition of Martin Sherman's *Bent* (1981), translated by the author.

38 Heger, *The Men with the Pink Triangle*, 48–49.
39 Kogon, *Der SS Staat*, 274–5.
40 Levi, *Questo è un uomo*, throughout; Kogon, *Der SS Staat*, 75; Des Pres, *The Survivor*, 53–71.
41 Letter from L.W. to the author, May 1980.
42 Reminiscences of former camp inmate K.R., as reported in personal correspondence to the author by W.K., September 1, 1978.
43 Lautmann, *Gesellschaft und Homosexualität*, 339–40.
44 Hoess, *Kommandant in Auschwitz*, 101–5.
45 Stümke and Finkler, *Rosa Winkel*, 292–94, translated by the author. See also Harthauser in Schlegel, *Das Grosse Tabu*, 9–13.
46 Lautmann, *Gesellschaft und Homosexualität*, 350.
47 Kogon, *Der SS Staat*, 183, 270–71, 283; and Johe, *Neuengamme*, 14.
48 ITS, Arolsen, folder 418, contains incomplete statistics on homosexual detainees from April 1942 to June 1944. The number of homosexuals fluctuates in this period between 60 and 35.
49 Harthauser in Schlegel, *Das Grosse Tabu*, 30–31.
50 See Mitscherlich and Mielke, *Medizin ohne Menschlichkeit*, for further treatment of this topic.
51 Kogon, *Der SS Staat*, 183, 200, 270–71.
52 Ibid., 184–90, 200–5.
53 ITS, Arolsen, book 36, folder 172.
54 Precise data have become essential because in 1950 the West German government began restitution payments to survivors of these tests. According to Heinrich Siebel, the Arolsen documentation expert, fifty-nine types of experiments were undertaken. SS physicians coined the phrase "expendable experimental" for individuals they knew would die during or soon after such tests. Interview with Siebel by the author, June 1976. See also Johe, *Neuengamme*, 36–37, and Kogon, *Der SS Staat*, 182–205.
55 ITS, Arolsen, book 36, folder 405.
56 Kogon, *Der SS Staat*, 182–201.
57 The following chart can be found in Lautmann, *Gesellschaft und Homosexualität*, 351.

# Notes

58  Letters to the author from former prisoners H.R. (April 26, 1980) and W.L. (April 24, 1980, and June, 1980).
59  See various testimonies in Stümke and Finkler, *Rosa Winkel*, 276–337.

### CONCLUSION

1  Haffner, *Anmerkungen zu Hitler*, 155–203.
2  Gilbert, *Auschwitz and the Allies.*
3  Arendt, *Eichmann in Jerusalem*, 232.
4  Boswell, *Christianity*, 292.
5  Evans, *Witchcraft and the Gay Counterculture*, 92–93.
6  As quoted in Rubenstein, *The Cunning of History*, 31.
7  Keller, *Die Psychologie der Folter*, 31–55.

# SELECTED
# BIBLIOGRAPHY

Anonymous. "Celebration of Those Killed in Camp Neuengamme." *Applause* (July 1978).

——. *Concentration Camp Dachau 1933–1945*. Brussels: Comité International de Dachau, 1965.

——. *Der Homosexuelle Nächste. Ein Symposion*. Hamburg: Furche Verlag, 1963.

——. *Nürnberg: das Urteil von 1946*. Munich: Deutscher Taschenbuchverlag, 1961.

——. *Plädoyer fur die Abschaffung des Paragraphen 175*. Frankfurt: Suhrkamp, 1966.

——. *Roehm-Memoiren des Stabschef*. Saarbrücken: Uranus Verlag, 1934.

——. *Rosa Winkel? Das ist doch schon lange vorbei*. Materialien zu dem gleichnamigen Film Bielefeld: AJ2 Druck & Verlag, 1976.

Ackermann, Joseph. *Heinrich Himmler als Ideologe*. Göttingen: Musterschmidt, 1970.

Adler, Alfred. *Das Problem der Homosexualität und sexueller Perversionen*. Frankfurt: S. Fischer, 1977.

Allport, Gordon. *The Nature of Prejudice*. Chicago: Addison-Wesley, 1954.

Arendt, Hannah. *Antisemitism*. New York: Harcourt, Brace & World, 1968.

——. *Eichmann in Jerusalem*. New York: Harcourt, Brace & World, 1964.

——. *Imperialism*. New York: Harcourt, Brace & World, 1968.

——. *Die Kontroverse: Hannah Arendt, Eichmann und die Juden*. Munich: Nymphenburger Verlagsbuchhandlung, 1964.

——. *Macht und Gewalt*. Munich: Piper, 1971.

——. *Sechs Essays*. Munich: Piper, 1948.

——. "Social Science Techniques and the Study of Concentration Camps." *Jewish Social Studies* 12 (1950): 49–64.

——. *Totalitarianism*. New York: Harcourt, Brace & World, 1968.

——. *Über die Revolution*. Munich: Piper, 1974.

Aronson, Schlomo. *Reinhard Heydrich und die Fruhgeschichte von Gestapo und SD*. Stuttgart: Deutsche Verlagsanstalt, 1971.

Auerbach, Hellmuth. "Die Einheit Dirlewanger." *Vierteljahreshefte für Zeitgeschichte* 10, no. 3 (July 1962): 250–63.

Ayçoberry, Pierre. *The Nazi Question*. New York: Random House, 1981.

Bailey, Derrick Sherwin. *Homosexuality and the Western Christian Tradition*. London: Longmans, Green, 1955.

Bailey, George. *Germans: Biography of an Obsession*. New York: Avon, 1972.

Becker, Howard. *German Youth: Bond or Free*. New York: Oxford University Press, 1964.

Bernstein, Eduard. *On Homosexuality*. Dublin: Athol Books, 1977.

Besgen, Achim. *Der Stille Befehl*. Munich: Nymphenburger Verlagsanstalt, 1960.

Bettelheim, Bruno. *The Informed Heart*. New York: Avon Books, 1971.

——. *Surviving and Other Essays*. New York: Knopf, 1979.

Birenbaum, Halina. *Hope Is the Last To Die*. New York: Twayne, 1977.

Bleibtreu-Ehrenberg, Gisela. *Tabu Homosexualität*. Frankfurt: S. Fischer, 1978.

Bleuel, Hans Peter. *Sex and Society in Nazi Germany*. Philadelphia: Lippincott, 1973.

Bloch, Charles. *Die SA und die Krise des NS Regimes*, Frankfurt: Suhrkamp, 1970.

Bollé, Michael, ed. *Eldorado: Homosexuelle Frauen und Männer in Berlin 1850–1950*. Berlin: Frölich & Kaufmann, 1984.

Borkin, Joseph. *The Crime and Punishment of IG Farben*. New York: Free Press, 1978.

Bosch, Herrmann. *Heeresrichter Karl Sack im Widerstand*. Munich: Gotthold Müller, 1967.

Boswell, John. *Christianity, Social Tolerance and Homosexuality*. Chicago: University of Chicago Press, 1980.

Bracher, Karl Dietrich. *The German Dictatorship*. Middlesex: Penguin University Books, 1980.

Bracher, Karl Dietrich, Gerhard Schulz, and Wolfgang Sauer. *Die nationalsozialistische Machtergreifung*. Frankfurt: Ullstein, 1960.

Brandenburg, Hans-Christian. *Die Geschichte der H.J.* Köln: Verlag Wissenschaft und Politik, 1968.

# Selected Bibliography

Bringmann, Fritz. *Neuengamme: Berichte, Erinnerungen, Dokumente.* Frankfurt: Röderberg Verlag, 1981.

Broszat, Martin. *German National Socialism 1919–1945.* Santa Barbara: Clio Press, 1966.

———. *Der Staat Hitlers.* Munich: Deutscher Taschenbuch Verlag, 1976.

Bullock, Alan. *Hitler.* New York: Harper & Row, 1964.

Bullough, Vern L. *Homosexuality and History.* New York: Meridian Books, 1979.

———. "Homosexuality and the Medical Model." *Journal of Homosexuality* 1, no. 6 (1975): 99–110.

Canetti, Elias. *The Conscience of Words.* New York: Seabury Press, 1979.

Cargas, Harry James. *The Holocaust: An Annotated Bibliography.* Haverford, Pennsylvania: Catholic Library Association, 1977.

Churchill, Wainwright. *Homosexual Behavior Among Males.* New York: Prentice-Hall, 1967.

Clébert, Jean-Paul. *Das Volk der Zigeuner.* Frankfurt: S. Fischer, 1967.

Cocks, Geoffrey. *Psychotherapy in the Third Reich.* New York: Oxford University Press, 1985.

Craig, Gordon A. *Germany 1866–1945.* New York: Oxford University Press, 1978.

Crompton, Louis. "Gay Genocide: From Leviticus to Hitler." Address delivered to Gay Academic Union, New York University, November, 1974.

Dannecker, Martin and Reiche, Reimut. *Der gewöhnliche Homosexuelle.* Frankfurt: S. Fischer, 1974.

Dannecker, Martin. *Der Homosexuelle und die Homosexualität.* Frankfurt: Syndikat, 1978.

Dawidowicz, Lucy S. *The War Against the Jews 1933–1945.* New York: Holt, Rinehart and Winston, 1975.

Delarue, Jacques. *The Gestapo.* New York: Morrow, 1964.

Des Pres, Terrence. *The Survivor: An Anatomy of Life in the Death Camps.* New York: Oxford University Press, 1976.

Deutsch, Harold C. *The Conspiracy Against Hitler in the Twilight War.* Minneapolis: University of Minnesota Press, 1968.

———. *Hitler and His Generals.* Minneapolis: University of Minnesota Press, 1974.

Diels, Rudolf. *Lucifer ante Portas.* Stuttgart: Deutsche Verlagsanstalt, 1950.

Doucet, Friedrich W. *Homosexualität.* Munich: Lichtenberg, 1967.

Eissler, Wilfried. "Sexualpolitik der beiden grossen Arbeiterparteien der Weimar Parteien." Ph.D. thesis, Free University of Berlin, 1978.

Evans, Arthur. *Witchcraft and the Gay Counterculture*. Boston: Fag Rag Books, 1978.

Feig, Konnilyn G. *Hitler's Death Camps*. New York: Holmes & Meier, 1981.

Fénelon, Fania. *Playing for Time*. New York: Atheneum, 1977.

Fest, Joachim C. *The Face of the Third Reich*. New York: Pantheon, 1970.

————. *Hitler*. New York: Harcourt Brace Jovanovich, 1974.

Flitner, Andreas. *Geistesleben und Nationalsozialismus*. Tübingen: Rainer Wunderlich, 1965.

Freeman, Gilliam. *The Confessions of Elisabeth von S*. New York: Dutton, 1978.

Friedrich, Otto. *Before the Deluge*. New York: Avon, 1972.

Fromm, Erich. *The Anatomy of Human Destructiveness*. New York: Holt, Rinehart and Winston, 1973.

Gagnon, John H. and William Simon, eds. *Sexual Deviance*. New York: Harper & Row, 1967.

Gallo, Max. *The Night of the Long Knives*. New York: Harper & Row, 1972.

Garlinski, Jozef. *Fighting Auschwitz*. Greenwich, Connecticut: Fawcett, 1975.

Gay, Ruth. *Outwitting the Final Solution*. New York: Horizon, 1977.

Geissler, Brigitte. "Die Homosexuellen-Gesetzgebung als Instrument der Ausübung politischer Macht." M.A. thesis, University of Göttingen, 1968.

Geve, Thomas. *Youth in Chains*. Jerusalem: Rubin Mass, 1978.

Giese, Hans. *Der homosexuelle Mann in der Welt*. Munich: Kindler.

Gilbert, Gustave M. *Nürnberger Tagebuch*. Frankfurt: Fischer Taschenbuch, 1962.

Gilbert, Martin. *Auschwitz and the Allies*. New York: Holt, Rinehart and Winston, 1981.

————. *The Holocaust*. New York: Holt, Rinehart and Winston, 1986.

Gisevius, Hans-Bernd. *Bis Zum Bittren Ende*. Zürich: Fretz und Wasmuth, 1946.

Gobineau, Arthur. *Selected Political Writings*. New York: Harper & Row, 1971.

Goebbels, Joseph. *The Goebbels Diaries 1942–1943*. Garden City: Doubleday, 1948.

Selected Bibliography

Gollner, Günther. *Homosexualität, Ideologiekritik und Entmythologisierung einer Gesetzgebung.* Berlin: Duncker & Humblot, 1974.
Gross, Leonard. *The Last Jews of Berlin.* New York: Bantam, 1983.
Grosser, Alfred. *Wie War es Möglich?* Munich: Carl Hanser, 1978.
Grunberger, Richard. *The Twelve-Year Reich.* New York: Holt, Rinehart and Winston, 1971.
Grunfeld, Frederic V. *The Hitler File.* New York: Random House, 1974.
Haffner, Sebastian. *Anmerkungen zu Hitler.* Munich: Kindler, 1978.
Hahn, Fred. *Lieber Stürmer! Leserbriefe.* Stuttgart: Seewald, 1978.
Hallgarten, George W. F. *Als die Schatten Fielen.* Frankfurt: Ullstein, 1969.
Hamilton, Alistair. *The Appeal of Fascism 1919–1945.* New York: Avon, 1973.
Harthauser, Wolfgang. "Der Massenmord an Homosexuellen im Dritten Reich." In Wilhart S. Schlegel, *Das Grosse Tabu.* Munich: Rütten & Löning, 1967.
Heger, Heinz. *Die Männer mit dem Rosa Winkel.* Hamburg: Merlin, 1972.
———. *The Men With the Pink Triangle.* Boston: Alyson, 1980.
Heiber, Helmut, ed. *Reichsführer!* ... Munich: Deutscher Taschenbuch Verlag, 1970.
Heiber, Helmut. *Goebbels.* London: Robert Hale, 1972.
Hillel, Marc and Clarissa Henry. *Lebensborn E.V.* Vienna: Zsolnay, 1975.
Hirschfeld, Magnus. *Die Homosexualität des Mannes und des Weibes.* Berlin: Louis Marcus, 1920.
Hitler, Adolf. *Mein Kampf.* Munich: Eber, 1925.
Hockerts, Hans-Günther. *Die Sittlichkeitsprozesse gegen Katholische Ordensangehörige und Priester.* Mainz: Mathias Grünewald, 1971.
Hoffmann, Gerhard. Analyse der Voraussetzungen und Bedingungen der Homosexuellenbewegung und der Diskussionen um den Paragraphen 175. Dissertation, Free University of Berlin, 1974.
Hoffmann, Peter. *The History of the German Resistance.* Cambridge: MIT Press, 1977.
Höhne, Heinz. *Canaris.* New York: Doubleday, 1976.
———. *Codeword: Direktor.* New York: Coward McCann, 1971.
———. *Der Orden unter dem Totenkopf.* Frankfurt: S. Fischer, 1969.
Hohenstein, Alexander. *Warthetändisches Tagebuch.* Munich: Deutscher Taschenbuch Verlag, 1963.

# Selected Bibliography

Hohmann, Joachim S., ed. *Der Unterdrückte Sexus*. Lollar: Andreas Achenbach, 1977.

Hoess, Rudolf, *Kommandant in Auschwitz*. Munich: Deutscher Taschenbuch Verlag, 1963.

Hossbach, Friedrich. *Zwischen Wehrmacht und Hitler*. Wolfenbüttel: Wolfenbüttel Verlagsanstalt, 1949.

Hughes, H. Stuart. *The Sea Change*. New York: McGraw-Hill, 1977.

Hull, David Stuart. *Film in the Third Reich*. Berkeley: University of California Press, 1969.

Humble, Richard. *Hitler's Generals*. Garden City: Doubleday, 1974.

Igra, Samuel. *Germany's National Vice*. London: Quality Press, 1945.

Johe, Werner. *Neuengamme*. Hamburg: Landeszentrale für politische Bildung, 1981.

Kalnoky, Ingeborg and Ilona Herisko. *The Guest House*. Indianapolis: Bobbs-Merrill, 1974.

Kalow, Gert. *Hitler—das deutsche Trauma*. Munich: R. Piper, 1974.

Katz, Jonathan. *Gay American History*. New York: Crowell, 1976.

———. *Gay Lesbian Almanac*. New York: Harper & Row, 1983.

Ka-Tzetnik 135633. *Atrocity*. New York: Lyle Stuart, 1963.

Keller, Gustav. *Die Psychologie der Folter*. Frankfurt: Fischer Taschenbuch Verlag, 1981.

Kempner, Benedetta Maria. *Priester vor Hitlers Tribunalen*. Munich: Rütten & Löning, 1966.

———. *Nonnen unter dem Hakenkreuz*. Würzburg: Naumann Verlag, 1979.

Kerscher, Ignatz. *Konfliktfeld Sexualität*. Darmstadt: Luchterhand, 1977.

Kersten, Felix. *The Kersten Memoirs 1940–1945*. New York: Macmillan, 1957.

———. *The Memoirs of Dr. Felix Kersten*. Garden City: Doubleday, 1947.

———. *Totenkopf und Treue: Heinrich Himmler ohne Uniform*. Hamburg: Robert Molich, 1955.

Kessel, Joseph. *The Man with the Golden Hands*. Freeport, New York: Books for Libraries Press, 1971.

Kieler, Wieslaw. *Anus Mundi*. New York: Times Books, 1980.

Kielmansegg, Johann Adolf. *Der Fritsch Prozess 1938*. Hamburg: Hoffmann und Campe, 1949.

Kiss, Edmund. "Germanenkunde und ihr Tieferer Sinn." *Germanien 9* (January 1937): 26–29.

# Selected Bibliography

Klare, Rudolf. *Homosexualität und Strafrecht.* Hamburg: Hanseatische Verlagsbuchhandlung, 1937.

Klimmer, Rudolph. *Die Homosexualität.* Hamburg: Verlag für kriminalistische Fachliteratur, 1965.

Koch, Hans-Joachim W. *The Hitler Youth.* London: Macdonald and James, 1975.

Kogon, Eugen. *The Theory and Practice of Hell.* New York: Berkley, 1968.

——. *Der SS Staat: Das System der deutschen Konzentrationslager.* Munich: Kindler, 1974.

——, Hermann Langbein, and Adalbert Rückert. *Nationalsozialistische Massentötungen durch Giftgas.* Frankfurt: S. Fischer, 1983.

Krich, Aron. *The Sexual Revolution.* New York: Delta, 1964.

Kröger, Peter. "Entwicklungsstadien der Bestrafung der widernatürlichen Unzucht." Ph.D. thesis, Free University of Berlin, 1957.

Kuckuc, Ina. *Der Kampf gegen Unterdrückung.* Munich: Frauenoffensive, 1975.

Kühn, Dieter. *Grenzen des Widerstands.* Frankfurt: Suhrkamp, 1972.

Langbein, Hermann. *Menschen in Auschwitz.* Vienna: Europaverlag, 1972.

Langer, Lawrence. *The Holocaust and the Literary Imagination.* New Haven: Yale University Press, 1975.

Langer, Walter C. *The Mind of Adolf Hitler.* New York: Basic Books, 1972.

Laqueur, Walter Z. *Young Germany.* London: Routledge and Kegan Paul, 1962.

Lauritsen, John and David Thorstad. *The Early Homosexual Rights Movement 1864–1935.* New York: Times Change Press, 1974.

——. "Forerunners of Gay Liberation." *The Civil Liberties Review* (Summer 1975): 81–102.

Lautmann, Rüdiger. "Nur nicht Anecken." In *Terror und Hoffnung in Deutschland, 1933–1945.* Hamburg: Rowohlt, 1980, 361–90.

——. *Seminar: Gesellschaft und Homosexualität.* Frankfurt: Suhrkamp, 1977.

Lautmann, Rüdiger and Hanns Wienold. *Das Sexuelle Abwehrsytem gegen sexuelle Abweichung, insbesondere Homosexualität.* Bremen: privately printed, 1978.

Lee, Patrick and Robert Susman Stewart, eds., *Sex Differences.* New York: Urizen Books, 1976.

Lehmann-Haupt, Hellmut. *Art Under a Dictatorship*. New York: Oxford University Press, 1954.

Leiser, Erwin. *Nazi Cinema*. New York: Collier, 1975.

Leonhardt, Rudolf Walter. *Wer Wirft den Ersten Stein?* Munich: R. Piper & Co., 1969.

Leslie, Peter. *The Liberation of the Riviera*. New York: Wyndam Books, 1980.

Levi, Primo. *Questo è un uomo*. Frankfurt: S. Fischer, 1961.

Levin, Nora. *The Holocaust: The Destruction of European Jewry 1933–1945*. New York: Schocken, 1973.

Lichtenstein, Heiner. *Warum Auschwitz nicht Bombardiert wurde*. Köln: Bund Verlag, 1980.

Lorant, Stefan. *Sieg Heil!* New York: Norton, 1974.

Ludwig, Carl. *Die Flüchtingspolitik der Schweiz seit 1933 bis zur Gegenwart*. Bern: Herbert Lang & Cie., 1966.

Luetgebruene, Walter. *Ein Kampf um Röhm*. Diessen: J.C. Huber, 1933.

Maltitz, Horst von. *The Evolution of Hitler's Germany*. New York: McGraw-Hill, 1973.

Manchester, William. *The Arms of Krupp*. Boston: Little, Brown, 1964.

Mann, Golo. *Deutsche Geschichte 1919–1945*. Frankfurt: S. Fischer, 1973.

Mann, Klaus. "Homosexualität und Fascismus." In *Heute und Morgen*. Munich: Piper, 1969.

———. *Mephisto*. New York: Penguin, 1983.

Manvell, Roger and Heinrich Fraenkel. *Dr. Goebbels*. New York: Simon & Schuster, 1960.

———. *Himmler*. New York: Putnam, 1965.

———. *The Incomparable Crime*. New York, Putnam, 1967.

Maser, Werner. *Hitler: Legend, Myth, and Reality*. New York: Harper & Row, 1973.

Masterman, J. C. *The Double-Cross System in the War of 1939–1945*. New Haven: Yale University Press, 1972.

Mayer, Hans. *Aussenseiter*. Frankfurt: Suhrkamp, 1975.

———. *Materialien zu Hans Mayers Aussenseiter*. Edited by Gert Ueding. Frankfurt: Suhrkamp, 1978.

McRandle, James H. *The Track of the Wolf*. Evanston: Northwestern University Press, 1965.

Meineke, Friedrich. *The German Catastrophe*. Boston: Beacon Press, 1950.

Selected Bibliography

Mills, Richard. "Wilhelm Jansen and the German Wandervogel Movement." *Gay Sunshine* 44/45 (1980): 48–50.

Mitscherlich, Alexander. *Die Unwirtlichkeit unserer Städte*. Frankfurt: Suhrkamp, 1959.

Mitscherlich, Alexander and Fred Mielke. *Das Diktat der Menschenverachtung*. Heidelberg: Lambert Schneider, 1947.

———. *Medizin ohne Menschlichkeit*. Frankfurt: S. Fischer, 1949.

Moll, Albert. *Perversions of the Sex Instinct*. Newark: Julian Press, 1931.

Mosley, Leonard. *The Reich Marshal*. New York: Dell, 1974.

Mosse, George L. *Toward the Final Solution: A History of European Racism*. New York: Howard Fertig, 1978.

———. *The Crisis of German Ideology*. New York: Grosset & Dunlap, 1964.

———. *Nationalism and Sexuality*. New York: Howard Fertig, 1985.

Neumann, Robert. *Hitler: Aufstieg und Untergang des Dritten Reiches*. Munich: Kurt Desch, 1961.

Nolte, Ernst. *Der Nationalsozialismus*. Frankfurt: Ullstein, 1970.

Nyomarkay, Joseph. *Charisma and Factionalism in the Nazi Party*. Minneapolis: University of Minnesota Press, 1967.

O'Donnell, James P. *The Bunker*. Boston: Houghton Mifflin, 1978.

Ovesey, Lionel. *Homosexuality and Pseudohomosexuality*. New York: Science House, 1969.

Paetel, Karl O. *Jugend in der Entscheidung 1913–1945*. Bad Godesberg: publisher unknown, 1963.

Pawelczynska, Anna. *Values and Violence in Auschwitz*. Berkeley: University of California Press, 1979.

Payne, Robert. *The Life and Death of Adolf Hitler*. New York: Praeger, 1973.

Petrow, Richard. *The Bitter Years*. New York: Morrow, 1974.

Picker, Henry, Heinrich Hoffman, and Jochen von Lang, eds. *Hitler Close-Up*. New York: Macmillan, 1969.

Plant, Richard. "Memoirs of the Holocaust." *Gay Tide* 3, no. 1 (1975): 6–11.

———. "Stumme Zeugen Sprechen Laut." *Aufbau* (September 1976):7.

———. "What the Nazis Did to the Gays." *Christopher Street* (January 1977): 5–10.

Plassman, J. O. "Zur Erkenntnis deutschen Wesens." *Germanien* 3 (March 1937): 65–68.

Pleck, Joseph L. and Jack Sawyer. *Men and Masculinity*. Englewood Cliffs: Prentice-Hall, 1974.

Poliakov, Leon. *The History of Anti-Semitism from the Time of Christ to the Court Jews*. New York: Schocken, 1974.

Poller, Walter. *Medical Block Buchenwald*. London: Corgi Books, 1961.

Presser, Jacob. *The Destruction of the Dutch Jews*. New York: Dutton, 1969.

Rabinowitz, Dorothy. *New Lives*. New York: Avon, 1976.

Reif, Adelbert, ed. *Gespräche mit Hannah Arendt*. Munich: Piper, 1976.

Reitlinger, Gerald. *The House Built on Sand*. New York: Viking, 1960.

———. *The SS: Alibi of a Nation 1922–1945*. New York: Viking, 1968.

Roehm, Ernst. *Geschichte eines Hochverräters*. Munich: Eher, 1933.

Rose, Franz. *Mönche vor Gericht*. Berlin: M.A. Klieber, 1939.

Rubenstein, Richard L. *The Cunning of History*. New York: Harper & Row, 1975.

Rückert, Adelbert. *The Investigation of Nazi Crimes 1945–1978*. Heidelberg: C. F. Müller, 1979.

Rudicki, Adolf, ed. *Lest We Forget*. Warsaw: Polonia Foreign Languages Publishing House, 1955.

Schellenberg, Walter. *Hitler's Secret Service*. New York: Harper, 1956.

Schilling, Heinz-Dieter, ed. *Schwule und Faschismus*. Berlin: Elefantenpresse, 1983.

Schnabel, Raimund. *Die Frommen in der Hölle*. Frankfurt: Roederberg, 1967.

Schoenberner, Gerhard. *Der Gelbe Stern*. Munich: Bertelsmann, 1978.

Scholl, Inge. *Die Weisse Rose*. Frankfurt: S. Fischer, 1955.

Schramm, Wilhelm V. *Aufstand der Generäle*. Munich: Heyne, 1978.

Scobie, W. I. "Death Camps: Remembering the Victims." *Gay Sunshine* 25 (Summer 1975): 28.

Seidler, Franz. *Prostitution, Homosexualität und Selbstverstümmelung*. Neckargemünd: Kurt Vowinkel, 1977.

Serpico, Joseph. *Piercing the Third Reich*. New York: Ballantine, 1979.

Shirer, William L. *The Nightmare Years 1930–1940*. Boston: Little, Brown, 1984.

———. *The Rise and Fall of the Third Reich*. New York: Fawcett, 1960.

Siemsen, Hans. *Die Geschichte des Hitlerjungen Adolf Goes*. Düsseldorf: Komet Verlag, 1947.

# Selected Bibliography

Smith, Bradley F. *Heinrich Himmler: A Nazi in the Making 1900–1926.* Stanford: Hoover Institute Press, 1971.

———. *Reaching Judgment at Nuremberg.* New York: Basic Books, 1977.

Smith, Bradley F. and Agnes F. Peterson, eds. *Heinrich Himmler Geheimreden 1933–1945.* Frankfurt: Propyläen, 1974.

Smith, Marcus J. *The Harrowing of Hell—Dachau.* Albuquerque: University of New Mexico Press, 1972.

Snyder, Louis L. *The Idea of Racialism.* New York: Van Nostrand–Reinhold, 1962.

———. *Encyclopedia of the Third Reich.* New York: McGraw-Hill, 1976.

Speer, Albert. *Infiltrations.* New York: Macmillan, 1982.

———. *Inside the Third Reich.* New York: Macmillan, 1970.

———. *Spandauer Tagebücher.* Frankfurt: Propyläen, 1975.

Staff, Ilse. *Justiz im Dritten Reich.* Frankfurt: S. Fischer, 1964.

Steakley, James D. *The Homosexual Emancipation Movement in Germany.* New York: Arno, 1975.

Stein, George H. *Hitler.* Englewood Cliffs: Prentice-Hall, 1968.

———. *The Waffen SS.* Ithaca, New York: Cornell University Press, 1966.

Steiner, Jean-François. *Treblinka.* New York: New American Library, 1979.

Stern, Fritz. *The Politics of Cultural Despair.* Berkeley: University of California Press, 1961.

Stern, J. P. *Hitler: The Führer and the People.* Berkeley: University of California Press, 1975.

Stieber, Wilhelm J. *The Chancellor's Spy.* New York: Grove Press, 1979.

Strasser, Otto and Michael Stern. *Flight from Terror.* New York: James McBride, 1943.

Stümke, Hans-Georg and Rudi Finkler. *Rosa Winkel–Rosa Listen.* Hamburg: Rowohlt, 1981.

Sydnor, Charles W. *Soldiers of Destruction.* Princeton: Princeton University Press, 1977.

Tennenbaum, Joseph. "Die Einsatztruppen." *Jewish Social Studies* 18 (January 1955): 43–46.

Thalman, Rita and Emanuel Feinermann. *Crystal Night: November 9–10, 1938.* New York: Coward McCann, 1974.

Theweleit, Klaus. *Männerphantasien.* Frankfurt: Roter Stern, 1978.

Toland, John. *Adolf Hitler.* New York: Doubleday, 1978.

# Selected Bibliography

Trevor-Roper, Hugh R. *The Last Days of Hitler*. New York: Macmillan, 1947.

Tripp, C. A. *The Homosexual Matrix*. New York: McGraw-Hill, 1975.

Vermehren, Isa. *Reise Durch den Letzten Akt*. Hamburg: Rowohlt, 1979.

Viereck, Peter. *Metapolitics: From the Romantics to Hitler*. New York: Knopf, 1941.

Vinnai, Gerhard. *Das Elend der Männlichkeit*. Hamburg: Rowohlt, 1977.

Vogelsang, Reinhard. *Der Freundeskreis Himmler*. Göttingen: Musterschmidt, 1972.

Wagner, Walter. *Volksgerichtshof im nationalsozialistischen Staat*. 3 vols. Stuttgart: Deutsche Verlagsanstalt, 1975.

Waite, Robert G. L. *The Psychopathic God: Adolf Hitler*. New York: Basic Books, 1977.

Walker, Lawrence D. *Hitler Youth and Catholic Youth 1933–1936*. Washington, D.C.: Catholic University of America Press, 1970.

Weinberg, George. *Society and the Healthy Homosexual*. New York: St. Martin's, 1972.

Weinberg, Gerald L. *World in the Balance*. Hanover, New Hampshire: University Presses of New England, 1981.

Weinberg, Martin and Alan P. Bell. *An Annotated Bibliography*. New York: Harper & Row, 1972.

Whiting, Charles. *Finale at Flensburg*. London: Corgi Books, 1973.

Wiesenthal, Simon. *Essays über Nazi Verbrechen Simon Wiesenthal gewidmet*. Amsterdam: Wiesenthal Fonds, 1973.

Wilde, Harry (Schulze). "Der Röhmputsch." *Damals Magazine* (1954): 336–60; 460–8; 534–56.

Wilde, Harry. *Das Schicksal der Verfemten*. Tübingen: Katzmann, 1969.

———. *Walther Rathenau*. Hamburg: Rowohlt, 1971.

Winkler, Lutz. *Studie zur gesellschaftlichen Funktion faschistischer Sprache*. Frankfurt: Suhrkamp, 1977.

Winterbotham, F. W. *The Nazi Connection*. New York: Dell, 1979.

Wulf, Joseph. *Heinrich Himmler*. Berlin: Arani, 1960.

———. *Aus dem Lexikon der Mörder*. Gütersloh: Sigbert Mohn, 1963.

Wykes, Alan. *Goebbels*. New York: Ballantine, 1973.

———. *Himmler*. New York: Ballantine, 1972.

Zassenhaus, Hillgunt. *Walls: Resisting the Third Reich*. Boston: Beacon Press, 1974.

# Selected Bibliography

## DOCUMENTS

Wiener Library. Bulletin No. 8, May–August 1954.

Baldur von Schirach, et al., Kriminalität und Gefährdung der Jugend. Lageberichte bis zum Stand vom 1. Januar 1941, Hrsg. vom Jugend führer des Deutschen Reiches, bearbeitet von W. Knopp (Berlin, n.d.).

Konzentrationslager Neuengamme, 1938–45. In Museum für Hamburgische Geschichte, No. 16. Hamburg, 1981.

Letter by survivor M.R. to author. Rome, October 1978.

Interview with a survivor. Wilfried Kühn interviews K. v. R. Winter 1978.

Letters by survivor Walter L. June 1980.

International Tracing Service. List of first names. Third list. Arolsen: 1974.

International Tracing Service. Thirty Years in the Service of Humanity. Arolsen: 1975.

International Tracing Service. The ITS: Its Origins, Tasks, and Activities. Arolsen: 1975.

International Tracing Service. Operations Reports: 1971–1976.

# INDEX

# Index

# Index

# ABOUT THE AUTHOR

RICHARD PLANT was born in Frankfurt and is a graduate of the University of Basel, where he earned his Ph.D. Since emigrating to the United States in 1938, he has contributed numerous essays and reviews to many publications, including *Esquire, The New Republic, The New Yorker, The New York Times,* and *Saturday Review.* He is also the author of a novel, *The Dragon in the Forest,* and coauthor of the opera *Lizzie Borden.* He currently teaches at the New School for Social Research in New York City.